ILLEGALIZED

Bordervisions

Vanessa Fonseca-Chávez and Yvette J. Saavedra, Series Editors

RAFAEL A. MARTÍNEZ

ILLEGALIZED

UNDOCUMENTED YOUTH MOVEMENTS IN THE UNITED STATES

THE UNIVERSITY OF
ARIZONA PRESS
TUCSON

The University of Arizona Press
www.uapress.arizona.edu

ISBN-13: 978-0-8165-4864-4 (hardcover)
ISBN-13: 978-0-8165-4863-7 (paperback)
ISBN-13: 978-0-8165-4885-1 (ebook)

Cover design by Leigh McDonald
Cover art from *Migrante Protejido* by Nicolas Gonzalez-Medina
Typeset by Leigh McDonald in Arno Pro 11/14, PF Fuel, and Social Gothic (display)

Publication of this book is made possible in part by the proceeds of a permanent endowment created with the assistance of a Challenge Grant from the National Endowment for the Humanities, a federal agency.

Library of Congress Cataloging-in-Publication Data
Names: Martínez, Rafael A., 1986– author.
Title: Illegalized : undocumented youth movements in the United States / Rafael A. Martínez.
Description: Tucson : University of Arizona Press, 2024. | Series: BorderVisions | Includes bibliographical references and index.
Identifiers: LCCN 2024000578 (print) | LCCN 2024000579 (ebook) | ISBN 9780816548644 (hardcover) | ISBN 9780816548637 (paperback) | ISBN 9780816548651 (ebook)
Subjects: LCSH: Youth movements—United States. | Noncitizens—Political activity—United States.
Classification: LCC HQ799.2.P6 M3655 2024 (print) | LCC HQ799.2.P6 (ebook) | DDC 305.2350973—dc23/eng/20240430
LC record available at https://lccn.loc.gov/2024000578
LC ebook record available at https://lccn.loc.gov/2024000579

Printed in the United States of America
♾ This paper meets the requirements of ANSI/NISO Z39.48-1992 (Permanence of Paper).

For Eliza

CONTENTS

ILLUSTRATIONS

PREFACE

I love my undocumented people . . . because we have constantly had to prove our humanity and have done it beautifully.

—YOSIMAR REYES, 2020

I T WAS A WARM DAY when I landed at the airport in Albuquerque, New Mexico, on August 4, 2012. Carrying no more than two large bags that contained all my clothing and personal belongings, I was excited to see the new city I was to call home. I was most excited to see the university where I would spend most of my time: the University of New Mexico. I had more questions than answers at that moment. I was feeling a blend of optimism combined with anxiety about venturing into uncharted territory. The fall semester started the following week, and this was the start of a future that I had never thought was possible. Graduate school felt like a safe bet to defer questions of a futurity never promised to me because of my undocumented status.

Higher education represented sanctuary to me. My undergraduate experience lasted eight grueling years. People looked at me with a superior stare when asking me why it took me so long to graduate with my bachelor's degree. I would always respond with a smirk, "Why graduate when you're having so much fun?" in a Van Wilder–type privileged response. Many would just dismiss my response with uncomfortable laughter. But in all honesty, my reality was quite the opposite. My true response, which very few knew, was, "Why graduate when there is no opportunity for a career or job at the end?"

I spent those eight years of undergraduate study in a California State University as an undocumented student from 2004 to 2012. When I entered the university, I was completely oblivious to the fact that undocumented students in California at that point had access to in-state tuition. I was unaware that undocumented students had been organizing in California since the 1990s for access to higher education and working with allied politicians like the late Marco Antonio Firebaugh to push California's congress to pass in-state tuition, which was done in 2001 through Assembly Bill 540 (AB 540).[1] Thanks to the efforts of undocumented organizers who came before me, I had access to in-state tuition in 2004. Graduating from high school, I was just happy that a state university would admit me and let me attend. Up to that point, my coming-of-age experience had been completely *illegalized*. That is, everything I had heard or known told me that my opportunities were slim because I was documented as an illegal alien.

I had gone through high school with friends who had obtained their driver's licenses and gotten their first cars, but during my time in California undocumented people were not legally able to get driver's licenses.[2] All my friends had started working and were excited that their earned income provided them with the material culture that naturally brings gratification to most youth. My parents forbade me from trying to get a job while in high school because they wanted to reduce the risk of possible detection and deportation, which could be increased by working with false documentation or no documentation. So, with no access to a driver's license, no opportunities to legally work, and a lack of mobility, my coming-of-age experience was determined by illegality rooted in my undocumented status. In this way, illegalization is embedded in a denial of documentation that restricts the natural privileges afforded to citizens. Undocumented youths' bodies are coded or documented as "other" to uphold the privileges of citizenship enjoyed by U.S.-born youth.

When I arrived in Albuquerque, New Mexico, in 2012 to start graduate school, I carried all of those traumas of illegalization. Migrating to New Mexico itself reminded me of the process of illegalization, from the Mexican matrícula (ID card) that I presented at the airport to the experience of looking up New Mexico's immigration policies on my phone while waiting for my flight at the airport terminal to see if I would even have an opportunity to exist, let alone go to school. Later I would find out that New Mexico was a leading pro-immigrant state for undocumented communities, offering privileges such as driver's licenses, in-state tuition, and state financial aid.[3] As such, I was able to get my first driver's license in New Mexico at the age of twenty-seven. I was able to apply for state aid such as state-funded scholarships. The time when I started graduate school also had significance because on June 12, 2012, just a few months before my move to New Mexico, President Obama had walked out to the lawn of the White House to announce the Deferred Action for Childhood Arrivals (DACA) program. DACA granted qualifying undocumented youth access to an employment authorization card (EAC) and a level of protection from deportation.[4]

All of a sudden in 2012, while going through the motions of the life-changing experience that was starting graduate school, I found myself with a level of *hyperdocumentation* that I had never known up to that point in my life. Hyperdocumentation is defined by Aurora Chang as added educational awards or titles that compensate for undocumented status.[5] My undergraduate experience in a way had been spent "in the shadows" without status.[6] Without my parents practicing what undocu-scholar Carlos Aguilar terms acompañamiento—the embodiment of parental engagement—such as working long hours and overtime to help me pay for tuition and offering emotional encouragement, my undergraduate experience would not have been possible.[7] Now, in graduate school and with DACA, I felt that avenues had been opened for me to step "out of the shadows" with a certain level of documentation in my immigration status. Having access to work authorization, I began working as a research assistant with professors in my graduate department, and I had access to fellowships, grants, and state funding that lifted the financial burden of tuition from my parents and myself. And, as mentioned earlier, for the first time in my life, I had the privilege of mobility thanks to a state driver's license. With the hyperdocumentation of DACA status, career-based employment, tuition coverage, and a driver's license, I felt visible, indivisible, free, and motivated. I thought to myself: How can I not thrive? Undocu-scholar Germán Cadenas and co-author Elizabeth Kiehne use the term "the undocumented advantage" to scientifically measure the connection between higher academic performance among Latinx college students and development of critical consciousness rooted in their undocumented status.[8] Cadenas and Kiehne argue that social oppression can be leveraged through a development of critical consciousness that provides meaningful purpose for undocumented Latinx students. I recognized that it was not just my newly DACAmented status that allowed me to thrive academically, but also the critical consciousness based on the literature I would be exposed to in graduate school and connected to my lived experience. When I say "DACAmented," this refers to undocumented youth with the privilege of having DACA status.[9]

During the first semester of my master's program at the University of New Mexico in the fall of 2012, several of my professors recognized the importance of my lived experience as an undocumented community member and my status as a graduate student, and they invited me to serve on a committee for a symposium being planned that same semester. It was one of the first times that I felt that my hyperdocumentation provided me access to being asked to contribute to an intellectual discussion based on my lived experience. I had organized and advocated at the institutional level and even at the state level in California. Having access to DACA facilitated a natural process of coming out of the shadows with my identity, which led to opportunities directly linked to my undocumented experience and newly attained DACAmented identity. That fall in 2012, the symposium changed my life and marked the beginning of a life's work that led to the long journey of research, academic training, and the publication of this book.

At the symposium, I had the opportunity to meet undocumented organizers whom I had heard about in my undergraduate years through social media networks. They were organizers who had stepped out of the shadows of the documentation conundrum rooted in illegalization to bring attention to the violence that undocumented communities face on a daily basis. My Myspace and Facebook feeds were filled with videos, images, digital artwork, music, and flyers informing undocumented communities of civil disobedience actions. There were several online platforms, portals, and chat groups formed by undocumented organizers inviting undocumented youth to participate and engage in activism. These online spaces were sites of critical consciousness formation for many undocumented youths like myself who had heard from our families that you must never reveal or document your undocumented status publicly.

The lineup of organizers who shared space at the symposium had been documenting their undocumented status publicly as an activist strategy for over a decade. Listening to the multiple organizers and academics at the symposium, I kept thinking of what it meant to document the undocumented experience in the United States. The use of documentation as a strategy to combat the denial of rights rooted in undocumented status inspired new directions for immigrant social movements that involved building collective political visibility toward the protection of marginalized groups. New technology like social media was used to construct public-facing messaging that documented the stories of undocumented communities, which otherwise were not told. The symposium of 2012 was only the beginning of an (un)documenting journey of research.

The endeavor to *(un)document* the historical importance and social contributions of undocumented youth movements (UYMs) in the United States motivated my master's thesis and my dissertation project and helped me land my first academic job at Arizona State University. Graduating with my doctoral degree in the spring of 2020 in the midst of the COVID-19 global pandemic was incredibly difficult, as I felt I did not get the opportunity to properly say my farewells and express my gratitude to communities in New Mexico that were part of my growth and development. The global pandemic impacted all aspects of daily life for most of humanity; it also served to highlight many societal injustices around race, gender, sexuality, and social class. Beginning my academic career in Arizona, which historically has been recognized as an anti-immigrant state, during the global pandemic has meant learning new abilities to navigate my DACAmented immigration status. Living in Arizona has reminded me of the importance of doing critical work at the service of our most marginalized immigrant community members. My journey to document the undocumented experience began with my life experience growing up undocumented in the United States, navigating graduate school, and beginning my academic career with the protection of DACA, and is now materialized in this book.

ACKNOWLEDGMENTS

T HIS BOOK HAS BEEN A journey, and as such, there are too many people to thank for being part of it. This book represents the majority of my adulthood and my formation of consciousness both as an intellectual and as an immigrant in the United States. I want to first thank the places where I have lived and that have shaped who I am. Moroleón, Guanajuato, in Mexico, is where I was born, and though I only lived there three years of my life, it is where my family's story begins. South Central Los Angeles was the place we migrated to and learned to call home. L.A. represents the pain and challenges of growing up undocumented, but also the resilience and strength of seeing beauty in the struggle. Albuquerque, New Mexico, provided the healing I needed with its blue sky, filled with cotton-like cumulus clouds that felt like a safe haven. Moving to Arizona during the COVID-19 global pandemic and a presidential election was not easy, but thanks to the many friends and community members who have helped my family and me find our niche, it has proven to be a place of professional and personal growth. Place shapes who we are, and this book has certainly been informed by the places I have grown to call home. And my family is my biggest inspiration and support for this book.

My beautiful daughter, Eliza Isabella Martínez Molina, was born when I was finishing my doctoral degree. My daughter has given me the strength and motivation to complete this book and begin my career as a professor. She has given me the inspiration to write with emphasis on contributing ideas to the world that can make it a better place for future generations. This book is a gift to my daughter to inspire her to fulfill her own intellectual aspirations. I am indebted to my beautiful partner, Adriana Molina, for her support and encouragement along my journey. Her love has given me the emotional and mental stability needed to complete the writing of this book. We have built a lovely family, which is my primary motivation in life.

I would like to thank my parents and family, because without their support, my education would have never been possible. Papá and Mamá, thanks for all the sacrifices and changes you both made for the well-being of our family. I know the road you both chose was not easy, but you have taught me to take on the world without fear and to take on all opportunities without reservations. To my sister, Karla, your life story is an inspiration to me and a motivation to continue to do what is best for our family. My nephew, Jayden Pedraza, and his cousin, Eliza, are the future of our family.

I would like to thank my mentor, role model, and advisor Dr. Irene Vásquez. Thanks to her guidance and support, my educational goals have been made possible. I thank her for all she has done for me and my family but also for all that she continues to do for all her students and community members. Her selfless dedication to education and to creating community has served as a model and inspiration.

I would like to thank my professor, mentor, and dissertation committee member Dr. Barbara Reyes for her mentorship and guidance over the years. Her passion for learning and teaching is something that has motivated me to become an educator. I will always be grateful for her time spent meeting with me to provide countless amounts of feedback and guidance along my project. I would also like to thank Dr. Antonio Tiongson and Dr. Ray Hernández-Durán for serving on my dissertation committee.

I would like to thank the Chicana and Chicano Studies (CCS) Department at the University of New Mexico (UNM). CCS has provided me with funding opportunities since I first arrived at UNM in the form of fellowships and teaching assistantships. Beyond funding opportunities, Chicana and Chicano Studies has served as an invaluable intellectual space where I grew as a scholar through the support and mentorship of several of the faculty and administrators in the department. I would also like to thank the Department of American Studies for providing me with the support to complete my doctoral degree. I received funding that helped support my doctoral degree completion. The guidance and mentorship I received from the faculty has shaped me into a better scholar today. In particular, I want to say thanks to Dr. Rebecca Schreiber in American Studies at UNM for believing in me since my arrival to the department and always pushing me to see the value of my work. My conversations with Dr. Schreiber will always be remembered and valued as informing a lot of my work.

At UNM, I would like to thank the Center for Regional Studies (CRS), the Southwest Hispanic Research Institute (SHRI), ENLACE New Mexico, UNM Student Affairs, and El Centro de la Raza for providing me with funding, mentorship, and guidance along my graduate degrees. These institutions demonstrated to me that there is an important academic community that cares about student and community growth. I would like to thank all of those friends and colleagues who have shown support along my journey of higher education. In particular, the Transnational Research Collective, composed of graduate students, was a formative experience in shaping my views on many of the themes that have gone into this book. I am indebted to the friendship of colegas in this group like María López-García, Alejandro Jara, Summer, Trisha Martínez, Froilan Orozco, Melisa García, and Moises Santos. Special thanks to Moises for reviewing and helping me edit several drafts of my book manuscript. I would also like to specially thank my brothers from Fi Iota Alfa Fraternidad Latina, for their friendship and the strength they have given me over the years. Friendship is crucial in accomplishing goals, and the community I have built is something that has helped me achieve my professional goals.

There are several creative and collective public-history projects that I helped create that shaped my views on the importance of bridging the gap between academia and community-based projects. The Humans of New Mexico collective was an oral history project composed of a collective of graduate students, undergraduate students, and community members. Thanks to Froilan Orozco, Christine Shell, Shradha Patel, and Georgia Rose-Elliott, and thanks to Dr. Vásquez, Dr. Reyes, Dr. Laura Belmonte, and Dr. Gabriel Meléndez for your mentorship and funding support of all of us in the collective. The UndocuTalks collective produced a podcast on immigrant topics often not discussed or covered by traditional media sources from the perspective of news, education, and culture. Thanks to my collective comrades: Froilan Orozco, Nancy Canales, Alejandro Mendiaz-Rivera, Cindy Nava, Mabel Arellanes, Melisa García, Moises Santos, and Elena Calderón. Finally, I also want to thank KUNM Radio in Albuquerque, New Mexico, for allowing me to be a volunteer contributor in the form of program host and show producer with the Raíces Collective.

Beyond UNM, I would also like to thank folks at my alma mater California State University, Dominguez Hills, in particular the Departments of History and of Chicana and Chicano Studies. Dr. Laura Talamante, Dr. Fawver, and Dr. Chris Monty served as inspirations to see myself in graduate school. Taking my first Chicana and Chicano studies course with Dr. Marisela Chávez served as an encouragement to learn about my own history and taught me the power of sharing it with others. I am a proud product of the CSU system, as it taught me the value of public education in the lives of diverse students and their families.

At Arizona State University (ASU), I have to start by thanking my home college, the College of Integrative Sciences and Arts (CISA), which has created a great space for me to start my career. Additionally, I want to thank some of the institutions that have helped with funding and encouragement during my time at ASU: the CISA, Knowledge Exchange for Resilience (KER), Institute for Humanities Research (IHR), and the Office of Veteran and Military Academic Engagement (OVMAE). Additionally, I want to acknowledge and thank the Humanities Institute (HI—formerly known as the Institute for Humanities Research) for awarding me a subvention grant for the indexing of my book. Finally, I want to thank the many colleagues and friends at ASU who have provided me the courage to grow as a scholar and who remind me of the importance of the work we do. Beyond ASU, a special shout-out to the community of Chandler, Arizona, which has welcomed my family and me and has made us feel at home.

I want to thank the entire team at the University of Arizona Press, who believed in my book project and saw fitting to include it as the first book in the Border Visions series. I want to give special thanks to editor-in-chief Kristen Buckles, who always followed up and made sure the project stayed on course toward publication. To the series editors of Border Visions, Yvette Saavedra and Vanessa Fonseca-Chávez, thank you for believing in the impact my work can have and for your close reading and feedback on my work. I have no doubt that Border Visions will become a reference point for all books border-related and a home to advancing critical conversations about borderlands. Additionally, I would like to thank copyeditor Matt Gleeson for his detailed and diligent attention to my manuscript.

Last but not least, this book would not have been possible without the bravery and actions of the organizers whose case studies are central. I want to thank all of those named, and those who are not named but have been part of the immigrant rights struggle. Your commitment to ensuring we imagine a better world served as the inspiration needed to write this book.

ILLEGALIZED

INTRODUCTION

The Rise of Undocumented Youth Movements

We knew that there was support for us that fit the criteria
of a DREAMer.
—ISAAC BARRERA, 2012

O N MAY 1, 2006, ON International Workers' Day, undocumented communities across the United States came out of the shadows in the millions to demand immigration reform and to protest anti-immigrant legislation proposed at the federal level. Five months earlier, in December 2005, H.R. 4437, dubbed the "Border Protection, Antiterrorism, and Illegal Immigration Control Act of 2005," aimed like many other predecessors to militarize the borderlands as a direct response to the 9/11 attacks just four years earlier. However, this new piece of proposed federal legislation attempted to move the borderlands to the interior of the country by funding and extending programs to detect, detain, and deport undocumented immigrants. Undocumented communities, mixed-status families, and allies recognized that if this piece of legislation passed, it could set in motion a witch-hunt atmosphere. Ethnic and multilingual radio stations became the vehicle by which people mobilized to spread word in households, car rides, and community spaces about massive public marches happening across major cities in the United States. Urban centers like Los Angeles, Chicago, New York, Las Vegas, Dallas, and Phoenix witnessed a wave of white T-shirts on diverse bodies waving multinational flags in a phenomenon many journalists described as "The Giant Awakens."[1]

May in Los Angeles features a bright, full-bodied sun shining across the concrete jungle. The skyscrapers cast a much-needed man-made shade for the millions of people who had taken over the streets of downtown Los Angeles by noontime. I remember exiting the Metro Blue Line station in downtown Los Angeles to what felt like the hum from a beehive coming from every direction. The energy from the crowd was contagious and motivating, but simultaneously disorienting and chaotic. Up to this point, as with many other fellow undocumented community members, my activism had been relegated to the shadows of traditional forms of civic engagement. Historically, immigrant communities were told by society and even long-standing activist organizations to not call attention to themselves, as their undocumented status placed them in a precarious position. However, the May Day immigrant rights marches, which became widely known and recognized as an annual event after 2006, flipped the narrative of undocumented immigrants remaining in the shadows and set in motion new possibilities outside of civic-engagement modes of organizing.

In the course of my education, in terms of my identity and politics as an undocumented scholar, I have come to value the ability to look back at pivotal moments in the history of undocumented youth social movements that have changed the ways in which immigrant communities are discussed in society and allowed people to see undocumented communities as knowledge producers. Situating my own positionality as an *undocu-scholar*—that is, someone who identifies as undocumented and as a scholar—is important in this research on undocumented youth activists.[2] I define undocu-scholars as individuals who are conducting research, writing, documenting, producing artwork, and developing public projects based on the lived experiences of being undocumented or formerly undocumented. As such, the history that I am charting in my research represents my experience in the United States as an immigrant with no status for the majority of my life, and recently with protection under DACA that opened the doors to pursuing a career in academia. Thus, my positionality is a central component in the analysis I perform in my research and case studies.

Like other undocumented youth of my time in the mid-2000s for me the May Day peaceful marches represented new possibilities in mobilizing for immigrant rights. For generations undocumented youth were subjugated to a vision of model citizens who were deemed worthy to the extent that they had potential in educational realms and could assimilate into American values. Politicians had begun categorizing undocumented youth as "DREAMers," positioning them in terms of a future that was promised or always deferred. Young people were seen for the future prospects they could offer the state. So the offering of a pathway to inclusion rested on the expected deliverables that made them desirable in the first place. However, DREAMers only constituted a small percentage of the larger undocumented immigrant population.

Undocumented youth activists began creating local, state, and national organizations a few years after the 2006/7 May Day marches with the aim of changing the discourse around immigrant rights in the United States. In doing so, these activists realized that it was not enough to fight for the incorporation of a small minority, and that they needed to exchange the cultural capital gained from the visibility of the DREAMer movement at the national level for the ability to advocate for the larger undocumented immigrant population. The beginning of the twenty-first century, when undocumented youth movements grew to prominence, also coincided with high numbers of detentions in the interior of the country, an increase in deportation numbers, and the separation of mixed-status families across borders. Undocumented youth would address the issues of detention, deportation, and family separation head-on in direct forms of activism. This book captures some of the stories of activism that changed how immigrant rights are discussed in the United States.

Illegalized: Undocumented Youth Movements in the United States departs from the idea of undocumented youth movements as a single linear, homogeneous, or united movement.[3] Instead, the case studies in the book characterize undocumented youth movements (UYMs) as a series of movements that are heterogeneous, diverse, and often contradictory, or that have frictions and limitations.[4] Additionally, UYMs never occurred in a linear progression, as history rarely occurs in a continuum; rather, I argue that the case studies in the book are events that represent assemblages of organizational performances and showcase important ruptures related to the U.S. immigration system and its treatment of undocumented immigrants. One such rupture is the disruption and interrogation of the "DREAMer" identity or narrative. Another rupture is represented by an illegalized framework, which allows for the exploration of case studies in which undocumented youth activists take their activism to sites often kept in the shadows by the U.S. state. This book takes an (un)documenting approach—that is, it builds an archive that documents the activism of undocumented immigrant populations who resist violent forms of repression such as detention, deportation, and family separation. Assembling (un)documents represents social imaginaries in which undocumented youth organizers offer a discourse alternative to that of official U.S. immigration systems of policing and control.

ARE YOU A DREAMER? A BRIEF LEGAL AND HISTORICAL OVERVIEW OF UNDOCUMENTED YOUTH

When I began graduate school as an undocumented student at the University of New Mexico (UNM) in 2012, telling people that I was a DREAMer was the easy way to get out of the uncomfortable and nerve-wracking experience of revealing my immigration status. Using the term "DREAMer" made me legible to educational institutions and ended in the favorable outcome of being recognized as a member of the university. I used the identifier to appease others, consciously, or unconsciously at times. Navigating my undergraduate experience as an undocumented student with no status or financial aid was quite an undertaking, but thanks to the generations of advocates and undocumented activists who organized and pressured the political system, undocumented youth like myself in the 2000s had become recognized political subjects with cultural capital and political clout in spaces like university campuses.[5]

When I speak about "undocumented youth," you might be wondering: Who does that include? Who qualifies as an undocumented youth? And how did this particular group become a visible and prominent political subject? Politicians and journalists have spent significant time trying to define undocumented youth in bordered ways. For decades, sociologists have been at the forefront of identifying and studying undocumented youth, using the term "the 1.5 generation" to identify immigrant children who arrived in the United States at a young age and grew up there during formative periods of their lives.[6] Many immigrant youth entered the country alongside their parents or family members. Some used a visa and stayed after its expiration. Others came into the country without documentation. Both of these scenarios lead to political subjugation in the form of being identified as *undocumented*—used to identify immigrants who do not have a lawful presence or the authority to be in the United States. Since this 1.5 generation became undocumented during childhood, mainstream society crafted the narrative that their undocumented status should be deemed no fault of their own because they were not capable of making the choice at the time. But the parents were the ones who consciously made the choice to bring them to the United States. As such, parents or adults were to blame according to mainstream societal narratives being formed as early as the 1980s. Parents, guardians, and family members have been criminalized. These became the parameters for political narratives behind attempts to craft legislation offering relief for undocumented youth while excluding nonyouth as unfit for protection from the state. This narrative has been formed over time in political, legal, and societal spaces.

In 1982, the landmark case *Plyler v. Doe* granted immigrant populations access to the K–12 public education system in the United States regardless of immigration status.[7] Undocumented youth were recognized as a political category and provided human rights including education and health care. In 1985, California became the site of another landmark case, *Leticia "A" v. The Board of Regents of the University of California*, in which undocumented students began pushing and advocating for educational rights—for in-state tuition and access to equitable resident resources.[8] In the *Leticia "A"* case, we see that media and education outlets as early as the 1980s were playing to the "good immigrant" narrative in which education was a merit scale for inclusion and parents or nonyouth without education were criminalized, even if passively, in rhetoric.[9] The fight for access to in-state tuition for undocumented students in California continued into the 1990s, with political figures like Governor Pete Wilson operating as gatekeepers, fighting to deny undocumented students access to higher education.[10] These two cases highlight not only undocumented youth's activity in organizing for decades leading up to the period of heightened visibility in the 2000s but also the media's formation of the political categorization of immigrant students.

FROM INDIRECT TO DIRECT FORMS OF ACTIVISM

During my undergraduate years, in the mid-2000s I had already participated in national marches in Los Angeles and done organizing advocating for undocumented students in statewide and institutional spaces. Most of the activism I was exposed to had to do with civic engagement—that is, working within the political structure or institutional framework to enact political change. Political scientist and law scholar Bernard E. Harcourt outlines that political actors who remain closest to the prescribed notions of normative behavior are determined to be "civil." Harcourt goes on to state that those who move away from borders or rules of "civility" get marked as "uncivil."[11] Growing up undocumented in the United States and participating in activism represented an inherent risk; as such, I initially chose to participate through approaches that stayed in a "civil" lane in order to not call attention to myself or my family. However, during my first semester as a graduate student at UNM in 2012, I was given the opportunity to join an organizing committee across academic units putting together a symposium on immigrant rights that would expose me to new approaches to organizing. The symposium was titled "Everyday Practices of Popular Power: Art, Media, Immigration," held at UNM on November 9, 2012.[12] It highlighted the innovative use of art, media, and civil disobedience among immigrant rights organizers throughout the United States. The event brought together immigrant youth organizers, *artivists*, and scholars who were actively engaged as advocates and activists for undocumented communities.[13]

The symposium welcomed national organizers who had participated in activism for over a decade with the intention of moving immigrant rights organizing from indirect forms of activism to direct forms rooted in civil disobedience. I draw on the definitions provided by Vélez et al. (2008) of *indirect forms of activism*: "a political act that expresses critical concern, but do[es] not focus on attempting [to] physically challenge public institutions and/or their actors." Subsequently, *direct forms of activism* are defined as "overt political acts of protest that often involve the physical body as a vehicle for protest, including walkouts, sit-ins, or wearing clothing with political slogans that represent the movement."[14] Harcourt's understanding of "civil" pairs well with the definition provided by Vélez et al. of indirect forms of activism in that concern is expressed over a political issue, but the body is not used to stage the direct kind of protest that can cause somebody to be categorized as "uncivil." The undocumented youth activists who participated in the symposium advocated for the use of direct forms of activism as a strategy of placing public pressure on the U.S. immigration system.

The year 2012 became highly significant for undocumented youth movements. Activism by undocumented youth had been going on for a decade, which resulted in substantial political pressure on President Barack Obama's administration to implement the Deferred Action for Childhood Arrivals (DACA) program on June 12, 2012.[15] DACA offered qualifying undocumented youth two important things: a level of protection from deportation and a work permit. Since DACA passed a few months prior to the "Everyday Practices of Popular Power" symposium at UNM, a question shared by the organizers and the participants of the symposium was, How would the movement advance post-DACA?

There were a few resounding messages shared across most of the symposium panelists and participants. First, DACA had only been a temporary "Band-Aid" solution to much larger issues of immigration. Second, DACA only included a small part of the estimated undocumented immigrant population of ten million.[16] And finally, organizers declared that the cultural capital and temporary protected status earned through DACA needed to be used politically by undocumented youth to advocate for the immigrant populations that continued to be marginalized and had not been included for protection.

While DACA is not perfect, it has come to embody much of the debate surrounding legal protections for undocumented youth in the twenty-first century, including age parameters around the definition of youth. For the purposes of this book, undocumented immigrant youth are considered to be those between about age fifteen (the time of entering adulthood) and age thirty. The categorization of youth is typically debated and discussed distinctly by different scholars and fields. In the case of undocumented youth and their rise to political visibility, the category of "youth" has been marked by federal programs like the Dream Act and DACA. While *Illegalized: Undocumented Youth Movements in the United States* offers important critiques of the Dream Act, DACA, and the DREAMer narrative, the book uses the demographic age that is defined as "youth" by federal programs to explore the ways in which the political subjugation of immigrant youth under the DREAMer narrative grew in political visibility after the 2000s.

During the mid-2000s, the scale and scope of immigrant rights organizing expanded in the United States. Immigrant youth played an influential role in changing the discourse and strategies employed to decry punitive legislation in the country. Rather than illustrating a set of shared strategies and a consensus of opinions about the purposes and outcomes of immigrant rights organizing, the UNM symposium revealed the heterogeneity among participants in twenty-first-century UYMs. Several symposium participants challenged the notion of seeking inclusion in the legal framework of the United States and called attention to the larger issue of the intersection between human rights, civil rights, and inclusivity of their intersectional identities.

(UN)DOCUMENTING: THE ACT OF DOCUMENTING THE UNDOCUMENTED

My beginnings as a scholar at the University of New Mexico involved crossing paths with the activists in the book's case studies, including Jonathan Perez, Isaac Barrera, and members of the National Immigrant Youth Alliance (NIYA), during the UNM "Everyday Practices of Popular Power: Art, Media,

Immigration" symposium in 2012. Meeting these activists changed my life in a significant way and filled me with a sense of a responsibility to document and write about undocumented youth activism from an *illegalized* perspective—that is, to write from the margins and at the service of the undocumented communities who are most marginalized. Being an undocu-scholar holds this responsibility and sense of urgency.

I add to the theorization of the term *illegalized* as an identifier that aims to highlight the process by which immigrant bodies are made illegal through political systems, legal systems, and social constructions. I heed the call of Nicholas De Genova and Nathalie Peutz when they ask scholars "to engage politically and theoretically in renewed ways with questions of *freedom*, in one of its most basic and meaningful senses: the freedom to traverse spaces and to make a place for oneself in the world," underscoring the ways in which our scholarship is focused on the restriction of mobility and the categorization of immigrant bodies as illegal.[17] De Genova and Peutz go on to define "illegality" as "official 'exclusion,' that inflames the irrepressible desire and demand for undocumented migrants as a highly exploitable workforce—and thus ensures their enthusiastic importation and subordinate incorporation."[18]

I contribute to the scholarship of illegality by using a new methodology that I call an *(un)documenting* approach. When the UNM symposium culminated in 2012, I asked myself: What does it mean for undocumented youth organizers to document their activism? What does it mean for me as a scholar who grew up undocumented to document the experience of undocumented populations in the United States? In answering those questions, I kept going back to the archives produced by the activism that undocumented youth at the UNM symposium brought up in their discussions.

The archival turn in the humanities and social science has been described as a move toward challenging the production of archives as an authoritarian form of producing historical narratives.[19] Michel Foucault offers a definition of the archive as "the system that governs the appearance of statements as unique events"—that is, gathered primary sources that an interpreter or scholar deems to be "unique events."[20] Foucault begins to grapple with the possibilities and limitations of defining an archive through his analysis of *archaeology*—that is, an attempt to make sense of the multiple ways in which Western societies organized, constituted, and regarded knowledge production. The archive becomes a tool for societies and governments to harness power through narrative formations by controlling the production of the archive. Foucault argued that control of the archive or records represented authority over the narrative. French theorist Jacques Derrida's *Archive Fever* (1996) began offering critiques of archives in relation to what scholars chose to include or exclude, forming a narrative. For Derrida, the control of narrative was constituted by what was included in official records or documents.[21] In this way, we see that scholars challenging archival productions are interested in accounting for gaps, silences, and omissions in narratives told over time.

Undocumented youth activists wanted to highlight the irony of documentation. On one hand, they wanted to place their undocumented status front and center alongside the broader discussion of immigrant rights. On the other hand, undocumented status is defined by lack of "papers" or documentation, which is a paradox considering the state's efforts to document an immigrant's absence of documentation.[22] John-Michael Rivera's work speaks to this contradiction when he states, "The person is sin papeles, but is simultaneously an inscribed object of government authority."[23] Rivera's work (2021) produces an important base for my methodological use of (un)documenting to think through the desire of postcolonial power structures that use documentation as a form of governmentality. Illegalization of immigrants is represented in the social, political, and rhetorical way in which they are documented. My methodological approach of (un)documenting takes advantage of the fact that undocumented youth used documentation both as an activist strategy and as an alternative to the state's narrative. The alternative narrative presented by these undocumented youth created the possibility of producing a new social imaginary.

Illegalized: Undocumented Youth Movements in the United States is an assemblage of temporalities and movements that does not follow ideas of history as a continuum but rather gathers case studies for theoretical interests and disruption, and offers decolonial opportunities for possible visions of future world making. Emma Pérez conceives of the *decolonial imaginary* as a site or a third space of consciousness from which marginalized communities offer alternative ways of existing outside of traditional societal norms.[24] Building on Anzaldúa's and Pérez's works, Alicia Schmidt Camacho develops her concept of *migrant imaginaries*, which aims to reconfigure the borderlands as a unique and empowering space through the analysis of literature, music, artwork, and activism.[25] Inspired by the work of Anzaldúa, Pérez, and Schmidt Camacho, my (un)documenting methodology captures the assemblage of digital archives from undocumented youth's activism as sites where critical consciousness rooted in an illegalized political identity is produced.

This site of critical consciousness is what Emma Pérez refers to as a *third space* or what Gloria Anzaldúa refers to as la facultad. La facultad involves an alternate way of seeing social phenomena beyond what is at the surface level, an ability to interpret structural analysis based on lived experience. Undocumented youth began activating their own facultad from their lived realities and organizing knowledge to attempt to subvert the lies produced in narrative form by the state. The official narrative of the U.S. government under Presidents George W. Bush and Barack Obama in the 2000s was that the country was only focused on deporting criminals and those considered to be a threat. However, undocumented immigrant communities knew otherwise, because they were witnessing detentions and deportations of family and community members at an alarmingly heightened rate. Undocumented youth activists knew this to be the case because of their local, state, and national organizing efforts. Many of the undocumented youth activists who participated in the UNM symposium mentioned that they knew these facts, but how could they prove them? They needed to document them. They needed to build counterarguments to the official narrative of the state. They needed to build a counterarchive.

Here is Jonathan Perez's statement at the UNM symposium speaking to the effect of strategizing to build a counterarchive:

> The statements that they [the government] say is that they don't get involved in these type of cases; DREAMers or students or people with no criminal record. We obviously knew through all of our communities that that wasn't true. We knew people like us were being deported because we would take on campaigns to try and stop them. We knew, and so we wanted to create, I guess, a scenario where that can be seen in the public sphere.[26]

The first part of Jonathan's statement above points to the building of the official narrative of the state, which is that they do not deport "DREAMers or students or people with no criminal record." Undocumented youth activists wanted to document that lie. Jonathan's statement "we wanted to create . . . a scenario where that can be seen in the public sphere" speaks to the recognition of building a counterarchive that offered an alternate narrative with factual evidence contradicting the state's narratives. This was crucial to building public memory.

My work draws on archival traditions to craft my (un)documenting methodology and analyzes the need for undocumented youth to cultivate new public memories while exposing the *counterfeit narratives* told by the state.[27] I see the assemblage of performances or actions by undocumented youth as challenging power structures, not only in societal representations but also internally within the broader immigrant rights movements. I draw on a genealogy of literature interested in the ways in which social movements and minorities within them used archival documentation strategies to document their actions and to exert changes both internally within their movements and externally in society.[28] More specifically, I am interested in the way in which those without documents document themselves and their movements' actions. I am in conversation with scholars who warn about the complexities of the term "undocumented" and the paradoxes, limitations, and challenges related to documentation and immigration status.[29] My use of an (un)documenting methodology aims to highlight the archival production of UYMs as creating knowledge forms and narratives alternative to state-based forms of inclusion.

The "document" in "(un)document" points to the need to create a distinctive archival process that goes against the grain of traditional academic methodologies and situates undocumented youth themselves as knowledge producers and undocumented youth movements as producers of new archives. The "un" in "(un)document" represents aims to break away from colonial and neoliberal paradigms that undocumented communities are expected to hold. Furthermore, the "un" points to processes of unlearning or undoing normative constructions of what undocumented immigrants are expected to perform, the spaces they are to (un)occupy, and the labor they are limited to. The parentheses around the "(un)" are figurative and real representations of the duality between factual limitations on immigrant rights organizing and borders that are challenged by the activism of undocumented youth. To (un)document as a methodology is to document the ways undocumented youth challenge prescribed identities like the "DREAMer narrative."

As undocumented youth move away from identifiers like "DREAMer" related to "good immigrant" narratives and ideologies of inclusion in the "American Dream," I argue that they have begun forming new identities embodied in the direct forms of organizing that compose the archive assemblage of this book. In this sense, I am interested in recovering the ways in which undocumented youth construct multiple archival materials from direct forms of activism. The archival records by undocumented activists aim to record instances of state violence against immigrant populations. As such, I analyze the multiple ways in which these activists seek to subvert power relations by organizing around their illegal status as an identity marker, documenting state violence, and redirecting the label of "illegal" onto the state for its violations of immigrant populations' human rights. *Illegalized: Undocumented Youth Movements in the United States* shows undocumented youth organizers producing new records that move state violence out of the shadows and into the public realm. The materials left behind by the direct actions produce a record or digital archive, which I set out to analyze, in addition to interpreting the forms and strategies of their performance as an archival assemblage as well.

I take a cue from Diana Taylor's *The Archive and the Repertoire* (2003), where she redirects scholars toward decolonizing written archives by making them less authoritative and looking at other forms of archival production such as performance—or in my case studies here, social movement organizing strategies—in what she terms the *repertoire*.[30] The case studies in *Illegalized: Undocumented Youth Movements in the United States* represent undocumented youth's repertoire of physical/digital archives, and I include a visual analysis of their performance. Taylor declares, "Civic disobedience, resistance, citizenship, gender, ethnicity, and sexual identity . . . are rehearsed and performed daily in the public sphere. To understand these as performance suggests that performance also functions as an epistemology."[31] The repetition of these epistemological practices is what Taylor identifies as "embodied practice," which produces multiple pieces of the archives through bodily actions that are assembled into a "whole" or complete document. As such, the chapters of this book implement a combination of textual and visual analysis methodologies, doing a close reading of the transcripts and intimately analyzing the digital performance recorded in the case studies. Digital collections across media platforms have been assembled to offer a wide analysis of the knowledge produced by undocumented youth movements through organizers' narratives.

Social movements are social phenomena in which a group of people come together toward a set of common goals. In this case, I establish that undocumented youth in the 2000s initially came together to make efforts at working within the political system to pass immigration policy, and when that proved impossible, the shared goal was to escalate their organizing efforts toward direct forms of activism. Demonstrating what sociologists Francesca Polletta and James Jasper refer to as "collective identity," undocumented youth began organizing in direct forms while upholding an illegalized identity that showcased the processes by which immigrant populations are rendered illegal.[32] Finally, I speak of movements in the plural and focus my attention on case studies of activism to highlight that social movement scholars are moving away from analyzing mass organizing efforts as single movements or movements with unified fronts; rather, we have to think of organizing efforts as heterogeneous, contributing to and advancing toward multiple fronts and directions.

The archival assemblages gathered in *Illegalized: Undocumented Youth Movements in the United States* offer alternative directions for immigrant rights organizing as well as pedagogical underpinnings for documenting the undocumented experience that help create a social imaginary. As philosopher Maurizio Ferraris showed in his work *Documentality* (2013), where he argues the necessity of leaving "traces" of lived experiences, documents have the ability to birth new social imaginaries.[33] For undocumented youth activists, the social imaginary produced in their documented actions represented not only questioning their subjugated status but also imagining an alternate world without the governmentality of the immigration system. Writing about social imaginaries as an undocu-scholar represents building community among scholars coming from similar and distinct perspectives to form new methods and approaches to writing about undocumented communities in a push to build undocumented youth studies.

MAPPING UNDOCUMENTED YOUTH STUDIES

Much of the scholarship created to capture the rise of undocumented youth social movements is associated with a DREAMer identity. As undocumented scholars grow in number and visibility, the aim is to use our disenfranchised experience to produce pedagogical forms of knowledge that are critical of the scholarship used to study immigrant populations. As a self-identified undocu-scholar, I subscribe to the theoretical formations and field development of what is being identified as undocumented youth studies. In their foundational anthology *We Are Not Dreamers* (2020), featuring authors who include undocumented, DACAmented, and formerly undocumented scholars and organizers, editors Leisy J. Abrego and Genevieve Negrón-Gonzales state a fundamental basis for undocumented studies: "The voices of researchers whose lives are shaped by the contemporary production of 'illegality' are critical in understanding the varied and complex ways that citizenship status shapes lived experiences."[34]

The *We Are Not Dreamers* anthology served to bring together diverse perspectives from immigrant scholars who generated four defining key characteristics of undocumented youth studies. One, the field acknowledges that access to higher education is a privilege but also produces a relationship that undocumented youth need to be critical of in their analysis. Second, it recognizes the heterogeneous nature of the 1.5 generation.[35] Third, it is necessary to recognize "life stages" that produce varied experiences for undocumented youth. Finally, there is a strong critique of the DREAMer narrative on ideological and political grounds.[36] As such, *Illegalized: Undocumented Youth Movements in the United States* aims to include foundational works from interdisciplinary fields that have contributed to the study of undocumented youth in the United States for decades, alongside new voices from undocumented scholars carving out space in the formation of undocumented youth studies.

The work by undocu-scholars has revolved around documenting the ways in which illegalization under neoliberalism has operated differently across undocumented communities.[37] That is, undocumented youth who demonstrate merit or worthiness according to neoliberal modes of value are offered certain levels of protection while the majority of the undocumented immigrant populations are not. Gabrielle Cabrera's work (2020) draws on women-of-color methodologies to disrupt the cultural capital that undocumented youth have gained through DREAMer narratives, which universities in liberal states like California have tapped into to embed their "diversity" work.[38] However, Cabrera's work warns that said narratives only further neoliberal structures on the part of the university and do not typically result in structural change for undocumented students and their families.[39] Joel Sati's work (2020) emphasizes moving the immigrant rights discourse past "appearances" and into structural societal changes that include the majority of the immigrant population and not just a "legitimate" few. For Sati, DREAMer activism produces an appearance that might have resulted in visibility for some immigrants, but not for a majority of the diverse community. He warns, "Recognizing how we can move from the appearance of legitimacy to actual legitimacy is critically important for those in immigrant rights."[40] Finally, Carolina Valdivia's work on the vulnerability that mixed-status families face in certain political climates, which pays attention to local community politics, provides an important direction for undocumented studies to focus our attention.[41]

Similarly, Carlos Aguilar's work "Undocumented Critical Theory" (2019) argues that while there has been significant accumulation of privilege, public visibility, and cultural capital by undocumented youth through actions like DACA, we must remember that "different experiences of liminality translate into different experiences of reality" and avoid grouping undocumented immigrant experiences as homogeneous.[42] Aguilar highlights that undocumented status in relation to legality varies according to multiple factors in an immigrant's lived experience. Undocumented youth who have been able to participate in higher education opportunities recognize that their narratives can open doors, but they are also beginning to question the position of the university and institutional integration in relation to broader undocumented communities.

Undocu-scholars in the realms of activism, literature, poetry, academia, and other fields have begun to publish their work in order to add to the theorization of, creative representations of, and discussions about undocumented immigrant communities based on our own lived experiences. The book *Eclipse of Dreams* (2020) serves as an example of undocumented scholars and organizers, along with allies, coming together to interrogate the DREAMer narrative in the context of the United States and its relationship to the Americas. The authors, a combination of activists and scholars, state that their intention is to pose a "challenge to this narrative of the 'good citizen,' the good neoliberal subject who embodies the values that keep the myth of the American Dream alive."[43] The book focuses on the term "DREAMer" in relation to youth's innocence and how it aimed to challenge the mainstream negative labeling of immigrants as "illegal." *Eclipse of Dreams* highlights the importance of interrogating the transnational elements of concepts like the DREAMer narrative, the good citizen, the model immigrant, and the American Dream, which are embedded in neoliberal systems.[44]

Undocumented youth from various walks of life and fields began contributing to intellectual and action-driven works that, like activism, aimed at pushing the discussions from normative spaces into spaces that tried to be inclusive of the larger undocumented immigrant population. Journalists like Jose Antonio Vargas and Karla Cornejo Villavicencio also write in their memoirs about navigating corporate U.S. spaces with the pressure of being undocumented and the need to come out to share their stories with the hope of serving as inspirations to other undocumented immigrant youth.[45] Communities from Asian to Latinx struggle to define and contest migration narratives. Vargas's and Cornejo Villavicencio's memoirs and stories also serve as a platform for rejecting the "model minority" trope that undocumented youth are placed in by society, often beginning with our own parents and families.

Just as activism requires the carving out of spaces in which to carry out actions and experiment with pedagogical directions for the crafting of new social imaginaries, undocu-scholars have also been at the forefront of carving out literary spaces through commercial, local, and independent publishers. Examples of this are the groundbreaking anthology *Somewhere We Are Human* (2022), edited by writer Reyna Grande and artivist Sonia Guiñansaca, which includes a combination of literary writers, artivists, poets, and scholars.[46] The anthology asks its contributors to wrestle with the paradox of the American Dream, which pushes undocumented immigrant populations beyond human limits to exist, survive, and thrive in a U.S. society plagued with contradictions in its treatment of immigrants. Similarly, the anthology *Dreaming Out Loud* (2022) serves as a call to action for undocumented immigrants to search for their own voices and speak up against the multiple injustices faced in U.S. society, with the support of national, state, and local networks created by immigrants.[47] These works represent the importance of documenting a literary tradition and forming an intellectual base for future undocumented immigrants in generations to come.

Digital humanities and media studies have been natural fields for immigration scholars to explore because of the use of online platforms as a medium for storytelling. First, Marsha Kinder's work (1993) introduced the term *transmedia narratives* to media studies audiences.[48] Kinder's work offers a study of how children and youth began engaging with popular-culture media productions to control, manage, and reproduce new meanings from the assemblages of multiple media materials. Building on Kinder's work, Henry Jenkins goes on to define transmedia as "the flow of content across multiple media platforms."[49] Specific to undocumented youth, media scholars like Sasha Costanza-Chock and Arely Zimmerman have added to the literature using the Latin American tradition of testimonio through transmedia narratives to engage immigrant communities in direct forms of activism.[50] In particular, Costanza-Chock adds to scholarship on transmedia narratives with their conceptualization of "transmedia mobilizations," which they say "[mark] a transition in the role of movement communication from content creation to aggregation, curation, remixing and recirculation of rich media texts through networked movement formations."[51] Costanza-Chock's transmedia mobilizations provide a direct link between online storytelling and the interest it generates in mobilizing immigrant communities into activism.

My (un)documenting methodology adds to the literature in media studies as well as social movement scholarship in conceiving of transmedia narratives as testimonios shared across multiple platforms for the purpose of rallying others to action but also as an assembled archival repertoire that aims to impact public memory. In her book *The Undocumented Everyday* (2018), American studies scholar Rebecca Schreiber uses a "counter-documentation" approach that draws on examples of artistic self-representation in photographs, documentaries, literature, and artwork to explore the ways in which undocumented immigrants wanted to "challenge anti-immigrant discourses and policies that associated undocumented immigrants with criminality and illegality within locations in which they were limited from participating in aspects of everyday life."[52] Schreiber's "counter-documentation" analyzes aesthetics and performance as a way in which immigrants challenge the immigration system in the United States. My book uses an (un)documenting methodology, extending Schreiber's analysis into the realm of social movements by exploring the relationship between undocumented youth activists and the U.S. immigration system in terms of documentation and power.

The case studies in this book represent both textual exploration of the written digital archive and visual-studies exploration of the performative record produced by the actions of undocumented organizers. The digital archival materials explored in *Illegalized: Undocumented Youth Movements in the United States* consist of, but are not limited to, videos, photographs, audio, interviews, podcasts, social media content, artwork, media coverage, blogs, journalistic pieces, poetry, memoirs, music, and academic materials. Performance studies scholar Diana Taylor reminds us that "embodied practice" consists of everyday actions assembled into legible forms of knowledge that produce a "whole."[53] Each chapter in this book highlights distinct strategies undocumented youth activists use as "embodied practices" to build an archival methodology I call (un)documenting—highlighting power relations between the immigration system and undocumented immigrant communities.

CHAPTER DESCRIPTIONS

Each one of the chapters here represents a watershed moment in the history of undocumented youth movements that changed how mainstream society talks about immigrant rights in the United States. The case studies selected for discussion in this book highlight particular assemblages and performances of direct forms of activism using the body to call attention to particular injustices plaguing undocumented communities across the United States. Read collectively, the actions analyzed in the chapters produce an assemblage of UYMs in the twenty-first century. Individually, each chapter represents physical sites, figurative spaces, or locations within the social imaginary produced by undocumented youth activism. Ultimately, each assemblage takes on the following themes, respectively: challenging civility politics in the immigrant rights movement and moving toward direct action; challenging detention centers as sites of violence; challenging the restriction of mobility inherent in undocumented status; and centering joy in social movements for undocumented immigrant communities.

Chapter 1, "Assembling the Power of Direct Action," situates the period in which UYMs grew to prominence in the twenty-first century through Elvira Arellano's story. Elvira was a single mother, migrant, deportee, and asylum advocate who became an international symbol between 2006 and 2007. Elvira took sanctuary in a church in Chicago, Illinois, after being served a detention notice. Her dual symbolic action as both a lawbreaker and a human rights advocate magnified her representation as an immigrant woman of color who defiantly navigated state pressures. In this chapter, I offer a historiography of the broader immigrant rights movements (IRMs) in which Elvira became a symbol through the birth of the new sanctuary movements after 2007. I argue that Elvira's story is crucial in telling the story of UYMs because she represents the many generations of undocumented organizers who fought for immigrant rights but, because they did not fit the mold of the DREAMer narrative, were not protected. Additionally, Elvira's story reveals the multifold manners in which, ideologically and politically, the immigration system in the United States steadily grew as a neoliberal project aimed at producing global capital connections while restricting people's mobility and increasing deportation numbers from the interior of the country. Elvira's story situates the time in which undocumented organizers began to imagine alternative social imaginaries rooted in direct forms of activism.

Chapter 2, "From Detention to Infiltration: Illegalized Assemblages," situates the social imaginary inside of a detention center. In this chapter, I argue that the post–Dream Act era (after 2010) represents a critical moment in which undocumented youth organizers used their *bodies* in civil disobedience protest in strategic *spaces*. Chapter 2 focuses on the first detention center infiltration action by undocumented youth activists in 2011. Jonathan Perez and Isaac Barrera decided to infiltrate a detention center in Louisiana and risk deportation with the aim of bringing news to the outside world on the *illegalized* conditions that exist inside of U.S. detention centers. This was an unprecedented moment in the history of UYMs considering that public knowledge about the treatment of immigrant populations inside detention centers was not as common as it is now in 2023, when I am completing this book. The civil disobedience performed by Jonathan and Isaac was successful in two important ways: it documented and exposed the violence experienced by undocumented populations inside detention centers, and it added to the repertoire of what was possible within UYMs. I use a visual analysis methodology to examine the primary-source video that captured Jonathan and Isaac's infiltration action. Additionally, I use textual analysis in close readings of post-release interviews with Jonathan and Isaac that highlight their experience while in detention. I read Jonathan and Isaac's action as parallel to that of other undocumented youth organizers who were escalating their public visibility and using their cultural capital as a way of calling attention to the management of immigrant bodies.

In chapter 3, "Illegal Borders: Immigrant Youth Challenging Detention, Deportation, and Family Separation," undocumented youth take the social imaginary to the physical location of the Mexico-U.S. border to stage a transnational action.[54] In this chapter, I argue that the organizing by the National Immigrant Youth Alliance (NIYA) exposed the multiple ways in which the immigration system separates families across different nation-states. The chapter focuses on the #BringThemHome campaign organized by NIYA during the summer of 2013, consisting of two phases. Phase one entailed six individuals who chose to return to Mexico to challenge family separation and the restriction of mobility for immigrants. During this action, NIYA decided to incorporate three youths living in Mexico who had previously been undocumented youth in the United States. The stories of these three youths added a new dimension to the action in terms of mobility—they represented the narratives of a growing transnational population of deportees and self-returned youth. As such, the chapter provides brief historical context and addresses new political identity formations resulting from punitive immigration policies and deportations: *deportees and* retornadxs. Phase one ended when the organizers marched across an official point of entry at the Mexico-U.S. border in Nogales, Arizona, and asked to be admitted back into the United States with humanitarian parole. The question on the minds of the organizers, their allied supporters, and the media was: Would they be allowed entry into the United States?

If they were allowed entry, the second phase of the #BringThemHome campaign would consist of infiltrating a detention center. I assemble the chapter's case study through the compilation of self-produced and self-distributed transmedia archives by NIYA, the wide media coverage that the action received, and video/audio interviews with participants. Organizing the transcripts of the archival material allows me to do close reading and textual analysis to offer critical insights into how NIYA altered the discourse of mobility-based actions in the broader immigrant rights movements. NIYA's #BringThemHome was a precursor of what we have come to know as migrant caravans, in which the power lies in numbers.

Chapter 4, "Partying as Political," represents a new direction for UYMs, centering the social imaginary on the figurative location of *undocu-joy*. This chapter captures the growth of the Cumbiatón cultural movement (2016–present) led by undocumented queer and transgender organizers. As the culminating chapter, the Cumbiatón case study represents a third decade of organizing history for UYMs. As such, its leaders are undocumented organizers who were involved with UYMs since the early 2000s as youth and are now taking immigrant rights organizing in new directions as adults. The first two decades of the UYMs were focused on building public-facing mass movements primarily centered on national networks, with the goal of producing political change. Cumbiatón offers new directions and discourse for undocumented youth, the broader immigrant community, and mixed-status community members, highlighting that movement building is also an internal process in which joy should be as much of a goal as political change. I explore the rich transmedia archival collection produced by the Cumbiatón movement across their social media outlets, website, and artwork. Additionally, using the approach of visual analysis allows for the examination of transmedia archives as a performative assemblage, in the form of Cumbiatón's party productions, musical playlists, and nightclub sets, built as new forms of movement messaging. I argue that Cumbiatón offers an alternate politics of belonging in the contexts of both the state and social movements.

In my conclusion, I sum up the legacy of the case studies in my research and their importance in building what I theorize as an *(un)documenting* framework: archival knowledge production through the activism of undocumented youth. I analyze the context of civil disobedience actions by undocumented youth during the three decades of UYMs and what their importance is in a *post-Trumpamerica* U.S. society.[55] As a critical social-movement scholar, I analyze the contributions made by undocumented youth social movements, but I also connect these actions to power structures and political mobilizations that reshaped anti-immigrant fervor in the United States under Forty-Five's presidency, thereby theorizing (un)documenting processes that constrain undocumented communities. I draw on critical race theory scholars like Eduardo Bonilla-Silva who call for scholars to develop countertheorization that challenges white-supremacist constructs, dominant narratives of citizenship by merit, and the political marginalization of queer people, trans people, youth, and communities of color.

As an undocu-scholar, I am indebted to the community of undocumented youth organizers who chose to document and produce an archival record of actions that would change the way we discuss immigrant rights in the United States in the twenty-first century. No pseudonyms are used in the case studies of this book. All the case studies involve activists who are consciously "out of the shadows" with their identities and statuses as a form of agency and an organizing platform. In chapter 2, I provide contextualization of the history of UYMs with a pivotal event, "Coming Out of the Shadows," held in Chicago in 2011, at which one of the slogans that emerged was "Undocumented and Unafraid." In organizing the book, I made the conscious decision to include only case studies involving organizers who were "out of the shadows" and who through their organizing campaigns have produced the public visibility allowing for the archival material used in this book.[56]

Part of the selection process in choosing case studies was understanding the power of narrative through the archival trail, which led to my methodology of (un)documenting. Following scholars in various disciplines and conducting a mixed-methods approach to documenting the undocumented experience, with (un)documenting I credit undocumented organizers for their intellectual and knowledge production through organized actions rather than hiding their contributions through a pseudonym. The activists highlighted in this book are organizers who remain public and "out of the shadows" with their identities and status as a form of organizing. Undocumented organizers have been at the forefront of documenting the oppressive tools of management and control that render immigrant populations illegal. The case studies assembled in this book aim to inform, inspire, and help motivate contemporary movements that work to bring attention to detentions, deportation, and family separations.

CHAPTER 1

ASSEMBLING THE POWER OF DIRECT ACTION

Thank God I have remained firm in my values, even
when I received ill treatment and bullying messages from
immigration officers.
—ELVIRA ARELLANO, 2015

LVIRA ARELLANO EXPERIENCED DETENTION, DEPORTATION,
and family separation multiple times in her migration to the United
States. She made her first attempt to migrate there when she was around
twenty-two years old. She was detained at the Mexico-U.S. border for trying
to enter without documentation, and subsequently deported. That experience
did not deter Elvira, and she eventually crossed the border successfully and
made her way to the state of Washington.[1] Two years after arriving in the
United States, in 1999, she gave birth to her son Saúl. Elvira was only twenty-
four years old and found herself a single mother as well as an immigrant
woman living in the United States. Like her immigration status, Elvira has
always left the status of Saúl's father intentionally (un)documented or unde-
fined. Elvira has always prided herself on being a single mother.

With a newborn child, Elvira found herself with the same need she initially
had when migrating to the United States—economic stability and prosperity.
Having a U.S.-born son now placed her in a *mixed-status family*—a family composed of members with diverse immigration statuses, including undocumented
family members and U.S.-citizen family members.[2] With limited options, she
reached out to the only family she had in the United States: Saúl's godparents
in Chicago. Elvira and Saúl migrated to Chicago in 2000. Initially, Elvira found
it challenging to secure stable employment in the Windy City, but eventually
she heard there were job opportunities cleaning aircraft at O'Hare International

Airport. And while it was a minimum-wage job, it offered the job security she needed at the time. Elvira supplemented her wage by cleaning homes for wealthy households in broader metropolitan Chicago.[3] While working in an international airport brought her job security, Elvira recognized there were risks to working in such a site. For one, immigration agencies have a strong presence in all airports in the United States. Secondly, working in a federal location like an airport requires the verification of documentation to legally work in the United States. When they lack this documentation, or what is often referred to as "papers," immigrants are left to acquire and present false documentation to work. As such, sites like airports become another extension of the physical borderlands, where systems are set up to detect, monitor, apprehend, detain, and deport those without legal documentation. Despite the risk, Elvira still made the choice to work at an international airport for the well-being of her newborn child.

Elvira worked and remained undetected by immigration authorities for two years. In what sociocultural anthropologist Ruth Gomberg-Muñoz calls "living under the radar," immigrants like Elvira find themselves trying to remain undetected by immigration enforcement agencies.[4] However, in 2001 the immigration system changed. The terrorist attacks on the United States on September 11, 2001, popularly remembered as "9/11," had an immense impact on U.S. society, and one of the areas they had immediate effects on was immigration. President George W. Bush signed the Homeland Security Act of 2002 on November 25, which created the Department of Homeland Security (DHS). The establishment of DHS is significant to Elvira's story for two reasons. First, under DHS, the employment authorization program E-Verify became used more regularly as a tool to lead nationwide workplace raids. Secondly, under DHS the enforcement branch of the agency was created, Immigration and Customs Enforcement (ICE), which was set up to detect, detain, and deport immigrants from the interior of the country. What is significant about ICE is that previously, under the Immigration and Naturalization Services (INS) office that existed prior to DHS, enforcement was managed under the Department of Justice (DOJ), which meant that under ICE the U.S. government shifted and expanded its capacity to detain and deport undocumented immigrants in the interior of the country. With the establishment of DHS, the number of detentions caused by E-Verify and the deportation of immigrants from the interior of the United States through ICE grew exponentially. Elvira was only one of thousands of immigrants who became caught in the immigration system's web.

On December 10, 2002, Elvira was arrested by immigration officers at her home in Chicago for using falsified documents to work. After a few days in custody, she was released and given a deportation notice scheduled for September 18, 2003. This would only be the beginning of Elvira's story of challenging the immigration system and advocating for her family's right to stay in the United States. Just two days before her deportation notice went into effect in 2003, Representatives Luis V. Gutiérrez (D–IL) and Dick Durbin (D–IL) introduced a private bill that not only protected Elvira from the original deportation but also granted her a work permit, social security card, and driver's license.[5] This private bill extended her deportation notice for three years to August 15, 2006.[6] This was an example in which Elvira witnessed the power of multiple organizations and community members organizing to put pressure on allied politicians like Rep. Gutiérrez and Rep. Durbin to move toward political action through policy.

However, Elvira would never show up to face an immigration judge. Instead, she took sanctuary inside of the Adalberto United Methodist Church located in Humboldt Park, a Latinx neighborhood in Chicago. She remained in sanctuary for one year (August 2006–August 2007) against the threat of detainment and deportation. While she remained confined within the walls of the church building, Elvira's story received national and global media attention and made her a common household name between 2006 and 2007. In the time between her arrest in 2002 and her court date in 2006, Elvira became an ardent immigrant-rights organizer in Chicago working with the organization she created, La Familia Latina Unida. Elvira used media outlets to share her story, a strategy that she learned through grassroots organizing training. When she took sanctuary in the church on August 19, 2006, she was already a locally known and recognized figure within Chicago's Latinx community. By December 2006, she reached national and international recognition when *Time Magazine* named her Person of the Year, under the category of "People Who Mattered."[7]

Elvira's case study is important because it sparked debates within broader immigrant rights movements (IRMs). Her case of sanctuary is commonly referred to by scholars as the birth of the new sanctuary movements (NSMs), which continued the legacy of over twenty years of the Sanctuary Movement (SM) up to that point. Most journalists covering immigration have written about Elvira's experience within the context of these two phases in the sanctuary movements. Scholars of feminist studies of color and Latinx studies have also written significantly on Elvira's activism in relation to her motherhood practices as a single immigrant mother of color. Scholars like Maura I. Toro-Morn and Nilda Flores González write about Elvira in the context of the growing analytical field of transnational Latina motherhood and immigrant activism. These two scholars build on the work of Latina feminist scholars Pierrette Hondagneu-Sotelo and Ernestine Ávila, whose work focuses on the gendering of migration patterns and complicates notions of motherhood in the context of immigrant women who might have children across multiple borders.[8]

My interest in adding to the critical literature on Elvira's activism is in relation to the rise of undocumented youth movements (UYMs). I argue that we can't tell the story of UYMs in the United States without first telling Elvira's activist story. Her activism began in the 2000s in parallel with the construction of civic engagement and political visibility for undocumented youth in the United States and moved toward direct forms of activism as undocumented youth were beginning to form organizations, networks, and organizing campaigns. When Elvira entered the scene of immigrant rights organizing, immigrant rights movements had been seen only in the context of labor rights, without regard for identity formations. As such, immigrant rights were controlled primarily by traditional organizations from the civil-rights-movement period that still felt the pressures of patriarchal structures. Those patriarchal structures also pushed undocumented immigrants into the shadows by not allowing leadership opportunities, and they mostly limited activism to indirect forms of organizing such as civic engagement. These traditional organizations kept immigrant leadership in the realm of "civility," defined by Scott Henkel and Vanessa Fonseca-Chávez as action that "remains within the boundaries of particular norms."[9] My interpretation of the IRMs up to the twenty-first century is that they were movements that relegated undocumented immigrants to staying in line with the norms of not speaking up or assuming leadership. Elvira's case study is significant in that it would break away from that and offer alternative possibilities rooted in direct forms of organizing.

Elvira's activism represents major shifts in the broader immigrant rights movements (late 1980s–present) and the new sanctuary movements (2006–present), and, as I will demonstrate, it intersects with growth and shifts in the undocumented youth movements (2000–present). Young immigrants transitioning into adulthood in the United States like Elvira did not qualify for protective political and administrative legislation like the Dream Act (2001) or Deferred Action for Childhood Arrivals (DACA, 2012). The introduction of the Dream Act set in motion the definition of immigrant youth not only in terms of age group but also in terms of merit. Young immigrants like Elvira were not considered deserving members of society because of their lack of educational attainment. Elvira's case study allows us to challenge the neoliberal construction of the DREAMer narrative, which is one of the parameters used to determine merit warranting inclusion into the national body. Despite civic engagement and political organizing by individuals like Elvira, many young immigrants aged out of qualifying for the Dream Act and DACA. Elvira Arellano's case study represents a shift in activism from *indirect forms of activism*—characterized as civic engagement or working with the political system—toward *direct forms of activism*, typified by the use of the body as a vehicle for change and the conducting of civil disobedience with aims of pressuring the political system toward societal change.[10]

I begin the chapter by providing background information on Elvira's migration journey, detailing the neoliberal moment in which she arrived to the United States. By understanding the social and political time period when Elvira migrated, we can understand what led her to pursue learning grassroots organizing strategies, which included indirect and direct forms of activism and the use of media outlets to craft *transmedia narratives*.[11] Immigrant organizers used traditional media outlets like television and radio before moving on to early forms of online platforms like blogs, chat rooms, and instant messaging to control their movements' messaging, and Elvira's case study represents an early form of transmedia narrative construction. Elvira became the face of the new sanctuary movements in the mid–2000s and began to put much of what she learned in her grassroots training into practice while in sanctuary. As such, the chapter moves to analyze Elvira's time in sanctuary between 2006 and 2007 as it relates to the new sanctuary movements and broader immigrant rights movements. Finally, the chapter ends by analyzing the conscious choice Elvira made to leave sanctuary in order to practice direct forms of activism that connect her to the undocumented youth movements that are discussed throughout the book.

BACKGROUND: ELVIRA'S MIGRATION JOURNEY AND THE RISE OF NEOLIBERAL POWER

The United States of America to which Elvira arrived at the end of the twentieth century had a neoliberal political and economic power structure. According to David Harvey, the rise of neoliberal power in the United States was predicated on four tenets: (a) the guarantee of the quality and integrity of money, (b) the establishment of policing entities and institutions to secure private property rights, (c) the creation of markets that had not previously existed, and (d) the reduction or elimination of state intervention in markets.[12] The neoliberal state, Harvey describes, impacts undocumented communities by placing no barriers on the movement of capital while restricting the mobility of immigrants. Additionally, the North American Free Trade Agreement (NAFTA, 1994) effectively eliminated state interventions in commercial interests across North America and allowed industries to operate in Mexico and Latin America without the checks and balances required in the United States. NAFTA caused local markets in Mexico and Latin America to tank, as they could not compete on an uneven economic playing field with the U.S. market.[13] This produced a steady flow of mass migration from Mexico, Central America, and Latin America as many lost their businesses, land, and economic stability.[14]

Elvira Arellano was only one of millions of immigrants who deemed it necessary to migrate to survive. In her hometown of San Miguel Curahuango in the state of Michoacán, Mexico, she was an accountant for a small business owned by four brothers who transported agricultural products to several different national markets.[15] When NAFTA passed on January 1, 1994, it had a drastic impact on the agricultural field and its distributors, and Elvira's bosses

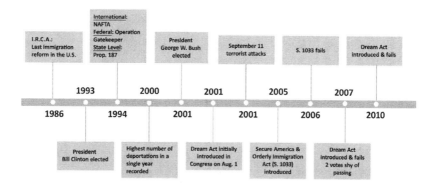

FIGURE 1 Immigration policy and neoliberal power. The tables and timelines in this chapter are constructed to illustrate some of the multiple entry points into the discussion of immigration policy, neoliberal power, and activism/organization.

lost their business. As a daughter from a small rural town in Mexico, she did not have the privilege of education and had to work at a young age to help financially support her parents. When she lost her job, migration seemed a viable option to find better economic opportunities and continue to financially support her family. In what Pierrette Hondagneu-Sotelo and Ernestine Ávila term a "gender-transformative odyssey," many young women like Elvira find themselves in financial predicaments and resort to migration from small rural towns to bigger urban cities in search of better economic opportunities.[16] In traditional frameworks in the field of immigration studies, the family narratives most often described by scholars involved men migrating with their family's economic progress as a pull factor. The "gender-transformative odyssey" framework developed by Hondagneu-Sotelo and Ávila points us to new migration patterns that require a focus on gender dynamics: young women being pushed to migrate out of necessity and not necessarily out of their own desire, with economic opportunities as the compelling motive. As an extension of these new gendered migration patterns, the Mexico-U.S. borderlands became a site that many young migrant women turned to out of necessity, while transnational businesses capitalized on these changing migration conditions.[17]

The border region in northern Mexico became an urban transfronterizo site. Cities along the borderlands that have shared histories of interrelated culture witnessed economic and industrial growth post-NAFTA. Many U.S. businesses set up giant maquiladoras—mass industrial assembly lines—that were dependent on low-wage female employees for maximum capital.[18] Women from small rural towns migrated en masse to the border region in search of steady income opportunities. Many scholars have documented the harsh working conditions, the constant sexual harassment, and the labor violations that occur in the maquiladora industry.[19]

Elvira migrated to the borderland region of Tijuana, Baja California, in search of a job as an accountant.[20] However, she realized that her lack of formal education and inability to speak English limited her opportunities. She was eventually forced to take an assembly-line job at a maquiladora where she witnessed firsthand the abuse that women faced on a daily basis. Work at the maquiladora was hard and did not pay enough for Elvira to continue supporting her family. Being in the borderlands, the natural next step was to continue her migration journey to the north, across the border to the United States in search of economic stability.

In the late twentieth and early twenty-first centuries, as industrial jobs transferred to Mexico, the United States moved to a low-wage service economy.[21] Neoliberal economic models are based on the free flow of business and the restriction of people's migration to maintain a racial and economic hierarchical status quo. As such, in the early 1990s the United States began to transform the immigration control system by expanding the militarization of the Mexico-U.S. borderlands, and implementing immigration policy that would restrict the mobility of migrants and limit their rights if they managed to make it to the interior of the country.

It is estimated that in the 1990s a total of 4.9 million Mexican migrants made their way to the United States as a result of neoliberal policies.[22] The U.S. immigration control system contended with these migration patterns south of its border by enacting immigration policies at the federal and state levels. California, the state that many Mexican migrants made their home, saw a rise of anti-immigrant political attention in the mid-1990s. Governor Pete Wilson viewed immigrants as a burden on the state's resources. That led to Proposition 187, which would have barred undocumented immigrants from using public state resources. Proposition 187 initially passed but was immediately challenged and taken to the Supreme Court, which ruled it unconstitutional, and it was never implemented in the state of California. State concerns and voices were raised to a national stage when Operation Gatekeeper was implemented in 1994 with the pretext that the Mexico-U.S. borderlands needed to be surveilled to protect the nation.[23] Operation Gatekeeper aimed at reducing the number of migrants crossing the Mexico-U.S. border at its busiest entry points: Tijuana, Baja California–San Diego, California; and Ciudad Juárez, Chihuahua–El Paso, Texas. Through the militarization of the border, Operation Gatekeeper forced migrants through harsh routes in Arizona's Sonoran desert.[24] Scholars describe these policies toward the control of capital output and labor organization as attempts to solidify neoliberal power.[25] Militarizing the borderlands appeased states located in the region, while facilitating similar federal policies for the interior of the country in nonborderlands states.

This anti-immigrant sentiment and rhetoric was carried into federal politics when President Bill Clinton campaigned on securing the Mexico-U.S. border and passing restrictive immigration legislation at the federal level, which would lead to the Illegal Immigration Reform and Immigrant Responsibility Act (IIRIRA, 1996). IIRIRA has been one of the most punitive immigration policies to date, as it made it possible to move the physical borderlands figuratively and effectively to the interior of the country. It did this by expanding the categories of crimes for which undocumented populations could be deported. Nicholas De Genova describes this encroachment on immigrant populations as "deportability." Eithne Luibhéid states that "the bills also stripped immigration judges of the power to consider mitigating circumstances, such as length of residence and community ties."[26] With IIRIRA two programs were begun that would subsequently be amplified and used vigorously with the birth of the Department of Homeland Security in 2002, which also coincided with Elvira's arrest: E-Verify and 287(g). E-Verify targeted immigrants who used false documents at their work sites, and 287(g) set the structure through which the federal government cooperated with local law enforcement to detain immigrants in the interior of the country. As a result, mixed-status families became much more vulnerable after the implementation of IIRIRA in 1996, and this act laid the groundwork for what unfolded in the 2000s.[27]

Criminalization through policy had the intention of rendering immigrant bodies "illegal." Susan B. Coutin describes this process as one that [made] "individuals . . . physically present but legally absent, existing in a space outside of society, a space of 'non-existence,' a space that is not actually 'elsewhere' or beyond borders but that is rather a hidden dimension of social reality."[28] Rendering undocumented populations nonexistent in a legal sense makes them disposable and deportable. Undocu-scholar Joel Sati also describes illegality as the process by which undocumented populations become invisible, not because of their lack of documentation, but because of legal interpretations that criminalize them and force them to operate outside of the purview of the nation-state. He states, "Undocumented immigrants become alien not only as a matter of phenotype, but also as a matter of understanding—citizenship is impossible for illegal aliens because they do not operate in the same cognitive, moral, or political space as citizens do."[29]

In 1997, then, Elvira migrated to a country that was going to extraordinary lengths and investing large amounts of money to render undocumented populations invisible while documenting them as "illegal." As the twentieth century was coming to an end, the focus in immigration enforcement was already moving toward the interior of the country. During the first two years of Elvira's life in the United States (1997–99), she remained undetected by immigration officials. However, in 1999, Elvira gave birth to her son Saúl and found herself a single mother in Washington. Distant from family or friends

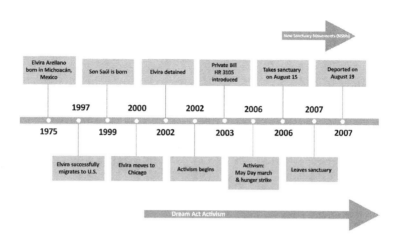

FIGURE 2 Timeline of Elvira's activism. This timeline is intended as a visual tool to allow the reader to follow the actions and key dates referenced in the chapter. Elvira's activism as an individual is not intended to represent all forms of activism that were happening in this time period but instead to highlight how she inspired and prompted undocumented youth and others toward direct forms of activism. This timeline represents only one story and one form of activism, which has its limitations.

who could offer support, she was forced to continue her migration journey to Chicago in search of economic stability and community support. However, nothing could prepare Elvira, or any of us in the United States, for the impacts that 9/11 had on the world and the changes it caused. After 9/11, the aspirations for immigration reform were overshadowed by a harsher reality in the form of the growth of immigration enforcement, but not without immigrants resisting and challenging neoliberal power structures.

LEARNING THE POWER OF DIRECT ACTIVISM

In the aftermath of 9/11, as the country mourned the events of that day, citizens and immigrants were aware that changes were coming. Immigrant communities across the United States felt the pressure and anxieties over 9/11; they knew the event would change the national discourse around immigration and immigration reform. These are years that are significant and critical in Elvira's life and activism. First, in 2002 the 9/11 attacks were still fresh in the

United States, and one of the immediate effects was increased deportations nationwide. When Elvira was served her deportation notice in December 2002, it propelled her to look for the spiritual guidance and strength that she needed at that moment. She found that spiritual guidance in the Adalberto United Methodist Church located in Humboldt Park in Chicago. Historically a Puerto Rican hub, Humboldt Park, like growing metropolitan Chicago, had witnessed the impacts of migration during the 1990s when new immigrant populations began looking for affordable housing in an integrated global city. Humboldt Park had also been the site of radical and political organizing by Latinx populations in the Midwest during the civil rights period in the 1960s and 1970s.[30]

Elvira was entering a city and neighborhood with a strong history of activism and of struggles for social justice for diverse groups. The Adalberto United Methodist Church, established in the 1980s, was a spiritual hub that had been part of this activist history. In an interview with the grassroots volunteer collective Chicago Independent TV, who covered Elvira's time in sanctuary in depth, Elvira states that her initial attraction to the church was that she "like[d] the way they did the prayers in this church."[31] She goes on to speak about her spiritual journey, saying, "I come from a Catholic background, but when I came here, they never said you have to believe in this or not. They said, 'You are a woman of faith, and you are welcomed in this church,'" speaking to the interfaith guidance and knowledge in which the traditional Sanctuary Movement is rooted. The second reason Elvira was drawn to and stayed in the church was the activism profile it combined with this spiritual guidance. She states, "I liked also that all the members of this church are active in the community. For this reason, also, I continue coming to this church."[32] Connecting with the Adalberto United Methodist Church was only the beginning of Elvira's journey and development as an activist.

Building on its established sanctuary roots from the 1980s, the Adalberto United Methodist Church was incredibly active in community organizing and part of several interfaith networks in the Chicago area. The church worked with diverse immigrant communities during the 1990s and strengthened their activism during the 2000s, when deportation numbers from the interior of the United States grew significantly. Attending Mass at Adalberto United Methodist Church also meant connecting to a community network organizing for immigrant rights. Elvira was drawn to that environment because it gave her an opportunity to meet multiple families like hers, composed of mixed-status

family members and women facing deportation. Eventually she was connected to the Coalition for African, Asian, European, and Latino Immigrants
of Illinois (CAAELII), which awarded her a scholarship and trained her in
foundational organizing rooted in civil-rights, intersectional, and interfaith
methods.[33] After the scholarship, Elvira became a full-time devoted organizer
with the community-center component of the Adalberto United Methodist
Church, Centro Sin Fronteras, originally established in 1987. In that same
interview with Chicago Independent TV, Elvira states, "That has been my
work for the last two years—learning how to organize."[34] The organizing curriculum from the CAAELII scholarship would result in Elvira creating the
organization La Familia Latina Unida in 2002.

La Familia Latina Unida was centered on helping mixed-status families
who were going through similar experiences of family separation at the hands
of the state, and on challenging the threat of deportation that was becoming
more common among immigrant communities post-9/11. Elvira's household
reflects what was becoming more common in the United States: mixed-status
households composed of undocumented family members and U.S.-citizen
family members.[35] Separation of mixed-status families via deportation often
meant U.S. children were left without parents or family members to care for
them. As a single mother, Elvira was aware that if she was deported, either her
son Saúl would have to leave with her or else they would be separated, which
meant he would not enjoy the privileges of U.S. citizenship. In the post-9/11
world, as detention and deportation numbers grew drastically in the interior
of the country, this was the conundrum of a growing number of mixed-status
families.[36] The physical border that migrants had once crossed to come to the
United States was encroaching on them and following them to the interior of
the country. Activism became the tool through which Elvira fought against a
punitive political immigration system.

The organization La Familia Latina Unida grew out of the civic engagement
of multiple organizations in Chicago and had the support of congressman
Luis G. Gutiérrez.[37] However, it eventually deviated from traditional forms
of organizing, going beyond indirect forms of activism like civic engagement
within the political system. In their article "Battling for Human Rights and
Social Justice," Veronica Vélez, Lindsay Perez Huber, Corina Benavidez Lopez,
Ariana de la Luz, and Daniel G. Solórzano provide the definitions of indirect
and direct forms of activism that I use in this book. They define indirect forms
of activism as "political acts that express critical concern, but do not focus on

attempting to physically challenge public institutions and/or their actors," and direct forms of organizing as "overt political acts of protest that often utilize the physical body as a vehicle for protest."[38] In the case of La Familia Latina Unida, the organization viewed working with politicians like Luis G. Gutiérrez as one avenue worth pursuing. However, they knew that to help mixed-status families in Chicago who were facing deportation, they needed to utilize other strategies that aligned with the lived experiences of immigrant families.

The year 2006 was another significant moment for Elvira's formation as an activist, when she and La Familia Latina Unida began to employ direct forms of activism focused on the use of their bodies, leaning on their grassroots training rooted in civil rights discourse. Elvira's escalation to direct activism took place in a moment of heightened criminalization and deportation of immigrants. The 2006 and 2007 national immigrant-rights marches became a focal point in the national immigrant-rights debate. Those years marked a shift in which large immigrant populations left "the shadows" to achieve new public visibility.[39] Major newspapers around the United States flooded their audiences with headlines intended to capture the fervor of activism experienced during the 2006 marches.

The *Los Angeles Times* ran the headlines "500,000 Pack Streets to Protest Immigration Bills" and "500,000 Throng L.A. to Protest Immigrant Legislation," capturing the magnitude of the marches in that California city.[40] The demographics of immigrant populations in Los Angeles explain why this city's demonstration was the largest in the United States, but the media's choice to focus on the number of participants points to the ways that immigrants are made invisible or visible by the media even in a large city such as Los Angeles. Similarly, the *Chicago Tribune* ran headlines stating that there was "Power in Numbers," hinting that numbers and visibility were the only power held by immigrant communities.[41] Another *L.A. Times* headline—"Immigrants Demonstrate Peaceful Power"—captured the admiration for "peaceful" forms of organizing by immigrant activists.[42] Other newspapers, such as the *Las Vegas Review-Journal*, ran nativist opinion pieces such as "Marches Full of Disturbing Irony," quoting people who critiqued the immigrants involved in the marches, saying that their authority as noncitizens with undocumented status to demand civil rights was "ironic."[43]

The years 2006 and 2007 were also a crucial moment in the broader immigrant rights movements and Elvira's activism because they represented new social and political directions for organizers who recognized that, amid heightened state violence occurring through detention and deportation, direct forms of activism were needed to put pressure on the immigration debate at a federal level.[44] It is important to highlight that the 2006 and 2007 national peaceful marches happened in a moment when criminalization and deportation of immigrant populations was particularly high, and when there were also national debates about immigration reform on the table. This moment would initially lead to indirect forms of activism within the broader immigrant rights movements, which included civic engagement and immigrant youth working within the system to try to pass comprehensive immigration reform or the Dream Act. However, the 2006 and 2007 national marches also fractured the broader IRMs as they led to the realization that groups, organizations, and individuals needed to put pressure on political systems to produce immediate results that indirect activism was not achieving. Immigrant populations were being detained and deported and families were being separated at alarming rates. Immigrant youth and certain factions within the broader IRMs realized that they had to organize to highlight the lived experiences of immigrants and use their activism to challenge the sites where surveillance, detention, and deportations occurred.

The 2006 May Day national peaceful marches became a pivotal moment in U.S. activism history, as they were the largest marches that some major cities across the country had ever seen, and they also marked a point of no return for many undocumented activists like Elvira who knew that visibility, collective power gained through direct forms of activism, and transmedia narratives had to be used as strategies moving forward.[45] As such, under Elvira's leadership, La Familia Latina Unida drew on traditional and historical forms of protest rooted in civil disobedience that used the body as a vehicle to generate awareness about political needs. La Familia Latina Unida used these methods to highlight the experiences of immigrant communities. An example of this was a hunger strike they organized in May 2006. In August of that year, Elvira was to report to her deportation hearing. She had exhausted all the extensions possible in her legal case. In May, as a last resort to bring political attention to her case, Elvira and another member of La Familia Latina Unida, Flor Crisóstomo, went on a nearly month-long hunger strike.[46] Flor had been apprehended in a work raid in Chicago in April 2006.[47] Elvira's and Flor's cases were not unique: workplace raids were occurring across the nation, and affecting immigrant women and mixed-status families most profoundly. The longtime Chicago-based socialist paper *People's World* reported that in the year 2001, a total of

1,187 employees of the corporation IFCO Systems were arrested nationwide, with twenty-six of those arrests happening in Chicago.[48]

Elvira and Flor's hunger-strike campaign was strategically crafted as a direct action that used intentional messaging focused on undocumented mothers. They began the campaign on May 10, the day on which Mexican and other Latinx communities celebrate Mother's Day. The two women staged the hunger strike in the heart of Chicago's Latinx center, Pilsen. The women ensured that the campaign took place in a public space where community members could witness the day-to-day impacts of their hunger strike and be rallied into collective action. The campaign also produced local, state, and national headlines from diverse media sources. Elvira and Flor used media outlets strategically to bring awareness to the high level of deportation rates affecting immigrant communities nationwide. They gave multiple interviews to diverse media sources with the goal of building and controlling the messaging around deportation. It is my interpretation that they wanted to frame deportation as a human rights issue that impacted undocumented women and mixed-status families including U.S.-citizen children. This hunger strike represented an escalation of organizing efforts by undocumented women, and one that I analyze as an effort by Elvira and Flor to take their activism to new sites that included public visibility and the use of their body as a vehicle for civil disobedience. Hunger strikes are a historical form of protest, and Elvira continued to build on such historical examples of organizing when she took sanctuary in Adalberto United Methodist Church.

Elvira participated and witnessed the power of mass mobilization in the marches that took place in Chicago on May 1, 2006.[49] They happened right before she was supposed to present herself to immigration court on August 15, 2006. Instead of working with the legal system and waiting for the political system to protect her, she chose to take sanctuary inside her church with the direct protection of her community. Elvira would go on to become the face of what scholars and journalists have begun to document as the beginning of the new sanctuary movements (NSMs) in the 2000s.

ASSEMBLING TRANSMEDIA NARRATIVES IN SANCTUARY

As mentioned earlier, the Centro Sin Fronteras organization and the Adalberto United Methodist Church where Elvira learned activism had long-standing ties to civil rights movements stemming from the 1960s onward to the 1980s. Elvira learned about the power of direct forms of activism as well as the importance of storytelling in media outlets; in the civil rights period of the 1960s, activist groups had used the strategies of testimonials and control of messaging by producing and accessing media resources. Elvira's story coincides with a historical moment in the beginning of the twenty-first century in which media productions were drastically changing. The internet was still in its infancy. Social media as we know it today did not exist. The independence that the internet provided for activists to produce individual and organizational content would begin later in the decade. Sasha Costanza-Chock details the positive impact that the Television Act of 1996 had on immigrant populations by giving them access to news and content in their native languages and how this facilitated mass movement building for the immigrant rights movements.[50] As Costanza-Chock explains, prior to the rise of social media and the ability of everyday people to produce their own content, television and radio stations made communication possible between immigrant communities.

Elvira's case study is wedged in that historical moment between the prevalence of traditional media outlets like television and radio stations and the rise of social media. Elvira's relationship to media channels began in late 2002 after she was released from detention. According to Elvira, she was approached by a journalist to share her story and was unsure whether it was a good idea to speak about her situation. At a conference presentation in 2010, Elvira recounted how her first experiences with media began: "The media outlets had begun to call me to talk about my case. And I would ask myself, 'What should I do?'"[51] However, she decided to tell her story after failing to receive help from the Mexican consulate in Chicago and other governmental agencies. In the presentation mentioned above, Elvira mentions that the Chicago-based journalist offered to connect her to organizations and networks that support undocumented people. She states, "I naturally began to think about all the people I was meeting during this time period that had also been detained [by immigration authorities]."[52] Elvira realized she could connect her struggle to those of other families that were experiencing similar situations and might not feel comfortable speaking out.

Elvira's link to the media outlets signified the moment when she made the conscious choice to "come out of the shadows"—that is, to publicly represent immigrant families, who were expected to stay in the shadows. Elvira stated, "It's these circumstances that we live through that practically obligate us to defend our human rights. That is what leads me to say to myself, 'I am going to speak to the media outlets.' It is now in God's hands. I am no criminal."[53] By sharing her story through the media, Elvira was pushing back against a heightened moment of illegalization in the United States, when immigrant families were being criminalized. Her rhetoric in these testimonials reveals that she saw the media as an outlet to publicize immigrant family stories when nobody was talking about the heightened criminalization experienced by mixed-status families in which parents were trying to make a living and provide for their children. Elvira's push to support mixed-status families became a foundation later for undocumented youth to push beyond family units and advocate not only for "noncriminals" but for all undocumented immigrants.

Elvira's strategic use of media outlets was learned through her apprenticeship with the CAAELII network. This training provided her with the knowledge to produce, control, and distribute messaging to various media outlets. The stories that Elvira produced and the use of media outlets to distribute mixed-status family experiences constituted what media scholars refer to as *transmedia narratives*. The birth of transmedia narratives coincided with the rise of new media, which represented modes of media production that allowed for independent production and the *spreadability* of independent messaging.[54] My work here is in conversation with scholars who use transmedia narratives to document the growth of the undocumented youth movements in the later part of the 2000s.[55] However, my interest in Elvira's case study is because it

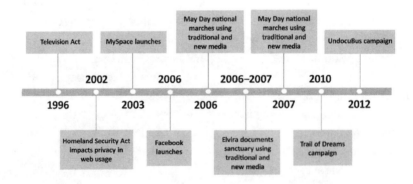

FIGURE 3 Timeline of media and communication in the United States in relation to undocumented youth movements.

helps me document earlier forms of testimonial production using traditional media outlets like television or radio stations prior to the new forms of media and new social movements. Elvira's case study represents an opportunity to understand how we can link the growth of transmedia narrative productions to direct forms of organizing rooted in controlling the messaging, which became the foundations of new social movements.

BRIDGING THE SANCTUARY MOVEMENTS AND THE IMMIGRANT RIGHTS MOVEMENTS

The immigration court in Chicago to which Elvira was supposed to report on August 18, 2006, is in the downtown corridor of the city. Elvira did not show up to said appointment. Instead, on that same day, a little over five miles away in the Humboldt Park neighborhood, in front of a multitude of people and cameras that created a makeshift press conference, Elvira announced her decision to take sanctuary inside of the Adalberto United Methodist Church. I read her decision to take sanctuary as a direct form of activism; she wanted to remain in control of her body and her future. In sanctuary, she claimed autonomy over her body to resist her deportation and challenge immigration systems. La Familia Latina Unida and Elvira recognized a cleavage in immigration policy. A memorandum by the Department of Homeland Security classified "locations of worship" as "sensitive locations" where immigration enforcement could not take place.[56] Elvira took sanctuary in the church to await a change in her immigration case or in policy. And while the decision to take sanctuary was to some extent an individual action for Elvira, it also represents a collective form of organizing with the support of the religious congregation and its diverse surrounding community, as it would take a whole village to perform the practice of sanctuary (as demonstrated later in the chapter).

I argue that Elvira's case study of sanctuary departs from traditional interpretations of the Sanctuary Movement of the 1980s and 1990s, in which immigrants and refugees who took sanctuary typically remained in "the shadows." In the traditional SM, it was the faith-based leaders or allied activists coordinating an immigrant/refugee's sanctuary who were in front of the cameras directing the messaging. Additionally, the majority of the academic texts written on the earlier SM of the 1980s/1990s are focused on the interfaith leaders who offered sanctuary in their religious centers, as opposed to the immigrants or refugees who took sanctuary. In Elvira's case, she was coordinating the messaging and was in front of the cameras while in sanctuary. That is not to say she did not receive aid and support from La Familia Latina Unida and community members, but Elvira's sanctuary case, along with other cases of sanctuary under the NSMs, placed the individual who was taking sanctuary in the driver's seat. Having the person taking sanctuary demonstrate that they were in control of their body and decision-making process was a new aspect introduced by the NSMs.

Elvira recognized that the only way to move her case forward was to craft her transmedia testimonial through diverse media outlets. As part of her strategy, she documented her experience as a single mother and immigrant woman, and that of her U.S.-citizen son who was forced to live in sanctuary. Ownership of story is a practice Elvira learned in her early days of organizing. Sanctuary was a historical example that Elvira had learned during her time organizing in interfaith spaces.

Sanctuary movements in the United States have a long colonial and racial legacy dating to the foundations of the nation-state. Two significant points in U.S. history are the colonial period and the period of slavery. In "Sanctuaryscapes in the North American Southwest" (2019), anthropologist Aimee Villarreal Garza details the ways in which Indigenous peoples took outcast refugees from the Spanish empire into their homes or "pueblos"—referring to the Pueblo peoples in present-day Arizona and New Mexico—as a form of protection or sanctuary.[57] U.S.-based immigrant rights activists learned lessons in creating local ordinances, organizing religious congregations, and creating a transnational network from the history of U.S. slavery. In the era of chattel slavery, religious congregations of escaped slaves and white allies created the well-documented Underground Railroad. Offering "sanctuary" for escaped slaves was a matter of life and death. It is important to situate IRMs and SMs in relation to the history of the United States and the faith-based communities that have objected to racial, colonial, and imperial domination.[58]

The Vietnam War was another moment when sanctuary became an important element in rejecting U.S. empire and developing activist platforms that would go on to inform contemporary SMs. U.S. citizens who rejected fighting in the Vietnam War, many of whom were people of color, took sanctuary in religious centers across the United States.[59] As the antiwar sentiment grew nationwide, so did the grassroots movement to protect conscientious objectors among faith-based communities. The U.S. government attacked said faith-based communities for protecting the war objectors, and went into these centers and physically dragged these individuals out in order to put them in jail. The public outcry was deafening, compelling the U.S. government to develop a policy related to sites they labeled "sensitive locations," which included religious centers, hospitals, schools, and other similar venues.[60] Only a decade later, as Central American refugees began arriving in the United States, and as U.S.-based activists learned about U.S. intervention in that part of the world and the inhumane approach of immigration/refugee law, many organizers began organizing locally within their congregations, and nationally by forming a network of faith-based institutions willing to take a stand.

The SMs developed out of progressive religious individuals and congregations in correlation to the inhumane treatment of migrants and refugees from Central America. Awareness of U.S. involvement in civil wars throughout Central America during the 1980s sensitized groups to the pressing need for asylum.[61] A growing number of concerned U.S. citizens began to critically ask why the government was involved financially and politically in foreign wars while inequalities continued to grow after the civil rights movements.[62] As Central American refugees arrived in large numbers in the United States, some U.S. citizens began learning firsthand about the horrifying experience these newly arrived immigrants faced in their nations as a result of U.S.-sponsored interventions. The number of arrivals generated an urgency among U.S. activists to create safe spaces where migrants would not be persecuted or deported and where they could petition for asylum.[63] Many requests for asylum were rejected when migrants were not able to present legally viable documents for court cases because they had been destroyed or simply could not be recovered from their countries of origin. Consequently, their experience as "illegalized" subjects began in the United States.[64] Devoted human-rights activists created the notion of sanctuary cities because they realized their efforts could not grant asylum status to each migrant; therefore, their strategies turned locally toward pressuring cities to pass ordinances to end collaboration with federal immigration offices.[65] Cities such as Tucson, Arizona; San Francisco, California; and Santa Fe, New Mexico, took the lead in providing aid for immigrants, publicly announcing they would harbor immigrants in safe spaces.[66] Immigrants in sanctuary cities lived within the confines of churches, with some protection given by devoted volunteers, but not without fear of harassment.[67]

Connecting the sanctuary movements to the immigrant rights movements is important to understand the long-standing tradition of activism on behalf of immigrants in the United States. Often, immigrant rights activism is perceived as a reaction to anti-immigration legislation.[68] While policymaking might have an impact on organizing, immigrant rights activism has an extensive trajectory in the United States, and immigrant organizers looked to past movements there for inspiration in how to organize in creative ways that were close to their lived experiences. Activists, in particular, paid special attention to the ways in which past movements used modes of communication to construct their internal and external messaging to grow their movements.

By controlling the messaging and documenting her family narrative, Elvira would show that the U.S. government was separating mixed-status families in which parents' only crime had been trying to provide a living for their families. Elvira's efforts were to document and produce transmedia narratives that actively countered the state's agenda to pursue immigrant populations for low-level infractions, thereby tearing families apart. A high percentage of undocumented immigrants in detention were placed there for low-level infractions like jaywalking, small traffic infractions such as failing to make a complete stop at a stop sign, or failing to have a driver's license in a state that did not offer them. And while Elvira's case study represents a focus on mixed-status families, she too would later see, thanks to undocumented youth activism, that there was a need to extend the focus to all undocumented members of the community, as criminalization went beyond normative family structures.

Elvira was aware that the creation of programs like E-Verify and sweeps in the interior of the country could only be countered through *hyperdocumentation*. Aurora Chang defines hyperdocumentation as the paradoxical way in which undocumented youth lack immigration status or documentation but in return produce an excessive amount of documentation in institutional ways.[69] Elvira recognized that she would need to bring attention to herself to build cultural capital and popular support if she was going to have a chance of winning her immigration court case. She also realized that she could generate awareness about many other immigrant women and mixed-status families that were living similar experiences. She states, "I started to give my testimonial to the media channels to not only defend my human rights and my son's, but also defend the human rights of the migrant," showing that she wanted to speak up for those who did not have a platform or feel comfortable doing so.[70] She goes on to say, "Just because we are in another country, it does not mean that said country has the right to violate those human rights and criminalize us," an active signaling of the criminalization rhetoric being constructed against immigrant communities at that moment. The multiple interviews that Elvira organized and agreed to give during her time in sanctuary were a form of transmedia testimonial, and should be regarded as a trajectory in transmedia archive building, which I define in my work as (un)documenting.

Elvira demonstrated a consciousness that the media coverage she was receiving was documenting her plight as an immigrant woman of color and single mother and shedding light on populations that otherwise were relegated to the shadows. The media coverage she received during her nearly one-year period in sanctuary creates an archival record that became one of the first instances in which intimate moments of sanctuary were documented. Sanctuary is a very personal, spiritual, and visceral experience for individuals who turn to a site of worship for protection from immigration authorities. In previous sanctuary movements, that space remained a personal and intimate one for the individual, a spiritual fort where immigration enforcement could not penetrate, and where typically cameras and reporters were not given access. Elvira, with the authority and permission of the church, wanted to flip that power dynamic and open the doors of her sanctuary experience to show people that she was not inactively awaiting her fate, but rather crafting her destiny by means of the narrative she constructed through various media outlets.

Elvira was open to having elements of her sanctuary experience captured and documented by media. In an interview conducted while in sanctuary with ChicagoTalks, a nonprofit organization aimed at producing a local neighborhood news source, she states, "The house of God cannot be a jail to anybody," letting folks know that she did not see the space she occupied in sanctuary as a jail cell because she was not a criminal.[71] I also read this statement as indicating agency in her choice to take sanctuary, as a form of taking control of her family's outcome instead of accepting deportation. The next part of the video footage captured by ChicagoTalks documents a regular day in Elvira's life in sanctuary. From the initial interview to the B-roll footage of Elvira's experience in sanctuary, the audience is let in and allowed to see that Elvira remains active in her role as an organizer and as a mother. By not accepting her deportation order, she refused to stop organizing and being a mother to Saúl.

The B-roll footage gives the impression of being a homemade production, a raw look inside Elvira's journey in sanctuary. The camera's frame captures Saúl sitting in a chair reading a book while Elvira helps him with some of the challenging words on the page. Elvira continues her emphasis on education, helping Saúl with reading and homework on a regular basis while in sanctuary.

Next, we see Elvira and Saúl near the exit of the church. Elvira is placing a large bright-orange puffy jacket on Saúl and proceeds to secure his backpack. We see Elvira, in keeping with her Catholic faith, draw the cross with her fingers across Saúl's face and tell him to have a good day. Saúl opens the door and is off to what we can assume will be a cold day in the Windy City, while Elvira remains in the warm confines of the church. The next shot shows a family friend walking Saúl to the school's front door. The video provides the viewer with the impression that Elvira will not allow school routines to be altered or dismissed while she is in sanctuary.

The video continues with another interview in which Elvira is asked more specific questions about her experience in sanctuary after six months in the Adalberto United Methodist Church. As usual, Elvira appears calm and collected when she declares, "For me, time has passed by so fast. I have always stayed in touch with the exterior through my computer and telephone. The work that I was used to doing, I keep doing it."[72] The serenity in her expression reveals a nonchalant attitude that performs full control and agency over her moment in sanctuary. The transmedia narrative that she is producing (un)documents the sanctuary experience. That is, she produces an alternative document or register for the public of what life in sanctuary in opposition to immigration enforcement can look like. In fact, she defies any limitations that the public might expect her to have in sanctuary when she goes on to say, "I remain in regular communication with leaders at the national level. We are talking about a possible protest on Día de los Niños [Children's Day] on April ninth," proclaiming her ongoing activism. She ends her thought with an expression that can be read as a shrug, saying, "And, well, we keep at it," in a way normalizing the sanctuary experience for undocumented populations.

Digging through several documentary video archives, one can find multiple sources capturing Elvira's experience in sanctuary with a similar tone: Elvira speaking out in defiance of immigration enforcement and giving power back to the community who supported her family. In the same interview described above, she highlights community support by informing the audience that she and Saúl are receiving cooked meals donated by restaurants and groceries from local markets.[73] In *MTV Cribs*–like fashion, Elvira walks the camera crew through various parts of her new home in sanctuary. The video shows Elvira beginning with the bed where she and her son sleep. It moves on to show the audience the kitchen, where we see Elvira and other women cooking collective meals. All these spaces are the intimate confines of home life, typically private for most people. However, Elvira's choice to produce a transmedia narrative using television, radio, print media, and the internet was a form of documenting the lengths to which immigration enforcement went to criminalize mixed-status families. In other words, Elvira's choice to give up her private life was consciously made in order to document a behind-the-scenes look at what mixed-status families facing detention and deportation had to go through to remain in the United States—a tactic to expose the violence experienced at the hands of the state. Immigration enforcement has no problem documenting and categorizing immigrants as "illegal aliens" or foreign criminals. Elvira's case study demonstrates that illegalization only works when it is the state documenting immigrants as criminals and controlling the messaging. Elvira's choice to document the violence inflicted on mixed-status families flips the script on the illegalization process.

These examples of coverage of Elvira's sanctuary experience represent favorable snapshots produced by media outlets, but not everything that was written about her was positive. In fact, some of the media outlets and journalists that covered Elvira's sanctuary experience used the rhetoric of "illegalization" to extend the argument that immigrants like her did not deserve any protection because they had broken the laws of the country, thus connecting arguments in favor of criminalization with processes of illegalizing immigrant bodies. For Lisa Marie Cacho, the construction of the *illegal* represents a change in discourse on the part of the nation-state.[74] The label "illegal" creates the face of the enemy and makes it justifiable to create *spaces of death* that determine which bodies live and which are made more valuable through what she defines as *social death*.[75] In other words, the rhetoric crafted by much of the anti-immigrant-toned coverage of Elvira's case—that she was an illegal alien who had broken the law when she presented false documentation to work, and that the punishment should be expulsion from the national body—supported a process of removal that represented social death.

Negative coverage of Elvira's sanctuary case was not just limited to her presence in the country and protection via sanctuary; it was also a direct backlash to her activism and, I argue, to her transmedia narrative. Journalists and U.S. citizens were upset that an immigrant woman was receiving so much coverage and attention. After all, immigrants were expected to remain "in the shadows" of U.S. society. We saw a similar pattern during the previously mentioned national peaceful marches of 2006 and 2007, which certain sectors of the media covered negatively because the expectation was that immigrants should not be public or vocal. Elvira shifted that script, and her boldness pushed against conservative and anti-immigrant agendas. The president of Chicago's Minuteman Project, Rick Biesada, states in an interview, "If she [Elvira] is allowed to stay in the country, every illegal alien that is in this country right now, all they have to do is run to a church somewhere and claim sanctuary." This highlights the threat that Elvira and the sanctuary movements represented for conservative political organizations and citizens.[76] The Minuteman Project was an instigator that drew hundreds of U.S. citizens with anti-immigrant sentiments to the Mexico-U.S. border, with the stated aim of securing it themselves because the government was supposedly not doing enough to protect its citizens from a so-called threat. The expansion of the Minuteman Project organization to the interior of the country to directly protest movements and individuals like Elvira demonstrates another way in which the borderland region was transferred to the interior of the country. However, this would not deter Elvira from continuing to tackle negative portrayals coming from the media and from anti-immigrant organizations.

Elvira's case study represents this battleground with its tug-and-pull between immigrant rights organizers pushing for immigration reform and conservative organizers pushing for stronger enforcement at the border and in the interior of the country. Lisa Marie Cacho argues that the "politics of deviance" are a battle between conservative entities that seek to maintain racial order through the enforcement of normative social values coded in the language of law and policy, and organizers who fight for alternate forms of political discourse.[77] Elvira became a symbol of defiance for using political modes and media representation to deviate from the normative constructions of immigrant communities as criminals. To add to the complexity of Elvira's representation in the media, Cacho also highlights the ways in which she was catapulted into national debates when she began to be compared to other historical civil-rights figures like Rosa Parks. Cacho focuses on the response by an African American columnist for the *Chicago Tribune* who was upset that Elvira was being compared to civil rights leaders. For this columnist, Cacho argues, "it mattered that Elvira Arellano and Rosa Parks had different relationships to U.S. law; in fact, on some level, she considered this difference to be all that mattered."[78]

And while there are examples of anti-immigrant sentiment on the part of people of color in the United States, such as the incident with the *Chicago Tribune* columnist that Cacho presents, Elvira herself also highlights the need for the undocumented community to work with migrant/immigrant groups that are more marginalized. Elvira's case study reminds us that our decolonial practices must not solely be directed outward but must also look inward to our individual reflections and toward the communities we represent.

DEPORTED: THREAT TO THE STATE

As mentioned earlier in the chapter, Elvira had a chance to participate in the 2006 national marches that took place in Chicago right before she entered sanctuary a few months later.[79] This experience allowed her to see the power of collective action and of transmedia narrative building when immigrants stepped out of the shadows and occupied public space in mass numbers. This certainly stayed with Elvira as a source of motivation through her journey in sanctuary. Elvira went from joining a collective action with millions publicly out in the streets of downtown Chicago to taking sanctuary in isolation in the confines of a church. The energy from the 2006 national marches was carried on to the next year as the immigration debate remained at the forefront of national politics. Elvira had a hard choice to make: Should she continue to foster her own visibility on behalf of immigrant rights from her position in sanctuary? Or should she take to the streets again in protest? Elvira chose the latter.

Elvira's choice to leave sanctuary to participate in marches and public organizing campaigns in 2007 was a choice to continue engaging in direct forms of activism in which she used her acquired cultural capital to fight against the immigration control system. So, in 2007, Elvira had her eyes on taking her activism to Los Angeles. In a reflective interview, when Elvira was asked why she decided to remain active within the movement, she declared, "I am not sitting with my arms crossed in my church. I am fighting, and thanks to media outlets, we can reach many homes to support those families still detained."[80] Her statement was a deliberate move to step out of the shadows of sanctuary and into a visible space of mobility through direct forms of organizing.[81] Again, she was using her body as a vehicle of change to confront immigration systems.

When Elvira decided to leave sanctuary in Chicago to participate in public organizing in Los Angeles, she did so knowing she faced deportation. She would indeed be deported after arriving in Los Angeles on August 19, 2007. It is reported that when Elvira arrived in Los Angeles, she made her way to one of the city's historical locations for the Mexican and Mexican American community: La Placita Olvera, near downtown Los Angeles. Elvira intended to participate in an immigrant-based event that was to be held there. She had left La Placita after an initial visit with her son and a few close friends who were accompanying her on the trip, and they were making their way through the busy streets of downtown Los Angeles, when the vehicle she was traveling in was intercepted by government trucks. She was ordered out of the vehicle and immediately placed in handcuffs, with her son witnessing the arrest. Saúl, only seven years at the time, cried in horror at seeing his mother treated like a high-profile criminal again. All this took place in the bustling streets of downtown Los Angeles.

In an interview shortly after her deportation, Elvira recounted the moment in which she was abruptly detained by ICE agents in downtown Los Angeles. She declared, "I am a little sad. When the agents arrived, he [Saúl] entered into a panic. I only asked them that they give me a minute with him to try to calm him down. I told him that everything was OK. I know what he is currently living through is hard on him."[82] Those words captured the traumatic impact her detention and deportation had on her son. In the interview, she came across as calm, collected, and confident in her response. A close reading of this interview as part of Elvira's archival repertoire indicates that her composure was part of her performance, ensuring that her transmedia narrative always communicated that she was in control of her body, emotions, and message. In front of the media, she would not break down, and she would not show weakness to immigration systems, even in the face of deportation.

In her interview, Elvira continued to perform calmness and serenity while critically analyzing the ways immigration systems produce a narrative of criminalization that justifies the action of deportation. She detailed her illegalized treatment at the hands of ICE, stating:

> They [ICE] did not allow me to contact anybody, including the Mexican consulate. This was what you would call an "express deportation." What they wanted to do was deport me as fast as they could. They think and know that I can be a threat to them. They know the pueblo can rise up! And that's what I want, for the pueblo to rise and fight for their rights![83]

Here we can see that Elvira's public visibility and her action of stepping out of the shadows of sanctuary and into a public space represented a threat and challenge to the nation-state. That threat resulted in the state using its tools and strategies of deportation. Elvira's case study is an early example from the beginning of the twenty-first century of an undocumented individual publicly challenging the nation-state's immigration system and attempting to use the cultural capital gained through transmedia narratives as protection against deportation. This was a lesson for undocumented youth, and one that they would turn to in their activist strategies by the end of the decade. Elvira had been influential in the switch from indirect forms of activism to direct forms that organized around immigrants' real lived experience and highlighted the human rights abuses being suffered at the hands of the state. Elvira's activism showed that mixed-status families were being criminalized, and that the finger needed to be pointed at the state for the violence inflicted on these families. Her activism aimed to highlight her humanity in contrast to the inhumane and illegalized treatment at the hands of the nation-state. Undocumented youth witnessed attacks on their families and undocumented community members, such as the example of Elvira, and recognized that messaging and media production can be an effective tool to more broadly represent the larger immigrant population. This chapter's epigraph highlights this activist strategy by Elvira:

> Thank God I have remained firm in my values, even when I received ill treatment and bullying messages from the immigration officers.[84]

CONCLUSION

This chapter has followed Elvira's trajectory to the direct forms of activism that would lead to her deportation and propel her into becoming an international figure. In the beginning of the chapter, I detailed how Elvira's path to activism began with discovering that her mixed-status family was not the only one being impacted by the growing number of deportation notices in the post-9/11 world. She would find strength in the collective action of organizing with families experiencing the realities of detention and deportation. Her case study is unique because it presents a moment when the sites of resistance in the broader immigrant rights movement shifted from indirect action toward a new use of direct action to call attention to a growing punitive immigration system that disposed of immigrants through a rigorous deportation regime.

This activist represents a trajectory of critical consciousness in which undocumented youth activists would develop new social imaginaries.

I approach Elvira's story through the lens of illegalization to highlight the way undocumented women of color such as Elvira are placed in vulnerable positions by global capitalist models that only value women's labor for producing a labor surplus, as historian Mae Ngai describes in *Impossible Subjects*.[85] In this way, Pierrette Hondagneu-Sotelo and Ernestine Ávila propose the framework of the "gender-transformative odyssey" to describe gendered migration patterns in which young women migrate out of necessity and also as a result of a global capitalist system that builds gendered labor models. From this system we see how the transnational migration patterns get coded for gender, from labor in the Mexico-U.S. borderlands in maquiladoras to eventual migration to the United States. Elvira's case study demonstrates that moving to the United States does not end the management of migrant women's bodies. Immigration legislation in the post-9/11 world represented a move of the borderlands to the interior of the country through new policing programs like E-Verify and 287(g), which were also gendered in their management of a growing body of immigrant women and mixed-status families.

Elvira spent a year in sanctuary; however, as soon as she stepped out of the protected space of her church and into public space with intentions to organize, the immigration system moved quickly to apprehend and deport her. In this chapter, I demonstrate that Elvira, along with other women of color and mixed-status families, became the target of a deportation regime. Once she began to organize publicly using direct forms, she was also criticized as a woman of color for stepping out of the boundaries prescribed in political advocacy for women. Women-of-color scholars doing work around transnational mothering highlight the incredible amount of pressure that immigrant women face, not only having the burden placed on them of financially providing for their children, but also being expected to do the work of mothering, including the emotional labor that goes into raising children. Scholars like Hondagneu-Sotelo and Ávila discuss this challenging balance between the "expression of care" and material goods.[86] In Elvira's case study, I read her activism in line with women-of-color scholars who have analyzed her activism as an extension of her practices of mothering her son and keeping her family together. The criticisms did not stop Elvira; in fact, she would apply the same strategies of direct forms of activism in sanctuary. She welcomed the media and strategically used them to control the messaging and narrative around her activism representing mixed-status families facing deportation. This radical-ized the traditional Sanctuary Movement and moved it into what scholars now call the new sanctuary movements.

The control of her transmedia testimonial while in sanctuary catapulted Elvira to being one of the most recognized figures, if not the most recognized, of immigrant rights movements during the mid-2000s. However, the level of attention was also being carefully monitored by the immigration control system. After the creation of the Department of Homeland Security as an immigration control apparatus, Elvira Arellano's activism would represent one of the most significant manifestations of public challenges to and questioning of the growing number of detentions and deportations in the United States.[87] Her choice to leave sanctuary to continue to publicly participate in the immigrant rights movements represents a crucial moment when DHS as an immigration control apparatus made a critical decision about how to handle that type of protest from immigration organizers.

Using the concept of what Michel Foucault terms "fearless speech," which refers to a subject's ability to transgress the expected norms, I analyze Elvira's case study as one in which her fearless speech aimed to spark a public debate with regard to the social imaginary of the United States about the violence that immigrant women of color and mixed-status families like hers were being subjected to.[88] However, as Foucault also highlights, fearless speech is typically received as a threat to a nation-state and is often met with violent responses. In Elvira's case, it led to an expedited deportation. My analysis of Elvira's case study demonstrates that she was deemed a threat to the nation-state because of the high media profile that resulted from her fearless speech. Deportation became the tool used to attempt to silence her and minimize her impact. Immigrant rights organizers paid attention to the fact that the response from the state was to deport those who stepped out of the norms of civility as Elvira had done. However, undocumented youth saw this break away from civility, coupled with their growth in cultural capital, as an important strategy, and continued to incorporate fearless speech into their direct forms of activism.

Elvira's activism and transmedia narrative productions would not end with deportation. Once she was deported to Mexico, her activism would expand into transnational dimensions. Her reach grew to global proportions when she began organizing Central American migrants who were making their journey across Mexico, heading north to the United States.[89] Continuing her activism in Mexico allowed Elvira to recognize that the immigrant's plight is not just a U.S. issue, but a systemic global issue in which multiple nation-states are involved. She organized in Mexico for seven years with multiple transnational organizations, interfaith groups, and migrant centers. In an interview during her time organizing in Mexico, Elvira declares, "I am part of the Mesoamerican migrant movement . . . as part of the caravan the movement follows Central American women and children."[90] Elvira continued her direct forms of organizing in Mexico and linked them to global migrant experiences.

Elvira remained active in Mexico while staying in transnational communication with political leaders and community members in the United States. She kept her attention on the United States and never lost sight of the fact that her son was being denied his rights as a U.S. citizen. As she was deported from the United States in 2007, undocumented youth organizers began entering the scene of the broader immigrant rights movements. The undocumented youth movements that rose in college campuses across the United States at first worked within the political system using indirect forms of activism, but this would soon shift when the Dream Act failed on its last attempt in Congress in 2010. Undocumented youth realized that if they wanted the political system to listen to their demands, they would need to take new approaches to calling attention to the issues they wanted addressed. Undocumented youth who had begun connecting with each other across the nation on social media sites like Myspace (launched in 2003) and later Facebook (public launch in 2006) began to realize that there was a need to come together. I read Elvira's case study as one that had a legacy in shifting the immigrant rights movements to direct forms of activism, and as representing an early form of (un)documenting—capturing transmedia testimonials and archiving them—which would be an important component of the rise of undocumented youth movements in the United States.

In fact, Elvira's story does not end in Mexico. I will continue her migration and organizing journey in chapter 3, where she begins to directly collaborate with undocumented youth organizers. Elvira became a symbol for immigrant parents who were raising mixed-status families and households in the United States. But for undocumented youth she also represented a generation of immigrants who did not meet the criteria for protection by the immigration policies introduced in the 2000s: the Dream Act (which saw attempts to pass it between 2000 and 2010) and Deferred Action for Childhood Arrivals (2012). Undocumented youth realized that the DREAMer narrative crafted to include and protect them did not apply to their parents. Elvira had connected with undocumented youths' parents and as such presented a symbol that could be used to organize the broader immigrant community.

Elvira witnessed the rise of undocumented youth movements in the United States while she was in Mexico. The energy generated by undocumented youth was the rejuvenation and paradigm shift that the broader immigrant rights movements needed. Like a virus, the contagious feeling of empowerment that was (un)documented by undocumented youth in their many actions across the United States would spread to migrants who had self-returned or who, like Elvira, had been deported to their home countries. In chapter 2, I transition from Elvira's case study and the broader immigrant rights movements to the rise of undocumented youth movements across the United States and the escalation they performed by taking their activism to sites that had previously been in the shadows of society: detention centers.

> The DREAMers have proven to us . . . me personally, they have opened my eyes to the fact that there is another way of fighting. Within the law, these young individuals have taught us how to fight.[91]

CHAPTER 2

FROM DETENTION TO INFILTRATION

Illegalized Assemblages

We challenged ICE directly, publicly, and they didn't want
to put us in deportation.
—ISAAC BARRERA, 2011

JONATHAN PEREZ AND ISAAC BARRERA are co-founders of the Immigrant Youth Coalition (IYC), an immigrant rights network operating out of the Inland Empire in Southern California. The IYC was born out of the collaboration of multiple immigrant-rights organizations in the region. Those organizations were led by undocumented youth who wanted to move immigrant rights activism in new directions. Primarily, IYC wanted to craft space for youth organizing and movement building. Secondly, they wanted to move immigrant rights organizing into intersectional identity building by ensuring that movements were led by queer and transgender individuals. Having youth and queer/trans activists take leadership roles meant that those often most marginalized at multiple levels by U.S. society and within organizations began addressing immigrant rights issues that had not been historically addressed within the broader immigrant rights movements (IRMs). Jonathan's and Isaac's leadership within IYC, and later in national networks, represents the moment in which undocumented youth activism grew to prominence in the United States after 2010. They shifted the ways immigrant populations were documented externally in mainstream society and internally within immigrant-rights organizing spaces.

Jonathan self-identifies as a queer undocumented Afro-Colombian asylum seeker; their work with the IYC focused on merging the intersections of their queer, trans, Black, and undocumented status to highlight the large gaps of intersectionality within the immigrant rights movement.[1] Isaac self-identifies as an Indigenous Mexican immigrant, and they began their organizing work focusing on the alarming surveillance by the Los Angeles Police Department (LAPD) and soon after on the collaboration of local law enforcement with federal agencies like Immigration and Customs Enforcement (ICE).[2] By the mid-2000s ICE began regularly setting up raids and picking up immigrants as they went about their everyday lives with the assistance of the LAPD. Jonathan and Isaac co-founded the IYC at the same time that other undocumented youth–based organizations grew after the failure of the Dream Act in 2010.[3] Regional networks across urban cities and rural towns grew out of the 2006 and 2007 national peaceful marches and continued growing into the early period of the 2010s.[4] These networks were composed of organizations, like the IYC, of youth who wanted to change the immigrant rights movements' trajectory. Youth organizers within the IYC shifted their organizing strategies to bring attention to the lived experiences of the most marginalized within undocumented communities. They operated along the lines of intersectionality and ensured that those most marginalized within immigrant communities were represented in the decision-making process.

In this chapter, I focus on the activism and organizing of Jonathan Perez and Isaac Barrera from 2010 to 2018, when they formed part of a national effort to bring attention to the human rights violations occurring inside of detention centers. I chose these two *actors* because their *performances* were a microcosm of larger mobilizations and because the events in which they participated received broad national attention. As organizers, their performances were carefully constructed scripts that revealed strategies of direct forms of activism.[5] Through their performances, Jonathan and Isaac confronted immigration control systems and documented sites that were previously kept out of the public eye. They were the first undocumented youth activists to successfully infiltrate an immigration detention center and publicly speak to the human rights violations they witnessed while there. In this chapter, I add to the theorization of *illegality* by incorporating woman-of-color and queer-of-color critiques of social movement approaches to understand the ways undocumented youth crafted an *illegal* identity and assembled archives and the documentation of *illegal sites*: detention centers.

After 2010, undocumented youth activists began to identify new sites of struggle to escalate strategic civil-disobedience actions aimed at exposing state-produced violent acts against immigrants. These activists took their grievances directly to sites of power and disciplinary institutions. The first part of this chapter will provide brief historical background that connects the early period of the 2000s with the broader IRMs and then covers the end of the first decade of the twenty-first century, when undocumented youth movements (UYMs) grew out of the fractures and new assemblages of the traditional immigrant-rights spaces. This first section also defines the framework of illegalization, building on woman-of-color and queer-of-color scholarship. The body of this chapter focuses on Jonathan and Isaac's activism in November of 2011, dividing it into two acts. In "Act One," I analyze video documentation of both activists successfully getting detained at a border patrol office in Mobile, Alabama. "Act Two" focuses on the organizing of their infiltration action once in detention in south Louisiana. In the final part of the chapter, I use textual analysis to analyze two archival videos: an interview produced just weeks after their infiltration action and a recording during a symposium panel that captures Jonathan's and Isaac's reactions after their infiltration. The conclusion or postscript discusses the legacies of their infiltration campaign.

UNDOCUMENTED YOUTH MOVEMENTS SHIFT TO DIRECT FORMS OF ACTIVISM

Chapter 1 analyzed Elvira Arellano's case study in the first part of the twenty-first century, following her trajectory toward direct forms of activism involving civil disobedience, embedded in traditions of the U.S. civil rights movements. As mentioned in the previous chapter, the 2006 and 2007 national peaceful marches were central to the development of consciousness for many immigrant communities but especially for undocumented youth.[6] For many undocumented youths, this was the moment when they realized there was power in mass organizing. However, their participation in mass organizing made them realize the constraints that existed in the traditional immigrant rights movements. As such, undocumented youth began creating their own organizations, a vision for collective movements, and new identities from which to create organizing platforms. Concurrently, the rise and growth of the internet and social media platforms facilitated the control of messaging, creative opportunities, and the possibility for like-minded undocumented youth to meet and share their visions for organizing.[7]

Undocumented youth had gone through the trials and tribulations of organizing collectively with their respective state political representatives and nationally across the web in attempts to pass the federal Dream Act on three occasions: 2001, 2007, and 2010. When those efforts failed to culminate as policy in 2010, the emotions of undocumented youth ranged from disappointment and disillusionment to anger and frustration. Many ultimately grew to distrust the U.S. political system. Many undocumented youth realized that they had been sold a dream and that the political system was not going to change unless they changed their approaches and relationship to that political system. Undocumented youth locally and nationally took to the streets and escalated toward direct forms of activism by using their bodies as a form of protest. Although the Dream Act failed, ultimately undocumented youth realized they had gained something important from organizing within the political system: *cultural capital*.[8] Undocumented youth had not achieved legislative success in ensuring a pathway to citizenship for undocumented populations, but they did gain a cultural status that was valuable as sociopolitical currency. Undocumented youth began to test that cultural capital and exchange it for protection while escalating their civil disobedience activism.

In chapter 1, the years 2006 and 2007 are crucial to Elvira Arellano's case study and the broader immigrant rights movements. This chapter highlights 2010 as a pivotal year in which undocumented youth movements escalated their direct forms of organizing in several civil disobedience actions. Before turning to this type of direct activism, organizers used civic engagement models—that is, working withing the confines of the political system to enact change. Many of these civic engagement models came from historically established organizations from the civil rights movements that stood to benefit from their control over immigrant rights platforms. Examples of civic engagement included working closely with politicians and lobbying in favor of legislation like the Dream Act. In "The Politics of Incivility," Bernard E. Harcourt argues that civility stands to benefit those with long-term, established power or privilege in a society.[9] Civility, according to Harcourt, is a colonial extension of assimilation to dominant ideas aimed at upholding societal norms. Established Chicana/o/x or Latina/o/x organizations stemming from the civil rights movements tended to control the messaging and thus controlled funding, resources, and directions for activism. When efforts to pass the Dream Act failed and indirect forms of activism rooted in civic engagement did not work, organizers like Jonathan and Isaac realized that they needed to organize around messaging that challenged the definition of undocumented.

Under neoliberal models, immigration control systems serve to inflict systemic and episodic violence on undocumented populations as a means of controlling labor systems and extending capital flows.[10] Neoliberal labor systems have developed alongside the modernization and increasing complexity of an immigration control system aimed at classifying and regulating immigrant bodies and restricting their mobility.[11] Thus, immigrant rights organizers and activists realized that their illegal status and their bodies could be used as means of resistance. Undocu-queer activists and artists (*artivists*) were influenced by their civil rights predecessors and by LGBTQ movements' strategies of resistance, in which aggrieved populations make strategic use of their bodies and identities in public spaces. However, undocu-queer organizers, like their civil rights predecessors, also had to learn about the blatant homophobia, transphobia, and anti-queer sentiments that existed in immigrant rights movements that had not dealt with identity formations but rather focused on labor organizing in a zero-sum-game model. Focusing on identity was something that was seen as detracting from bigger gains. These traditional organizations that controlled immigrant rights activism up to the 2000s upheld neoliberal paradigms focused on capital accumulation and did not provide space for youth to explore their identity formations as important sources of subjugation.

Woman-of-color and queer-of-color scholarship has spent significant time uncovering the internal marginalization of women, queer people, trans people, and youth in broader and historical movements like the Chicanx movements and Black power movements. I am reminded of Audre Lorde's words: "The 60s for me was a time of promise and excitement, but the 60s was also a time of isolation and frustration from within."[12] Lorde's words highlight how social movements can both be liberating and reinforce the systems of power they aim to decolonize. Similarly, the anthology edited by Dionne Espinoza, María Eugenia Cotera, and Maylei Blackwell, *Chicana* Movidas (2018), charts the development of a praxis of resistance created both in opposition to the broader U.S. society and also internally within the mainstream Chicano Movement of the 1960s and 1970s. Each chapter offers movidas, which "[operate] as . . . the generative 'other' of what is visible, accredited, and sanctioned as a strategy of subversion," and focuses on multifaceted archival sources inserting Chicana women's contributions to major events in the Chicano Movement.[13]

Queer-of-color scholars in conversation with woman-of-color feminists offer critical accounts of how globalization works as a set of exclusionary measures hindering mobility and restricting queer bodies. Being queer is often defined as being out of place, strange, unrecognizable; therefore, queer-of-color scholars argue that we cannot divorce the politics of migration and queer politics from global economic practices. Karma Chávez's scholarship pushes for an analysis of how gender and sexuality are performed in the framing of social movements. Chávez calls for comparative analysis that moves across woman-of-color feminism and queer-of-color critique to offer new interpretations not tied to one nation or ethnic/national group. Chávez argues that migrant youth who do not perform the role of the "good immigrant" are queering social movements and produce *counter-public enclaves*, or possibilities for developing and documenting coalitional moments and politics.[14] If immigrants are the *other*, or opposite, of what citizens represent for the nation, then we must understand immigrant bodies as inherently queer in the formation of nation-state and global paradigms.

Importantly, queer-of-color scholars have advanced our understanding of normative notions of citizenship, building on earlier woman-of-color feminist traditions to propose intersectional and interlocking analytical frameworks. José Esteban Muñoz's development of the term *disidentification* underscores how queers of color perform identity to survive a heteronormative, patriarchal, and racially normative globe.[15] Muñoz warns readers that *disidentification* does not equate to conformity or assimilation but rather highlights the ways in which queers of color recognize normative structures and perform acts of resistance. Similarly, immigrant youth are often placed in binaries of model citizenry dictated by neoliberal global capitalist structures that expect production. When migrant youth step out of expected parameters they are often labeled as deviant youth. Activism in the form of civil disobedience produced deep introspection about the definition of immigrants, how they were conceptualized, and who among them deserved citizenship and human rights.

Undocu-queer artivists created the mantra "Undocumented and Unafraid" and converted it into a messaging staple of the immigrant rights movement. This slogan tied together communities of struggle that crossed the lines demarcated by race, class, gender, and sexuality.[16] Claiming a forthright undocumented identity in public spaces empowered undocumented youth with a sense of independence, grassroots spirit, and dissidence against a political system that continued to relegate immigrants to the shadows.[17] The slogan

"Undocumented and Unafraid" offered a twofold discursive intervention. First, it was a self-empowering message aimed against the U.S. political system, which marginalized immigrants. Second, it propelled immigrant youth as the vanguard of the immigrant rights movement. Undocumented youth stepped out in front of and in defense of their communities.

Nicholas De Genova states that the use of the slogan "¡Aquí estamos, y no nos vamos!" (We are here, and we're not leaving) by the immigrant rights movements demonstrates an inclination toward an "irreversible presence."[18] Similarly, with the slogan "Undocumented and Unafraid," undocumented youth activists underscored their own "irreversible presence." The transmedia narratives and testimonials produced by undocumented youth were not being used to create a spectacle or sympathy in the viewer. Instead, they were used to assert undocumented youth's self-owned and self-directed identity. René Galindo, an education scholar doing research on undocumented students and movements, demonstrates how this assertion helped immigrant committees construct a counternarrative against power structures. Galindo states, "Performances are critical for the construction of collective representation, since they are self-reflexive processes in which actors construct and communicate self-images through the use of verbal and nonverbal symbols."[19] The creation of new messaging correlated with undocumented youth activists' switch to acts of civil disobedience and a leadership spearheaded by undocu-queer artivists.

A critical aspect of undocu-queer activism centered art as a political strategy. Activists used art to educate audiences about the importance of applying intersectionality to immigrant rights activism. Queer artivist Nicolás (Nico) González participated in the first-ever "Coming Out of the Shadows" event organized in Chicago, Illinois, on March 10, 2010. The event was organized as a way for undocumented youth to publicly "come out" and announce their undocumented status and identities in public spaces. Activists were effectively "coming out of the shadows" to which immigrant communities are relegated. The event was a manifestation of pride in their undocumented identities and a reclaiming of their humanity in a public space. Nico describes the tensions that developed over representation and inclusivity during the planning of the action. The "Coming Out of the Shadows" campaign responded to and reflected disagreements over immigrant rights organizing and discourse. In a podcast interview Nico states, "It was a lot of fighting with the people who had been organizing and doing immigrant rights. A lot of them were politicians. A lot of them were directors at nonprofits . . . they were the ones telling undocumented people to stay in the back."[20] Nico directly refers to the tensions that existed between politicians and nonprofit directors on the one hand, and undocu-queer youth on the other. The youth felt pushed back and repressed in national immigrant-rights organizing. Thus, their activism against repressive federal and state policies also fought the barriers they faced in organizations led by nonprofits. The "Coming Out of the Shadows" event marked a turning point in organizing efforts by undocumented youth activists. Their politics, unlike that of previous generations of immigrant rights activism, involved direct action, intersectional discourse, and grassroots organizing.

"Coming Out of the Shadows" in 2010 was a coalitional event conducted by the Immigrant Youth Justice League (IYJL).[21] The IYJL was an organization founded in Chicago in 2009 by undocumented youth organizers who wanted to operate through direct forms of activism. Like other local and regional organizations, the IYJL later connected with national networks like the National Immigrant Youth Alliance (NIYA) to escalate civil disobedience actions. "Coming Out of the Shadows" became a trademark event for the IYJL. The public event drew on testimonial practices and aimed to capture widespread national coverage in both English and Spanish media outlets. The activists claimed public space while revealing themselves as undocumented youth. The activists' presence, identity declarations, media coverage, and sensational tactics marked a turn toward acts of civil disobedience. In both their organizational approaches and their slogan "Undocumented and Unafraid," undocumented youth declared the movement's disregard for abusive and repressive local, state, or federal authority.

The "Coming Out of the Shadows" event in 2010 spoke to audiences both within and outside of the movement. Undocumented youth were also challenging the practices and approaches of immigrant rights organizers who had assumed leadership over the undocumented communities most impacted by authoritarian legislation. Nico's words also denounce that old leadership's co-optation of the immigrant rights movements up to the mid-2000s and the limited flexibility to work outside of the political system. In the podcast interview referenced earlier, Nico reflects on the spark that led to organizing the first "Coming Out of the Shadows" event:

> With the whole "Coming Out of the Shadows," many of us were queer and we started doing national organizing. So, the conversation was like, "Look, there is a whole bunch of queer people in this movement!" And a lot of the people

that are speaking for immigrants were really this homophobic machista men. So, we said we were going to go challenge them in their frame of thinking, because a lot of them were older Chicanos organizing . . . we were constantly told to stay in the back. At this point the community wanted to see young people as the leaders. That is what we do, and this is who we are, and we continue to empower young people.[22]

Nico discusses how the messaging for immigrant rights organizing had been traditionally controlled by nonprofit leaders and organizations with roots in the civil rights movements, such as Chicano men whose leadership practices marginalized undocu-queer activists and community members.

Following the "Coming Out of the Shadows" event, undocumented youth continued to form national and regional networks and escalate their direct forms of activism through civil disobedience actions. One of the stories most covered by journalists and scholars of undocumented youth activism is the sit-in action in the late Arizona Republican senator John McCain's office in Tucson on May 18, 2010.[23] The undocumented student activists organized the sit-in to try to convince McCain to support the Dream Act. Senator John McCain had initially been a supporter of the Dream Act in its earlier stages, but later decided not to support the bill. As a result, he came under pressure by undocumented youth when the Dream Act came before Congress once again in 2010.

The sit-in action at Senator McCain's office is recognized as one of the first moments when undocumented youth escalated the intensity of their organizing efforts through targeted and direct forms of activism. It was also the first time this type of activism received heightened media attention. Headlines about this act of civil disobedience appeared in major newspapers across the United States, including one published in the *New York Times* on the same day of the action, May 18, 2010. Julia Preston, the journalist, summarized the sit-in with the headline "Illegal Immigrant Students Protest at McCain Office."[24] She states, "It was the first time since 2006 that students directly risked deportation in an effort to prompt Congress to take up a bill that would benefit illegal immigrant youths."[25] Preston references the 2006 national peaceful marches, one of the first episodes in which undocumented youth walked out in the streets to demonstrate. The organizing of the sit-in, and the public discourse used by undocumented youth, challenged conventional ideas about undocumented youth activism and the public use of immigrant bodies. Public discourse often represented immigrants as living in the shadows of society and as passive victims of immigration regulation and policy.

The action at Senator John McCain's office was anything but passive. Five known activists participated: Lizbeth Mateo, Mohammad Abdollahi, Yahaira Carrillo, Tania Unzueta, and Raúl Alcaraz.[26] Lizbeth Mateo and Mohammad Abdollahi were recognized members of the National Immigrant Youth Alliance. NIYA was among the first national networks formed in 2010 by undocumented youth through online portals where they met to organize national actions, and it connected with Jonathan Perez and Isaac Barrera to collectively organize the 2011 infiltration action central to this chapter.[27] NIYA was among the first undocumented youth collectives that tested the use of undocumented youth's cultural capital as a form of political protection to organize civil disobedience actions. They reached out to and recruited undocumented youth organizers from across the nation for political actions in strategic locations like Senator McCain's office.

NIYA and the undocumented youth who organized the actions did so with full awareness of the inherent risks of participation. Four out of the five activists in the Tucson sit-in—Lizbeth Mateo, Mohammad Abdollahi, Tania Unzueta, and Yahaira Carrillo—were undocumented youth risking deportation. The fifth participant, Raúl Alcaraz, was a legal resident at the time of the action and a Tucson high-school teacher.[28] The undocumented youth conducted the sit-in while symbolically wearing blue graduation caps and gowns, demonstrating their status as students in the United States and highlighting the potential that the United States was rejecting by not passing the Dream Act. Various traditional and online media channels referred to the participants in the sit-in as the "Dream Act 5."[29] This sit-in earned notoriety and gained even more cultural capital for undocumented youth.[30] Julia Preston continued to cover the "Dream Act 5" for the *New York Times* and published a follow-up article on August 8, 2010, that indicated that two of the activists from the sit-in at Senator McCain's office had been arrested for criminal trespassing by the local police, who then informed ICE.[31] However, neither of the two activists was charged with anything in federal immigration court. The sit-in received wide media coverage as well as attention from politicians outside of Arizona, and many public voices advocated for the activists' release. Because of this, the students were not placed in deportation proceedings.[32] The sit-in at Senator McCain's office, then, marked a focal moment in immigrant rights movements. For the first time, undocumented activists saw the Department of Homeland Security decline to pursue the deportation of undocumented youth. The activists strategically used the fact that, in the hierarchy of categorization of immigrant bodies, they had been designated as low priority for deportation from the country. The DHS's reluctance to place the undocumented activists in deportation proceedings surprised both pro- and anti-immigrant organizers alike.[33]

Anthropologist Laura Corrunker, one of the first scholars to cover this moment in undocumented youth organizing history, highlights the fact that the action was led by undocumented youth who identified as queer.[34] Corrunker states, "In the United States many undocumented youth have followed a similar strategy, influenced by the 'coming out' actions of the Lesbian/Gay/Transgender/Queer (LGBTQ) Movement," highlighting the ways youth who self-identified as undocumented and queer wanted to use their intersectional identities to inform organizing strategies. These youth realized that the immigrant rights movements at this point were not inclusive of all identities. As such, undocumented youth recognized the need to organize intersectionally across race, ethnicity, gender, and sexuality. This approach became one of the important distinctions in terms of leadership differences between the traditional IRMs and the UYMs. Undocu-queer organizers—individuals who self-identify both as undocumented and queer—have been at the forefront of the leadership and messaging in UYMs from the beginning.

Many academics and journalists have written about the empowering messages of the "Undocumented and Unafraid" and "Coming Out of the Shadows" slogans for undocumented youth. These terms also spoke discursively against the constructions of the "model citizen" that undergirded U.S. immigration policy and rhetorical practices. Immigrant youth were expected to aspire to be model citizens in order to deserve citizenship and its rights. The "Coming Out of the Shadows" slogan and related political action were about queering the immigrant rights movement. They were also meant to combat the ways immigrant communities continued to be illegalized by the dominant society and by the very same movements that supposedly existed to defend them. As such, a move toward civil disobedience was not only a switch to radical politics but also a type of activism that reflected the lived intersectional realities experienced by immigrant communities.

And while the "Coming Out of the Shadows" events that produced the "Undocumented and Unafraid" mantra in the UYMs carried forward across many undocumented youth circles, it is important to note the limitations of said strategies among diverse undocumented immigrant communities. For one, while the events were happening in public and urban metropolitan centers like Chicago, Los Angeles, New York, etc., there were other undocumented youth living in much more conservative and anti-immigrant states like those in the South, Midwest, or Pacific Northwest, where it was a risk to reveal not only your immigration status but also your identity as a queer individual.[35] The research by Jesús Cisneros and Christian Bracho (2019) examines how undocumented queer individuals navigate the boundaries of immigration status and identity, including multiple factors such as survival tactics, opportunities, and family rejection.[36] Undocumented youth activism revealed that intersectional movement creation was possible but also needed to be adapted and strategized differently according to location and individual differences.

The move toward a civil disobedience strategy was accompanied by new identity markers that rejected the "model minority" categories that undocumented youth had been expected to adopt during the early 2000s and that were carried onward with the creation of the DREAMer narrative. Undocumented youth grew frustrated with a political system that aimed at preserving racial and classist hierarchies and only included a selected few. Immigrant youth wanted to change immigration politics, but they realized they also needed to shift organizing spaces within the broader IRMs. They did so by staging political actions like the "Coming Out of the Shadows" event. In response to their criminalization by the immigration control system, undocumented youth organizers embraced the term "illegal" and turned it into an identity marker of defiance that propelled their activism to spaces where they could document the violence experienced by immigrants who had been rendered "illegal."

UNDOCUMENTED YOUTH MOVEMENTS THROUGH THE LENS OF WOMAN-OF-COLOR AND QUEER-OF-COLOR CRITIQUE

On November 6, 2013, Jonathan Perez posted a picture of themself on Facebook wearing a shirt that read, "I AM ILLEGAL." Beneath the bold all-caps text on the T-shirt that reads, "I AM ILLEGAL," there is a phonetic spelling that informs the viewer how to pronounce the word "illegal." This is done to highlight the word and emphasize to a non-undocumented audience how to refer to undocumented youth. The caption below the picture states:

Interesting story here. I wear this shirt and get high fives and over 60 likes. When a younger person Yessica Gonzalez (the designer) wears it, they get backlash for wearing it. #maleprivilege #sexism #patriarchy #our movement #adultism.[37]

The post underscores the need for an intersectional perspective that analyzes the way immigrant rights struggles reproduce systems of patriarchy that produce sexism and other forms of discrimination. Most importantly, Jonathan's caption critiques the power structures that render women and queers of color illegal within undocumented youth social movements. Like the "Coming Out of the Shadows" event, Jonathan's Facebook post was not only speaking outwardly to a general audience about their conceptualization of "illegal," but also inwardly to undocumented youth who were part of immigrant rights organizing.

FIGURE 4 "I AM ILLEGAL." T-shirt image. Photograph by Yessica Gonzalez.

Jonathan's photograph and post provide an example of how undocumented youth activists crafted transmedia narratives to communicate their political perspectives to mass audiences during the rise of undocumented youth movements in the twenty-first century. Undocumented youth organizers sought to encourage activists to go beyond civic engagement and build inclusive intersectional models that advocated for those most marginalized in diverse undocumented communities. In other words, undocumented youth organizers like Jonathan Perez recognized that documenting the undocumented community meant peeling back several layers of their identities to go beyond the "undocumented" label. I take a cue from organizers like Jonathan and Isaac when I underscore that (un)documenting requires us to think about intersectional identities, multiple issues, and diverse backgrounds to acknowledge that immigrant rights are not a homogeneous process. (Un)documenting— producing an archive of the undocumented experience—requires an extensive process of navigating multiplicity. In this book, I argue that to (un)document requires us to use methodologies such as visual analysis in a critical manner that allows us "to see" beyond the borders of traditional organizing and look beyond the margins, analyzing illegalization processes as they are inscribed in undocumented bodies.

The T-shirt worn by Jonathan, and designed by the artivist Yessica Gonzalez, exemplifies a shift in rhetoric and consciousness among some undocumented youth who lay claim to the term "illegal." I argue that this shift signifies the undocumented person's move away from seeking inclusion in the U.S. nation-state and toward pushing against the boundaries of inclusion and exclusion that are produced through the regulation and management of bodies and citizenship—what scholars have referred to as a process of illegalization.[38]

The Facebook photograph posted by Jonathan Perez also highlights how undocumented youth used the self-identifier "illegal" as a way to combat negative social imagery around "undocumented" immigrants. Jonathan wears the shirt in defiance of outward identification processes. By embracing the term "illegal," Jonathan and Yessica (creator of the T-shirt) resist being identified by societal norms and instead aim to take ownership of self-identification. Again, this messaging speaks outwardly to a general audience, but also inwardly to an undocumented youth audience, telling them to self-identify and not allow themselves to be labeled or identified by others.

The "I AM ILLEGAL" T-shirt also represents a queering of undocumented youth movements. At first glance, the T-shirt's statement may produce a visceral reaction from both a general audience and an immigrant community audience, causing people to ask themselves, "Why would undocumented youth choose to identify as illegal?" Chicanx studies and jotería studies scholarship helps us answer that question.[39] Gloria Anzaldúa's theorization of a *mestiza consciousness* employed an interdisciplinary and untraditional historical approach to exploring the subjectivity of Chicana lesbian women in the borderlands. In this exploration of subjectivity, Anzaldúa points to the contradictions and ambiguity that arise when individuals are made the subjects or objects of study in order to offer important critiques of how archives, knowledge, and narratives are similarly full of contradictions and ambiguity. Cherríe Moraga's "Queer Aztlán" addresses the sexism, patriarchy, and homophobia that have historically existed in the Chicano Movement and argues that we must recognize this past to be able to offer alternative futures.[40] Those alternative futures are work that Emma Pérez and Chela Sandoval develop into a framework for a jotería *consciousness*.[41]

A jotería consciousness is a focus on what jotería studies scholar Daniel Enrique Pérez defines as a "critical site of inquiry centering on nonheteronormative gender and sexuality as related to mestiza/o subjectivities and identities."[42] Pérez's work in jotería studies extends to his analysis of a mariposa *consciousness*, which aims to reclaim negative stereotyping of terms like mariposa (butterfly) in Chicanx, Latin American, and Latinx communities that historically used it as derogatory terminology to refer to gay, lesbian, trans, and queer communities. Pérez argues that the adoption of said terms by queer Chicanx individuals has represented the formation of a consciousness that creates sites and opportunities of empowerment through its decolonial oppositionality. A genealogy of jotería studies is critical to begin to understand the oppositional consciousness formed in an undocu-queer identity and the positionality employed in the activism of UYMs.

Juan D. Ochoa's work (2015) links the artivism of undocu-queer artist Julio Salgado to the scholarship of Chicanx feminists who reclaimed the derogatory Spanish term "joto" or "jota" to turn it into the positive term "jotería."[43] Yessica's art and Jonathan's post similarly reclaim the negative term "illegal." Undocumented youth converted "illegal" into a self-identifying term rooted in resilience that aims to highlight how immigrants resist illegalization processes. Read another way, the T-shirt conveys that the individual wearing it refuses to be sanctioned by the oppressive U.S. nation-state and therefore is not complicit with the inhumane treatment of vulnerable people.

Reclamation of negative terminology is a political and academic project that moves beyond inclusion, and it is also a way of naming and recuperating specific identifiers toward the crafting of new forms of knowledge. Chicana feminist Yvette Saavedra strategically uses the term "lesbian/queer" rather than separating the terminology according to the way traditional European and Western feminist waves of literature have divided these marginalized groups.[44] In doing so, Saavedra situates the intersections of these identities as being connected to the formation of Chicana feminist traditions. Saavedra extends these decolonial practices as coalitional opportunities between queer studies, jotería studies, and Chicana feminisms. Taking a cue from Saavedra's work, I argue that the adoption of an illegalized political identity by undocumented youth like Jonathan Perez and the example of the "I AM ILLEGAL" T-shirt represent coalitional moments in which the analysis offered by jotería studies, Chicana feminism, and queer-of-color critiques can inform the development of undocumented youth studies. Subverting negative terminology like "illegal" has the potential to produce new social imaginaries.

Juan D. Ochoa's article "Shine Bright Like a Diamond" connects jotería studies with the inclusion of undocu-queer activism within broader immigrant rights activism, and builds on a woman-of-color and queer-of-color genealogy in employing "jotería analytics." Speaking of undocu-queer artivist Julio Salgado, Ochoa declares that "Salgado's digital image provides an alternative migrant story: The migrant can also be queer," highlighting the way artivists like Salgado complicated immigrant rights narratives and pushed for inclusivity in undocumented youth movements.[45] Julio and Jonathan are contemporaries who collaborated and worked together in pushing the messages of undocumented youth movements beyond traditional immigrant-rights narratives of inclusion to instead advocate for intersectionality as a mode for the liberation of all people. In fact, Jonathan is one of the community members featured in Julio's original artwork series *I Am Undocuqueer*, originally published on their website in January 2012.[46] This series, like Jonathan's T-shirt Facebook post, pushes toward a queering of the archive: the intersections of being queer and being undocumented began to be archived in Julio's artwork.

Scholars like Melissa Autumn White have written about the limitations of seeking visibility, as in works like the *I Am Undocuqueer* series. White argues that "such representational tactics—in the form of announcing a new 'identity' formation—risk subtending the radical potential of such convergent politics within a register of visual containment: normativizing by definition."[47]

Similarly, undocumented youth were advocating for the inclusion of diverse identities as part of their organizing principles. These new organizing principles were present in the artwork, fashion, messaging, etc., but as White highlights, without the push for political action that shifted everyday forms of existence for multiple marginalized communities within the larger undocumented communities, they can easily remain normative. My analysis here aims to show how Jonathan's and Isaac's activism pushes the boundaries of organizing, not only externally and publicly through actions like the T-shirt discussed in this section, but also internally within the movement by questioning leadership that reinforces sexism, patriarchy, ageism, and racism.

Another aspect of Jonathan's post is its criticism of sexism and patriarchy. Jonathan's post quite literally embodies a push toward recognizing a double standard that exists within undocumented youth movements: namely, how a male-presenting individual like Jonathan can wear an "I AM ILLEGAL" T-shirt and receive recognition and approval, while the designer of the shirt, Yessica Gonzalez, a female-presenting activist, receives "backlash for wearing it." Jonathan is speaking directly to other undocumented youth activists and calling out patriarchal systems that produce inequalities within undocumented youth organizing spaces. A jotería analysis of the "I AM ILLEGAL" T-shirt builds on the adoption of the term "illegal" as oppositional consciousness that signals radicalization and decolonial and oppositional politics by undocu-queer youth. This oppositional consciousness adds to the illegalization framework that undocumented youth incorporated into their civil disobedience strategies.

An illegalization framework highlights how immigrant youth, similar to young women of color and queers of color, are criminalized, marked, and labeled disruptive when they step out of the normative parameters of society. Self-identified illegalized youth like Jonathan and Isaac felt that it was not enough to come out of the shadows with their undocumented status; rather, they felt the need to organize in ways closer to the sites where immigrants are rendered "illegal," as demonstrated in their marked flesh. Beyond the Facebook post including the photograph with the "I AM ILLEGAL" T-shirt, Jonathan continuously referred to themself with the "illegal" identifier on social media, producing a new discourse or transmedia narrative for UYMs.[48] Neither identity nor social movements are static or fixed; rather, they are fluid, and they grow and change over time. As such, social media posts should be analyzed as a construction of transmedia narratives producing reflections about an "illegal" identity that is not linear in time. Their reframing of the "illegal" identity works across time and space to produce a new form of reality rooted in immigrant bodily experiences.

Working across the intersections of activism and multiple identities represented within the undocumented immigrant communities, we can see that the intention of Jonathan's post is not only to call out the nation-state's power structures but also to highlight the internal tensions that exist within undocumented communities and their organizing sites. Jonathan's and Isaac's work also centers a critical race analysis within immigrant rights organizations. Illegalized youth organizers remind us that an undocumented person might eventually receive status, but if that person is Black or Indigenous, the perception of their illegality remains, because of anti-Black or anti-Indigenous racism prevalent in the logic of the nation-state. In a nation-state where Blackness is most closely associated with criminalization, achieving status does not equate to liberation for Black undocumented individuals in the same manner that it does for others who are undocumented.[49] And internally, in immigrant communities hailing from places like Latin America where anti-Indigenous racial hierarchies exist from colonial pasts, Indigenous bodies are still marked as "other" even after obtaining citizenship. Undocu-queer identity also highlights the ways in which receiving documented status does not necessarily transfer to societal liberation. Rather, the social hierarchy that separates and divides people based on race, class, gender, and sexuality remains in place, particularly for undocu-queer, undocu-Black, transgender, and Indigenous immigrant bodies.[50]

In the post–Dream Act era, undocumented youth like Jonathan and Isaac recognized that there was a need to escalate actions by organizing in spaces like U.S. detention centers to expose the very "illegalized" sites that rendered immigrant bodies disposable. After the failure of the Dream Act in 2010, queer- and trans-led networks like the Immigrant Youth Coalition began connecting with national networks like the National Immigrant Youth Alliance to bring together undocumented youth activists from across the nation who were willing to push the boundaries of legally prescribed sites of activism. Jonathan and Isaac had already taken their organizing to states like Arizona and Alabama that were passing anti-immigrant policies between 2009 and 2010 and criminalizing undocumented communities. In an interview reflecting on their activism in Alabama, which led to their infiltration action, Jonathan states that they wanted to "shift the balance of power" between immigration enforcement and undocumented populations who were housed inside of detention centers.[51] In the next section, I aim to (un)document their action—to provide visual and textual analysis of the archival video footage produced by Jonathan, Isaac, and NIYA of their detention at a border patrol office in Mobile, Alabama, on November 20, 2011.

ACT ONE: PERFORMING ILLEGALITY TO BE DETAINED

A theater performance contains multiple acts that produce an assemblage that is the total body of the work. This assemblage of acts is carefully curated to create a narrative the audience is to engage with. For historians, a similar relationship might be found in the multiple archives that the scholar assembles to produce a work of history. The documents are the tools with which historians tell stories that relate the meaning of particular events.[52]

Diana Taylor's work *The Archive and the Repertoire* (2003) suggests that other forms of documentation such as "performance" have been overlooked in traditional Western academic interpretations, with the effect of upholding white supremacy. She argues that civic disobedience is performed by marginalized communities in particular ways across everyday rituals that she terms "embodied practice."[53] Drawing on gender and critical theorists like J. L. Austin, Jacques Derrida, and Judith Butler, Taylor shows how *performativity* registers the way the process of socialization across intersections of gender and sexual identities regulates said identities. The realms of performance studies literature and social movement scholarship can find analysis of performativity particularly useful in uncovering the performance of organizers who challenge societal norms. In the digital world, Taylor extends her analysis to what she terms "technologically mediated performance," to uncover "productive frictions" that can reveal particular sites that systems of power aim to keep hidden.[54] Drawing from Taylor's work, my (un)documenting approach analyzes Jonathan and Isaac's "technologically mediated performance" in infiltrating a detention center as an act of resistance aimed at bringing sites of violence to the public imaginary.

In this section, I conduct a visual and textual analysis of the infiltration video footage captured by Jonathan Perez and Isaac Barrera at a Border Patrol office in Mobile, Alabama, on November 20, 2011. Such an analysis is useful to unpack the performativity of a social movement campaign like this one. The textual analysis of the transcripts highlights Jonathan's and Isaac's choice of words in their infiltration action performance. A visual analysis of the archival video footage for tone, words, body language, and distinct performance elements helps us understand the complex power exchange central to their action.[55]

On November 20, 2011, Jonathan Perez and Isaac Barrera walked into a Border Patrol office in Mobile, Alabama. They walked in separately and at different times, but their performance was similar and used the same strategy of pretending to be lost and disoriented. NIYA had already attempted infiltration but had been unsuccessful because Border Patrol agents did not take the bait. By the time Jonathan and Isaac signed up for their collaboration with NIYA, they realized that they needed to incorporate a performance element to ensure that they were placed in a detention center. Jonathan's recording of the infiltration was publicly broadcast and disseminated on social media through NIYA's YouTube channel.[56] Jonathan's video is approximately three and a half minutes long and was recorded with a cell-phone camera hidden in their front shirt pocket. Isaac's video recording did not work due to technical issues with the cell phone used.

The curated and edited video presented to the public begins by naming the national networks that participated in the action, which include NIYA and the Dream Activist Undocumented Students and Resource Network.[57] Next, we see a new rendition of the popular slogan "Undocumented and Unafraid," with the addition of another word to make "Undocumented, Unafraid, Undercover." The addition of "undercover" signaled these undocumented activists' escalation toward civil disobedience in their organizing. In other words, it was not enough to pronounce one's identity as undocumented; it had to also be followed with action.

"Undercover" specifically refers to Jonathan's and Isaac's performance of an illegal identity for the border patrol agents in order to be successfully detained and thus begin their incognito operation of reporting inside of the detention center. Sociologist Angela S. García's work *Legal Passing* (2019) describes the tremendous amounts of effort that undocumented immigrants make to not call the attention of police and immigration officials across their local, city, and state jurisdictions. García states that "daily adjustments demanded by legal passing incrementally unfold and become habitual, they expand to shape the textures and rhythms of immigrants' everyday lives, as well as their bodies, behaviors, and minds."[58] As such, in my analysis, Jonathan and Isaac's infiltration action is based on performing the opposite of *legal passing*; that is, they are counting on *(il)legal passing*—Jonathan and Isaac needed to perform an illegal identity in order to be detained and accomplish their infiltration intentions. Stated differently, Jonathan's and Isaac's performance of illegality in the eyes of immigration authorities meant presenting themselves with the characteristics that undocumented individuals are assumed to have.

Angela S. García's work also talks about the choices and decisions that undocumented communities have to make to remain invisible across a landscape of policing and monitoring. In the case of UYMs, undocumented youth like Jonathan and Isaac realized that DREAMer narratives had positioned undocumented youth bodies to be read differently than those from broader undocumented immigrant communities that did not enjoy the same cultural capital. As such, UYMs aimed to use their visibility to (un)document the broader undocumented immigrant populations that did not have the privilege of visibility. Becoming more visible, then, was a tactic used by undocumented youth, and they turned it toward sites in the United States that contained and managed immigrant bodies. Jonathan and Isaac were aware that they were only going to be detained by Border Patrol if they appeared to be disoriented, vulnerable undocumented individuals, and so their strategy was to play the role expected by Border Patrol agents on their encounter. Additionally, the "undercover" component signals the countersurveillance action to produce a narrative to share widely across multiple social media platforms.

What follows should be read as a script encapsulating the effects of Jonathan's staged performance in their transmedia narrative video. Both activists, Jonathan and Isaac, perform a script that is inscribed in illegalization by the state. Through an illegalized framework, we can begin to understand the practices of escalation and civil disobedience that immigrant youth implemented to bring visibility to the most vulnerable members of the immigrant community and expose the dark perils of empire.

My visual analysis of the infiltration video is not meant to be an in-depth account but rather a theoretical exercise in understanding the important ways in which undocumented youth decided to use their bodies as vehicles of awareness in highlighting the processes by which undocumented immigrants are illegalized in sites of detention, deportation, and dehumanization in the United States.

In the video distributed by NIYA, after the title card "Undocumented, Unafraid, Undercover" fades, we see a video feed captured by a cell phone.

The first part of the video footage is captured in a limited horizontal frame and shows the inside of a moving vehicle. We hear someone outside the frame ask:

Last words?

Then we hear Jonathan laugh and respond in a comical tone:

Take this, ICE!

Jonathan continues to laugh. The cell-phone video fades, and we see a still photograph of Jonathan and Isaac with text that reads:

To begin a week of direct action against anti-immigration policies, undoc-umented youths Jonathan Perez and Isaac Barrera walked into the Border Patrol office in Alabama to ask a few questions . . .

This text informs the audience that the infiltration action that they are about to witness was part of ongoing organizing efforts, which had begun earlier in June 2011, to challenge anti-immigration legislation in Alabama.[59] States in the U.S. South had been targeting immigrant communities using punitive legislation, and Alabama was central to the fight against anti-immigration policies.

The last phrase of the text, "to ask a few questions," sets the tone for the audience and prepares them for what they are about to experience in Jon-athan's performance. The photograph accompanying the above text is also important because it captures Jonathan and Isaac posing proudly and hap-pily. We see Isaac on the left posing with a big smile and a thumbs-up. Jona-than has their right arm around Isaac's shoulder, making a peace-sign gesture with their hand. Jonathan's bodily posture is laid-back, to give a sense of full control and dominance to the audience. Both activists are front and center in the frame of the image. The background is faded and not easily made out. There appears to be a flash from the camera capturing the image, because we see a reflection in Jonathan's glasses and their skin tone is lit brightly without their dark complexion captured. Both organizers are wearing black T-shirts with screen-printed messages that are unidentifiable due to the framing of the photograph. Overall, the image conveys Jonathan's and Isaac's confidence and decisive posture going into the infiltration action.

I read the inclusion of this photograph as a deliberate performance of celebration of an unapologetic assertion against traditional representations of undocumented immigrants. In *Imprisoned in a Luminous Glare* (2013), Black studies scholar Leigh Raiford analyzes the use of photography by Black social movements "as a liberatory tool of black self-representation" that aims to engage discussions in the realm of public and private societal discourse.[60] Raiford's work also employs Diana Taylor's work on performativity to understand the ways in which alternative records captured by technology like photographs provide different registers of race, gender, and sexuality. Analyzing Jonathan's and Isaac's expressions of joy and comfortable and confident pose offers a different reading of Black, Indigenous, and queer undocumented immigrant bodies offered in public discourse. In other words, this photograph, combined with the performance elements in the video, offers a new register for a possible new social imaginary. A decolonial imaginary, as Emma Pérez highlights, offers new interpretations of racialized, queer, and gendered bodies.

The photograph fades at the thirty-second marker of the video, and we hear dramatic music as we see the cell-phone feed return.[61] Jonathan is walking in front of a white cement-textured building that has pillars decorating its front entrance. The building appears to be an office, but it is not until Jonathan

FIGURE 5 Screenshot from "Undocumented Youth vs. Border Patrol Round 1—Mobile, Alabama," posted by DreamActivistdotOrg.

reaches the front entrance that the audience can briefly make out a floor mat that reads, "U.S. Border Patrol," and below that the word "Mobile," indicating the city in Alabama where the office is located. The audience can see Jonathan's hand stretching out to open the glass front door of the office. The photograph followed by this footage captured by Jonathan's cell-phone camera provides what Diana Taylor describes as the first of the six elements of a scenario—a "scenario" being the set of social structures or factors that construct the stage or site for specific scenes to unfold.[62] The *scene*, as she states, "suggests both the material stage as well as the highly codified environment that gives viewers pertinent information, say, class status or historical period."[63] This initial thirty seconds provides the viewer with the physical location where the action is taking place; the information that this is a Border Patrol office also alerts the viewer to the authoritarian nature of the space.

The second element of a scenario that Diana Taylor's work points us to is the *social actors*. In the next thirty seconds of the video footage captured inside the Border Patrol office, Jonathan will embody the social construction of the disoriented and disarmed undocumented immigrant. Jonathan will encounter other social actors representing the immigration apparatus who embody power and authority over undocumented immigrants. Jonathan carefully assembles a script around the embodiment of diverse social constructions of the immigrant body. Their performance rests on the normative performance by the three social actors from the Border Patrol captured in the infiltration video.

At first, we see Jonathan being greeted by a female-presenting office staff member. There is a thirty-second exchange between the office assistant and Jonathan. In that brief time, Jonathan performs being lost and disoriented; the audience can see the confused expression on the office assistant's face. Jonathan's performance has left her in a state of puzzlement that the audience can infer is making her feel uncomfortable and unsure about how to proceed. The office assistant exits the frame slightly after the one-minute mark, and we do not see anybody appear in the frame for about twenty seconds. She does what is perhaps expected in a hierarchical and patriarchal structure like a Border Patrol office: she calls on male superiors with authority to manage the situation.

Although it may be an unintended or unscripted element of Jonathan's performance, the infiltration video has captured or recorded another gendered layer of the immigration apparatus with the character of the office assistant. She is visibly uncomfortable in the exchange with a Black male-presenting individual standing in her workplace lobby. Immigration studies scholars and historians have long written about the perceived threat of men of color in proximity to white women in personal and public spaces. The (un)document produced by Jonathan's video reaffirms the white panic around proper sexual interactions across racial hierarchies as something sustained over time. This is where Jonathan's identity as undocu-Black and undocu-queer is not legible to the office assistant, who only sees and registers a Black, male-presenting individual standing in front of her. The (un)document created by this exchange affirms precisely what undocu-Black activists and scholars argue: that even if a Black undocumented immigrant achieves documented status, their racial phenotype is still read as a threat to the state. This threat naturally leads to the entrance of two Anglo, male-presenting superiors, with the female-presenting office assistant never to return.

We see two male-presenting individuals walk into the office lobby. The first officer who leads the conversation with Jonathan is wearing a sport-style royal-blue collared shirt and appears to be an administrative officer. Additionally, this first officer has a royal-blue lanyard with a badge hanging over his chest, giving a sense of administrative and building access. The second officer is wearing an avocado-green shirt with a bright gold badge, the unmistakable Border Patrol uniform. Both men have visibly white phenotypes and blond hair. They both walk up and stand about a couple feet away from Jonathan.

In their initial exchange, Jonathan continues to perform the character of a disoriented immigrant. However, it is at the minute-and-a-half marker that we hear Jonathan's tone change and their performance switch from a lost immigrant to a character affirmatively "out" in their immigration status. In the elements of narrative, it is at this point of the performance by Jonathan that we see the storyline reach its *climax* or moment of highest tension. To bring Taylor's analysis into play again, she says that the "colonial 'encounter' contains a theatrical scenario structure that is meant to be predictable and formulaic so that it can be repeatable and applicable by governing power in different sites."[64] Jonathan and Isaac were counting on this prescribed response from the immigration officers, anticipating that the officers would respond to their disoriented immigrant roles by treating them as individuals to apprehend and detain.

This leads us to Taylor's third statement about scenarios: they produce expected action but leave room that "allows for reversal, parody, and change."[65] Jonathan's change in character, signaled by their tone and reverse-questioning approach toward the agents, represents a rupture that queers or estranges the power structures, even if only momentarily. Additionally, this rupture also shows that these systems of power are not unidirectional but instead afford opportunities for immigrants to invert those relationships. Finally, I read this momentary change of authority as a key moment in which the transmedia narrative produced represents a social imaginary of alternate possibilities in the structures of power. By using civil disobedience in their infiltration action, Jonathan and Isaac were able to connect with other undocumented youth who viewed the video to present direct forms of activism as viable strategies to disrupt hierarchical relationships of power between immigration enforcement and undocumented immigrant communities.

More specifically, in the transcript of the exchange captured in the video, Jonathan defiantly states:

> Yeah, you know what? I am actually not lost. I'm just kind of pissed off. What are y'all doing here?

Jonathan's question not only puzzles the two officers but also catches them off guard. In a short amount of time, Jonathan is able to invert the balance of power with his performance, assuming a position of authority by being the one posing the questions. In other words, Jonathan's question momentarily reverses the order and hierarchies of power, and it intends to place the two officers in an illegalized positionality that undermines their authority. This planned and scripted performance mirrors the ways that the immigration system questions and labels immigrants' presences as unlawful.

The two agents look straight at Jonathan with puzzled faces for two very long seconds. Finally, the first officer who has been doing the talking returns Jonathan's question in a confused-sounding tone:

> What are we doing here?

At this point Jonathan has the two immigration officials repeating questions in a state that reveals their estrangement from the scripted exchange. Jonathan continues to question the officials about their role in deporting immigrants, to which the agents answer that that is the role of federal judges. We can see the two agents standing firmly but uncomfortably, in particular the first officer, who had led the conversation up to this point of the video. The officer's discomfort is evident from the constant shuffling of his feet and the change in his tone of voice. Jonathan's change of tone, from a state of disorientation to a posture of control in a short amount of time, hints to the audience the performative element of their infiltration video.

Unable to establish dominance with his questioning, the first officer is disarmed. The second officer finally speaks two minutes into the video, stating:

It is our mission to protect the border.

The first agent tries to follow the statement with a question to establish authority:

What's it to you?

The first officer's attempt at regaining authority with the question, "What's it to you?" reveals a sense of being disarmed and a fragile masculinity that are unknowingly performed. The officer is confused as to why this dark-skinned individual is choosing to question his authority and what his job entails. In a way, Jonathan has managed to *queer* and to *estrange* the situation for the officers. The officers' uncomfortable body language in the video reveals that they have been forced to feel the kind of anxiety that immigrant bodies experience at the hands of the immigration control system. This discomfort disarms their positionality—a positionality that is otherwise typically filled with privilege in U.S. society, that of white male-presenting bodies.

The two officers become further confused at the two-minute-and-sixteen-second mark when Jonathan announces his status and identity in the "undocumented and unafraid" fashion, declaring:

I am undocumented too.

The first officer is confused and asks:

You're what?

In a reaffirming tone, Jonathan proudly goes beyond immigration status and embodies their identity, declaring:

I am an illegal too.

In an incredulous tone, the first officer asks:

You're illegal?

Jonathan continues the interrogation of the officers by demanding:

So, do you think I should get deported?

Finally, the first officer presses forward with perhaps the most expected question:

Why don't you show us some ID?

The first officer moves outside the video's frame, but we can assume he is to the left of Jonathan, waiting to be shown some identification. The second officer wearing the avocado-green Border Patrol uniform stands in front of Jonathan looking at them straight-on. After the first officer (still out of frame) receives the ID that Jonathan presents, we see him share the identification with the second officer.

The video thus ends with the agents performing the perhaps expected rhetorical response of asking for "papers" or documentation. Jonathan's performance in the video is an example of what Karma Chávez refers to as *social movement rhetoric*. Chávez states, "I offer rhetorical analysis of social movement rhetoric, internal activist strategizing, and media commentary drawn from textual as well as ethnographic sources. Rhetorical analysis of these texts illuminates the logics—what Lugones describes as the comments among meanings—whereby powerful imaginaries are created, sustained, and challenged."[66] Using social movement rhetoric as one of its source materials, Chávez's work points us to the need for multiple interdisciplinary, intersectional approaches to illuminate diverse imaginaries. Social movement rhetoric describes the creative and unique outlooks and practices that immigrant activists use to challenge power. Chávez also conceptualizes a "rhetoric of the streets," with a focus on how activists emphasize demonstrations in public spaces as a strategy for organizing. In other words, undocumented youth activists build rhetoric using their lived experience as undocumented people instead of the rhetoric used in traditional approaches to organizing in immigrant rights movements. Chávez's social movement rhetoric is present in

Jonathan's infiltration video. Jonathan's and Isaac's move toward direct forms of activism on behalf of the most marginalized immigrant groups is an example of "rhetoric of the streets" in action.

NIYA distributed Jonathan's video through the social media platform YouTube. This infiltration video marked the first time undocumented youth turned themselves in to Border Patrol to infiltrate a detention center. Like the "Dream Act 5" sit-in action in 2010, the infiltration event and video were sensationalized by the media. This represents Diana Taylor's fourth descriptor of a scenario: "passing it on" in the form of an archive and repertoire.[67] The archive in this case is Jonathan's performance and script, producing a repertoire that is transmittable across platforms to inspire direct forms of activism. By studying Jonathan's video, we see the fragmented answers to the question of how undocumented youth use their bodies as vehicles of communication to extend transmedia narratives. Detention centers are sites where the nation-state extends its power and defines its exclusionary and inclusionary logics. In other words, organizers like Jonathan and Isaac aimed to change the narrative of detention by infiltrating these centers to expose the multiple processes that the nation-state performs to render human beings illegal.

Infiltrating the Alabama Border Patrol office was the first step in Jonathan's and Isaac's strategy of escalation. The second act was to organize undocumented individuals inside of a detention center to expose the U.S. government's illegal practices. It was Jonathan's and Isaac's goal to expose the shadows of the nation-state that existed in the illegal practices inside of detention centers.

ACT TWO: ORGANIZING INSIDE THE DETENTION CENTER

Act one was accomplished by Jonathan and Isaac being detained by Border Patrol in Mobile, Alabama. The second act was to organize inside of the Basile Detention Center in south Louisiana, to which they were transported westward across state lines. I primarily use two post-infiltration videos that serve as archival records of Jonathan's and Isaac's accounts of their organizing strategies inside of the detention center and what they encountered there. The first video, titled "Interview w Jonathan Perez and Isaac Barrera," was recorded by scholars and community members in Albuquerque, New Mexico, on December 3, 2011, as the two organizers were driving back from Louisiana to California after being released from detention just a few weeks prior.[68] The second video is a recording from the archival records of the "Everyday Practices of Popular Power: Art, Media, Immigration" symposium that took place almost a year after Jonathan and Isaac's infiltration action, on November 9, 2012, at the University of New Mexico (UNM) campus.[69]

In their panel forum for the 2012 symposium, Jonathan and Isaac revealed that they had three goals for their infiltration action. First, they wanted to expose the human rights violations that were occurring inside of detention centers. Second, they aimed to collect and publicly share the stories of detained migrants. And finally, they hoped to offer help to detained migrants who might want to organize against the oppressive conditions faced inside detention centers.[70] With the number of detained migrants and deportees reaching unprecedented levels under the Obama administration, immigrant youth like Jonathan and Isaac realized that the only thing that the Department of Homeland Security and the political administration responded to was public negative media pressure.[71]

Undocumented youth organizers like Jonathan and Isaac, organizations like the Immigrant Youth Justice League, and networks like the National Immigrant Youth Alliance wanted to use the cultural capital and visibility gained through the civil methods and indirect forms of Dream Act–era activism to escalate their direct forms of activism. They produced transmedia narratives to transmit messages that countered official governmental records. Undocumented youth built a counternarrative, or an archive, that went against the official state—what I have been referring to in this book as an (un)documenting process. I use these two post-infiltration videos offered by Jonathan and Isaac, in which they reflect on their action inside of the south Louisiana detention center, as examples of the production of new transmedia narratives.

The first video is important because it captures Jonathan's and Isaac's reflections on their release from detention only a few weeks afterward. In the video, Jonathan states, "Our intention was to show the country what Obama has been doing in terms of these lies."[72] They continue:

> ICE does not pursue our cases when it's a public action. So we wanted to escalate to see how far we can take it.[73]

Pushing the boundaries of organizing strategies while also putting pressure on immigration enforcement defines the escalating philosophy behind Jonathan's, Isaac's, and NIYA's actions.

When the duo walked separately into the Border Patrol office in Mobile, Alabama, strategically looking to be arrested and placed into deportation proceedings, they did so knowing that they would be deemed a low priority. They were fully aware that even inside of detention centers there are hierarchical structures that dictate which immigrants are a priority for deportation, and in their case they were considered "low priority" according to immigration control system mandates because they were undocumented youth with no prior criminal record. Jonathan and Isaac used this low-priority status to buy them time inside of the detention center, while NIYA's network of organizers used this time to organize a transmedia campaign that would gain widespread coverage of the infiltration and lead to their cases being dismissed. Jonathan states:

> The best part is that we were counting on them doing their job. And they did it fine. They did an awesome job. They did what they had to do, and they put us on deportation proceedings. And so, mission accomplished.[74]

Jonathan's and Isaac's actions highlight how the U.S. deportation regime is driven by a capitalist model that profits from the exclusion, removal, and imprisonment of immigrant bodies. Jonathan commented on the experience of being processed after their apprehension:

> They kept saying, "We got to hurry up because we got to be out by five." It's their job. [*Laughs.*] It was also interesting for us to see that, that they have jobs, and they are just people, but they just don't have that [consciousness]. They don't know what they are actually doing.[75]

Jonathan's comment highlights that Border Patrol agents were performing a "business-as-usual" work routine without critically engaging with the real-life consequences of their actions. Jonathan recognizes the lack of critical thinking that law enforcement, in this case Border Patrol agents, have: "They are just people, but they just don't have that [consciousness]." These words expose the lack of consciousness needed to perform a job that pushes workers to treat human beings without human dignity. In other words, I interpret Jonathan's words as pointing to the ways in which an immigration control system requires its enforcers to see those whom they are imprisoning as not being worth the effort to consciously think of as humans. The daily needs of the officers supersede the human needs of detained migrants.

In the two post-infiltration videos that I analyze, Jonathan and Isaac discussed the impact of being detained and the difficult conditions of detention. They also spoke about the mental health impact of witnessing immigrants being treated like objects and denied basic communication with their families and loved ones. In this instance, illegalization refers to the ways in which a deportation regime generates the birth of a new legal and political subject—to borrow Mae Ngai's term, an *impossible subject*.[76] This refers to a subject who is unable to gain recognition from the state as legitimate through the immigration system while at the same time being recognized as an illegalized subject marked for expulsion and deportation from the state. As such, detention centers themselves serve as sites where citizenship is reinforced through the physical and mental violence inflicted on immigrant bodies: by building the category of the illegalized alien, citizenship is preserved. Detention centers are sites where those unworthy of citizenship are not only excluded and "otherized" but are also not afforded human rights. Jonathan and Isaac's infiltration action confirmed that human rights were being violated inside of detention centers. There is a long-standing tradition in which activists and allies have attempted to disrupt and expose the human rights violations inside of detention centers. Jessica Ordaz's work *The Shadow of El Centro* (2021) offers examples of how immigrants have historically resisted incarceration and organized inside of detention centers to counter violent repression. In chapter 3 of her work, Ordaz documents multiple times when detained migrants successfully ran away or managed to "disappear" as a form of survival faced with the violence endured inside the El Centro detention center on the border of California and Arizona next to the Mexico-U.S. border.[77] Jonathan's and Isaac's actions in 2011 represents an example in the twenty-first century in which detention centers, historical sites of repression where many recognized there were continued human rights violations, worked to limit access. Undocumented youth activists realized it would take civil disobedience actions like organizing infiltrations to document such violence publicly.

My conceptualization of illegalization and its application to detention center interventions builds on the tradition of immigration studies scholars who study race as a defining characteristic in the state's administration of which immigrant bodies are allowed entry and which need to be managed. Mae Ngai and Aviva Chomsky explore how laws not only reflect legal categories and exclusion but also serve the interests of racial capitalism through the concept of "illegality."[78] Categorizing immigrants as "illegal" or "law breakers" serves to criminalize immigrant populations through ideological practices even before the law intervenes as an enforcement mechanism. In other words, Ngai and Chomsky argue that if immigrant bodies can be made "illegal," or undeserving of legal protection or privileging, then there is no need for legal processing. Jonathan and Isaac came across many individuals in detention who were not afforded legal protection. Jonathan reports on what they saw inside of the detention center:

> Being in there [the detention center] is a constant struggle against depression. I think if I were in any of their situations, not knowing when I was going to get out or when I was going to be deported, it's depressing. I think going in there, we were better prepared than most people and we knew that because we had the funds to be able to call frequently. I think if we were in a different situation . . . looking back, I think we were ready to stay there if need be.[79]

In this passage, Jonathan's words acknowledge the privilege that they held when going into detention and also the psychological trauma that exists for immigrants in detention. Their infiltration action highlights the multiple ways in which illegalization is part of the subjugation that goes undocumented—in this case, I refer to the process of (un)documenting, as the violence inflicted by the state is intentionally not documented or recorded. Illegalization is documented when it comes to the qualities that justify an immigrant's expulsion. But the process of illegalization or of managing immigrant bodies for detention and expulsion is undocumented—not publicly visible, kept intentionally in the shadows by the state. Jonathan, Isaac, and NIYA's infiltration strategy was to (un)document—to document, archive, and create public transmedia narratives about—what happened behind the scenes and went undocumented by the state: the human rights violations, violence, and trauma that immigrants were experiencing in detention centers.

Unpacking the processes and structures behind how undocumented populations are rendered illegal requires a position of privilege. Jonathan and Isaac publicly rejected the DREAMer narrative that allowed the further criminalization and illegalization of undocumented communities to continue. Jonathan's and Isaac's post-detention interviews reflect a recognition of their privilege and the guilt they felt about not having the ability to change the fate of the people detained. Most undocumented people in detention do not have the means or the necessary support to fight the multiple barriers put in place by the immigration system. Jonathan's and Isaac's infiltration revealed how expensive the phone calls were from inside the detention center. The high price of phone calls created isolation and idleness for immigrants, whose mental health suffered at the hands of these violent structures. Many of the detained immigrants also did not have access to lawyers or legal aid to advise them on their cases. Furthermore, Jonathan and Isaac highlight that immigrants would often sign their expedited deportation removals out of desperation and necessity, as they might be their household's main source of income and feared for the well-being of their families.[80] Isaac remembers helping immigrants inside of the detention center with their expedited deportation cases:

> That's one of the toughest things I had to witness. Many people, they were just signing off [on expedited deportations], and I had to help one of them do that. It was heartbreaking and it made me angry, but I did it. I understood why. It's a warehouse, there's like seventy bunk beds, the calls are very expensive, most of the people there don't have the means to contact their family or even information of when their court hearing is. They're just kept there, they're being controlled, they're being dehumanized, they take away your clothes, your sense of freedom.[81]

Much of what Jonathan and Isaac talk about in the two video interviews that compose my archive and are referenced in this section reveals that detention is a strategic game of waiting and uncertainty at the expense of immigrants' mental health.

Toward the end of their post-infiltration video interview, Isaac revealed that this action was one of the hardest ones they had undertaken, in particular because of the realities they learned about while in detention. Isaac commented on their inability to directly help detained migrants and remedy their treatment:

> It was really hard to go through that . . . I remembered it messed with my mental health a lot. I cried myself to sleep sometimes. The way I saw these people being warehoused and ordered around as if they were some type of animals.[82]

Isaac's words reflect the impact of their organizing on their mental health and the trauma of witnessing inhumane treatment. Jonathan's and Isaac's mental health was also impacted by the helplessness they witnessed while in detention. The recognition of their privilege weighed heavily on them. Their guilt stemmed from having the protection acquired through cultural capital and the possibility of visibility. This was in stark contrast to other immigrants, who were relegated to the shadows, housed in detention centers, and facing deportation.

Trauma and guilt are experienced differently by the diverse generations of immigrant communities. Grace Cho's concept of *generational haunting* explains how trauma, or what she theorizes as a "haunting," not only works transnationally and is transported across borders but also is embedded across a family's generations.[83] Cho argues that the traumatic violence inflicted on immigrant bodies is dismissed because of the supposed benevolence of the United States in bringing democracy and the promise of the "American Dream" to families from many countries. Generational hauntings are present among both documented and undocumented youths who experience violence and multiple levels of oppression. These "hauntings" are felt in immigrant families for multiple generations. Undocumented youth expose the impossibility of the ideology of the American Dream. For immigrant families, achieving citizenship status does not equate to full freedom because the violence experienced continues to impact them for generations. Trauma and violence impact undocumented communities differently over time and space, and this is rarely discussed in activist circles. Campaigns like Jonathan's and Isaac's infiltration are rarely placed in the context of the impacts on the mental health of activists. Trauma is not glamorous. In their post-detention video interviews, Jonathan and Isaac repeatedly advised against sensationalizing their efforts or glorifying their practices.

As I write this book, it is my intention to honor Jonathan's and Isaac's wishes and ensure that their organizing efforts are not sensationalized, praised, or considered heroic. Jonathan and Isaac highlight the undeniable privilege they knew they had going into the detention center. Both organizers had to grapple with being face-to-face with immigrants experiencing horrible conditions in the flesh. Isaac declares:

> A lot of people have told me, "You are so courageous. You are fearless." I reflect and I realize I can do all of that, but it's me because . . .

Isaac's words and pause midsentence in the statement above represent to me a recognition of the inherent privilege earned by undocumented youth. This was a privilege unafforded to nonyouth, immigrants of color, and queer immigrants because they are *illegalized* differently. As demonstrated in chapter 1, Elvira Arellano was not afforded the same levels of privilege despite the public attention she received, and her illegalization led to her expedited deportation. Similar to practices of racialization and "othering," the public visibility of undocumented youth has presented a paradox in the process of illegalizing immigrant bodies. While immigrant youth lacked immigration status, which limited their access to certain societal institutions, the cultural capital and visibility gained in mainstream U.S. society has produced a political subject granted access and protection under a deportation regime that does not treat immigrants equally. Jonathan and Isaac might have not been deported as a result of the cultural capital gained by undocumented youth, but their post-release interviews reveal that their biggest challenge was being released and seeing that nonyouth would not be afforded the same privilege.

Jonathan and Isaac's infiltration accomplished many of the goals they set out to fulfill. Ultimately, their infiltration action provides insight into the ways in which illegalization processes categorize immigrant bodies as deserving or undeserving and manage them according to race, nationality, ethnicity, gender, sexuality, and age. Their action highlights for immigrant communities as well as for citizens that the privilege of visibility and recognition is invested in the exclusion of others from enjoying said freedoms. These privileges are not afforded to all immigrants in detention. Jonathan and Isaac wagered their public visibility and cultural capital to expose the inhumane treatment and violence endured by countless immigrants at the hands of the state. Their civil disobedience action serves as an example of countersurveillance, in which they turn the gaze back upon the state and use technological tools of vigilance against its oppressive regime.[84]

Jonathan and Isaac's infiltration was a watershed moment in the immigrant rights movements. Without notice, Jonathan and Isaac were released on November 24, 2011—Thanksgiving Day, of all days. Looking back at Elvira's case study in chapter 1, we see that she was detained in Los Angeles and rushed into deportation without any explanations or much of a process. We see that she was not afforded the same protection or relief, being a nonyouth, nor did she have the protection of the cultural capital that had been gained by undocumented youth by 2011. Jonathan and Isaac expressed the confusion and mystery that surrounded their release from the detention center. Jonathan remembers that, upon being released from the detention center, when we went back, because they kept our phones, they were looking at us kind of scared I think. [*Laughs.*] When we went back, they asked, "You're back?" We went to sign to release our phones and they all just kept looking at us. When we left, they were still looking at us through the windows. They found out who we were connected to and that it was part of an organizing effort and so they were a little more cautious this time. It was fun, at the end of the day.[85]

In this passage Jonathan recounts the sense of urgency and distrust that ICE agents had toward them after learning that their detention had all been an organizing effort. Their infiltration toppled systemic power, even if only at that moment of resistance. Jonathan's ironic and comic tone reveals the sense of pride they earned through the action.

Later the two organizers would hear about a conversation between ICE agents that was overheard by another detained migrant who was released at the same time. The warden of the detention center was contacted by the Department of Homeland Security and ordered to immediately and personally see that the two activists be released from detention as soon as possible.[86] As Jonathan and Isaac were released on Thanksgiving Day, the warden had to interrupt her Thanksgiving plans to return to the detention center and see to it that the two organizers were released. This top-down command speaks volumes about the visibility and cultural capital that undocumented youth had gained. But it also speaks to the privilege certain immigrants are provided, as Jonathan and Isaac reflected earlier. The celebration of the colonial and genocidal holiday of Thanksgiving was cut short for the warden of the detention center, and priority was given to undocumented youth who at that moment were a danger to the state inside of a detention center. Jonathan and Isaac's infiltration exposes the ironic condition of detention. In that moment, capital stopped for two undocumented youth organizers from California who were miles away from home and had threatened the government in ways that the state could not tolerate.

CONCLUSION: POSTSCRIPT

The act of (un)documenting produces a new archive. Jonathan and Isaac's infiltration was an instance where the UYMs were able to bring news to a general public about the human rights violations experienced by immigrants facing detention and deportation. The capturing of human rights violations inside of detention centers represents a new archive or new knowledge, because in 2011, when Jonathan and Isaac staged their infiltration action, these injustices had not yet been recorded and were not part of public knowledge in the United States. Their infiltration of the detention center in Alabama in 2011 catapulted Jonathan and Isaac into the national spotlight—a position that they would not particularly enjoy.

As a follow-up to the "Everyday Practices of Popular Power: Art, Media, Immigration" symposium at UNM in 2012, the Chicana and Chicano Studies and American Studies Departments hosted an art exhibit on October 5, 2018, titled "'Illegal' Lives: Immigrant/Refugee Struggles for Love and Freedom," by undocumented artist/photographer Blue-Green. Blue-Green is the gender-fluid artist's name that Isaac Barrera goes by today.[87] During the exhibit, Blue-Green talked about the undocumented youth networks that have grown regionally across state lines to organize against detention centers.[88] Blue-Green talked specifically about the work that has gone into organizing around ending the detention of transgender migrants. Jonathan has also been involved with Blue-Green and the push to support a growing movement under the motto #AbolishICE. Jonathan and Isaac's infiltration action led them to new social imaginaries including abolition work.[89] The public knowledge, or the (un)document produced, was the model for organizing around ending detention and deportation practices in the United States.

CHAPTER 3

ILLEGAL BORDERS

Immigrant Youth Challenging Detention, Deportation, and
Family Separation

We decided to come back [to Mexico]. We made the sacrifice
knowingly because it's a right that everyone deserves.
—MARCO SAAVEDRA, 2012

THE NATIONAL IMMIGRANT YOUTH ALLIANCE was founded in
2010, along with many other undocumented youth–led organizations
that challenged the normative discursive and structural spaces that
produced violent realities for immigrant communities. NIYA's motto was
Empower, Educate, and Escalate. Their website declared that to "empower" is
to embrace their identity as undocumented youth, and to "educate" means to
spread information through social movement discourse. They used "escalate"
to signify the way that the "movement . . . will use mindful and intentional
strategic acts of civil disobedience to be effective."[1] As a result, NIYA was at the
forefront of controversial events that frequently captured national headlines
between 2010 and 2013. NIYA's actions to "escalate" were aimed at putting pressure on the limitations that the immigration system had historically placed on
undocumented communities using the threat of detention and deportation.[2]

From earlier actions such as their 2010 sit-in at Senator John McCain's office
in Tucson, Arizona, and Jonathan Perez and Isaac Barrera's 2011 infiltration
campaign in Alabama/Louisiana, which they helped coordinate, NIYA learned
to push the borders of organizing strategies by bringing their activism to sites
and experiences closest to the undocumented experience. The #BringThem-
Home campaign would represent a new form of escalation by NIYA in 2012.
In an interview, NIYA co-founder Mohammad Abdollahi states, "I remember

calling Lizbeth and asking her if she was interested in doing something crazy, and she, as always, says, 'Yes.'"[3] In that same interview, Lizbeth Mateo adds, "It was almost a joke. I mean, I think we just started talking about it, we didn't think it was going to happen."[4] Lulu Martínez highlights the personal connection that would drive her to finally see the feasibility of the action, saying, "On a personal level too . . . I really wanted to know Mexico. I really wanted to go back and see where my parents were from."[5] In other words, while the #BringThemHome campaign began as a crazy idea and an organic discussion among the organizers, the seemingly radical idea had very personal significance. It was radical because it seemed ludicrous on the surface, but it was badly needed because it addressed a root problem that all undocumented populations face: legal access to free movement across political borders. NIYA began to carefully craft and strategically organize the action, involving lawyers, organizers, and political experts who were part of its support system.

The core intent was to assist the return of three activists to Mexico to reunite with their families after many years of being separated. The campaign reached widespread audiences at the local, national, and international levels. NIYA worked with media groups to give it wide reach through social media, using the campaign name in a hashtag: #BringThemHome.[6] As the campaign reached more people through media and social media coverage, NIYA was contacted by six individuals in Mexico who asked to join the action. These six individuals had either self-returned to Mexico or had been deported. NIYA incorporated them into the campaign as a way to challenge family separation and deportation practices. The participants in the campaign became known as the "Dream 9," and the campaign used the hashtag #Dream9.[7]

This chapter focuses on how, in the #BringThemHome campaign, also known as the Dream 9 campaign, organized by NIYA during the summer of 2013, undocumented youth used their bodies to reclaim space, conducting highly performative and symbolic acts of civil disobedience, to call attention to and challenge family separation, deportation, and detention. The campaign had a twofold objective to challenge restrictive immigration policies. First, activists traveled to Mexico to be reunited with their loved ones across the border, to challenge family separation and the restriction of mobility for immigrants living in the United States. Second, after their visits with family in Mexico, the activists returned to the United States through an official port of entry, where they expected to be placed in detention, an opportunity they would use to organize a detention infiltration action.

Spaces like detention centers, which serve as an extension of the militarized borderlands, became a site of strategic infiltration by undocumented youth. By infiltrating these sites, undocumented youth exposed the human rights violations and state violence that up to that point had not been publicly documented. Using an (un)documenting methodology allows me to trace the digital archives produced by NIYA in its #BringThemHome campaign, and to demonstrate how undocumented youth produced a counternarrative challenging the neoliberal capitalist system, which prioritizes the mobility of goods while restricting the freedom of migration, resulting in family separations. I argue that the #BringThemHome campaign was not only contributing important political and social commentary but also creating a new archive that I name an *(un)document*. To (un)document, in this case, is to produce public knowledge of state violence that was long kept out of public discourse. The (un)document produced by NIYA's actions exposes a history of family separation and human rights violations by the state, and produces a base for public knowledge of the state's detention and deportation practices.

It is important to recognize and understand the context in which the #BringThemHome campaign occurred and the impact it had. The first part of this chapter will provide a brief historical contextualization of important policy at federal and state levels, as well as the response by undocumented youth activists. Second, I will contextualize the #BringThemHome campaign by discussing the organizing strategies that NIYA used to coordinate the action. Then I use a visual analysis and textual analysis methodology to unpack the actions taken by NIYA activists upon their return to the United States and their infiltration of the Eloy Detention Center in Arizona in 2013. A visual analysis allows me to understand the symbolic references, representations, and messaging that demonstrate the deep level of strategic action NIYA used to connect with a broader U.S. and international audience. I analyze primary sources, such as digital video produced by NIYA, as well as video-journal check-ins from detention, and post-release media materials of the activists. A close reading of the transcripts of these self-produced videos reveals the complexities and interpersonal intricacies of the act of civil disobedience. In the latter part of the chapter, I briefly contextualize the campaigns that followed the Dream 9 campaign. Finally, I end the chapter with a postscript that discusses (un)documenting, the outcomes, lessons, and knowledge produced by the Dream 9 campaign, the limitations of direct activism like that performed by NIYA, and what some of the activists are up to today.

RETORNADXS, DEPORTEES, AND ASYLUM SEEKERS UNDER THE OBAMA ADMINISTRATION

The number of immigrants being detained and deported in the interior of the United States grew exponentially after 9/11. The numbers were sustained by the neoliberal policies implemented from the mid-1990s to the first decade of the twenty-first century and spanning the presidencies of George Bush Sr., Bill Clinton, George W. Bush, and Barack Obama. The policies implemented through the Illegal Immigration Reform and Immigrant Responsibility Act (IIRIRA, 1996) under President Bill Clinton laid the policy infrastructure that would make mass detention and deportation possible in the 2000s. September 11 became the spark needed to ignite the opportunity to build an industrial-size operation of warehousing and mass expulsion of immigrants from the interior of the country.

The Immigration Reform and Control Act (IRCA, 1986) was the last immigration reform that offered a pathway to citizenship. Passed under President Ronald Reagan, it helped legalize close to four million immigrants in the United States. With no subsequent immigration reform, the number of undocumented individuals had grown to an estimated eleven million as the United States entered the twenty-first century. Scholars widely see IRCA as an immigration reform because it provided undocumented residents a pathway to citizenship, while IIRIRA in 1996 did not provide a pathway to citizenship; the "reform" in its title refers to expanding neoliberal models of militarizing the border while restricting immigrant mobility and access to citizenship. The neoliberal agenda created a solution to a surplus undocumented population through a global capitalist model. As such, the United States turned its focus not specifically on the Mexico-U.S. borderlands, as it had done in previous decades, but on contracting these borderlands to the interior of the country. After 2002, the borderlands were contracted by means of legislation aimed at using ICE, the police enforcement branch of the newly created DHS, to encroach on migrants.

As DHS grew in size and power by the mid-2000s so did its reach and economic resources. It is reported that by 2007, DHS enjoyed a budget of over $30 billion, while there was a record number of detentions that same year at 311,169, and a record number of deportations at 319,000.[8] President Obama earned the title of "deporter in chief" from undocumented youth who grew disillusioned midway through his first term (2008–12), seeing that the Dream

Act failed in 2010 and their undocumented communities were being persecuted on a regular basis. By the end of the first decade of the twenty-first century, then, undocumented youth lost faith in the political and legislative process and were prepared to escalate their actions to new sites and heights with civil disobedience that better addressed the undocumented experience. They used transmedia narratives shared through various social media channels as a way to expose the political lies of the Obama administration when it insisted it was only deporting dangerous immigrants—a narrative that became popular after 9/11 and was only intensified by the 2007/8 economic recession.

The Pew Research Center reported that by 2011, net migration from Mexico to the United States had fallen to zero percent.[9] This means that the number of Mexican migrants coming to the United States was practically static by 2011. However, as mentioned above, the number of detentions and deportations grew exponentially by the end of the first decade of the twenty-first century. Most importantly, for the purposes of this chapter, that same Pew Research Center report indicated that approximately 1.4 million Mexican immigrants and their children returned to Mexico between 2005 and 2010. These two crucial sets of data—the growth in both number of deportations and number of self-returned immigrants—created two new identifiers that I associate with new renditions of illegality as a flexible and extending category. The first was the identifier *deportees*—those prioritized for deportation and deemed unworthy of inclusion into the U.S. political body. The second was the identifier retornadas/os/xs: undocumented individuals who chose to return to their country of origin.[10]

Illegalization had reached a new scale by 2010 with the growth in the number of deportees and retornadxs. Deportees and retornadxs were impacted by immigration policy, and many shared their stories of trauma caused by family separation and expressed their frustration at not being able to travel to see their loved ones. Deportees and retornadxs often belong to mixed-status families—families consisting of undocumented members along with members who are U.S. citizens. Undocumented youth realized that they must use the cultural capital they had earned through activism and public visibility in the United States to fight for undocumented communities—not only those in the United States but also deportees and retornadxs.

NIYA's #BringThemHome campaign planned to have the three original NIYA activists make their way to their home country of Mexico and then attempt to return: Lulu, Lizbeth, and Marco. But the hashtag

#BringThemHome took on a new meaning once deportees and retornadxs began reaching out to NIYA asking to join the campaign and return to the United States. The transmedia narratives produced by the campaign, which I analyze in this chapter, demonstrate the need to conceptualize mixed-status families as transnational undocumented families. NIYA wanted to challenge family separation and mobility restriction using a *cleavage* in immigration policy: *humanitarian parole*.[11]

By 2010, the number of Latin American refugees seeking asylum in the United States had also begun to grow as neoliberal systems produced economic and political instability throughout the hemisphere, causing many to flee violence, political turmoil, persecution on the basis of gender and sexuality, and poverty. By that year the U.S. immigration courts were flooded with petitions for asylum by refugees who were leaving their home countries and making the dangerous journey to the United States with typically nothing more than the clothes on their backs. The U.S. immigration system relied on historical processes that prioritized documentation when deciding whether to allow admission into the country. However, most refugees migrating to the United States left their home countries to escape grave danger and did not typically carry with them the necessary documentation to plead their asylum cases for admission into the country. And these refugees were coming from undesired national backgrounds: the U.S. quota system established in 1965 did not leave much room for Latin American migrants.[12]

According to immigration policy, an asylum seeker who can demonstrate with paperwork in immigration court that they have a "credible fear" of persecution under such categories as ethnicity, religion, political beliefs, gender, and sexuality is able to receive "humanitarian parole," which grants a legal stay in the United States along with work authorization. The NIYA team had for a long time received pro bono legal support from allied lawyers. As more members of the NIYA network expressed the frustration of not being able to travel to have a physical connection with the loved ones they were separated from and their country of origin, the idea began to grow to organize a campaign that could push the boundaries of immigration policy based on the cleavage of humanitarian parole. The legal team supporting NIYA warned them of the inherent dangers of such an action—namely, potentially being denied reentry into the United States and being banned from returning to the United States for a minimum of ten years. However, this cleavage identified by NIYA organizers represented the level of "escalating" that undocumented youth movements were looking for—that is, taking their civil disobedience to new sites where they could test their cultural capital to bring light to undocumented populations typically not afforded the same visibility and to places that the immigration system keeps in the shadows.

PHASE ONE: TRANSMEDIA NARRATIVES OF IMMIGRANT YOUTH RETORNADXS

NIYA's philosophy of *escalation* pushed the boundaries of the immigration system in terms of policy, ideology, and the physical borderlands. NIYA's organizing escalation was in line with a high-energy period among undocumented youth starting at the beginning of the twenty-first century. The #BringThem-Home campaign represented the next step in the escalation of activism to highlight the cruelty of restrictions on mobility and family separation while also providing a voice to the growing numbers of deportees and retornadxs. The transmedia narratives transmitted publicly by NIYA through its You-Tube channel and social media pages offered an opportunity to share heartfelt testimonials aimed at showing how the nation-state produced violence through the separation of families across borders, and at (un)documenting the direct correlations between detention and deportation of undocumented immigrants and profit. Their campaign aimed to disrupt these power balances between the immigration system and capitalist models.

The #BringThemHome campaign was coordinated by NIYA in the summer of 2013 and centered on one simple premise: family reunification. Within the NIYA network, undocumented youth shared testimonials internally with each other in meetings, workshops, and organizing spaces, about their experiences of growing up undocumented in the United States. Many of them shared how they had missed funerals, weddings, and other special events in their families' lives.[13] Others shared what it was like to be part of transnational families in which some members still resided in their countries of origin while others lived in the United States, and to form transnational connections with those relatives through regular phone calls, social media, and economic ties. Others spoke about not knowing or having any sort of relationship with their families in their countries of origin, or any physical or personal connection to their native lands. As such, NIYA thought family separation across borders could be the premise of its next escalating action.

During Jonathan Perez and Isaac Barrera's detention center infiltration, NIYA realized that their escalation action was premised on the fact that immigration policy considered them "low priority" in the detention and deportation hierarchy. Eventually, their accumulated cultural capital would result in their deportation proceedings being halted. The #BringThemHome campaign was centered on the technicality within the immigration system through which someone can request "humanitarian parole" if they have archived evidence to petition for asylum in the United States. NIYA's escalation actions used legal technicalities within the immigration system to challenge the illegalization of immigrants.

NIYA members reasoned that their unorthodox forms of organizing highlighted the real dangers that immigrants face when attempting to reunite with their families. Furthermore, the #BringThemHome campaign sought to raise awareness about the U.S. government interpretation of refugee laws. The number of refugee applicants from Mexico continued to rise, but the United States continued to reject applicants even when they met asylum requirements. As Mimi Nguyen mentions, "the language of evaluation and assessment of a people's competencies and their potential" is also a rule of measurement for refugees and immigrants who are applying to enter the United States legally.[14] As such, NIYA organizers who willingly self-returned to Mexico did so knowing the risks involved, in order to contest ideas of mobility limited by restrictionist immigration policies and instead make cultural claims of belonging across multiple borders.

NIYA's #BringThemHome campaign can also be understood as an escalation of their activists' previous efforts to infiltrate detention centers by voluntarily turning themselves in to Border Patrol, starting with Jonathan Perez and Isaac Barrera's infiltration in November 2011.[15] NIYA had continued these infiltration actions with other activists who were part of their network to bring to light and expose undocumented immigrants' experiences inside of detention centers. On August 5, 2012, NIYA successfully helped activists Marco Saavedra, from the East Coast, and Viridiana Martínez, from the U.S. South, to infiltrate the Broward Detention Center in Florida.[16] This organizing tactic brought the invisible and silenced population of detained migrants into the public imagination. NIYA sought to humanize these immigrants by sharing their stories of confinement and deprivation.

The goal of these infiltration practices is also to "educate" through any means necessary. I theorize this as the process of (un)documenting, or producing archives that construct public knowledge of sites that were not previously documented, such as detention centers. In particular, NIYA educated a public audience by (un)documenting the high number of deportations during President Obama's administration. Furthermore, NIYA organizers reported on the fact that detention centers operated under private contracts with the U.S. government in a way that dissolved government responsibility and allowed human rights violations to occur in a gray area of the law.[17] Organizations like NIYA, with their infiltration tactics, chose to organize at the margins, using acts of civil disobedience that showcase the lived realities of immigrant communities who are kept in the shadows of detention.

The original three #BringThemHome NIYA activists—Lizbeth Mateo, Marco Saavedra, and Lulu Martínez—self-returned to reunite and spend time with their loved ones in Mexico. This represented the first phase of the action, which was aimed at publicly challenging family separation and restriction of mobility. NIYA worked with volunteers who coordinated media and social media campaigns to focus on the impact of family reunification on these three activists.[18] NIYA ran a video campaign on its YouTube channel that began with videos of the three activists back in several states of Mexico and captured what it meant for each one of them to be reunited with their family after many years apart.[19] The emotional tone of these videos telling the stories of the original three NIYA activists returning to Mexico aimed to build empathy.

NIYA crafted, scripted, and produced the videos to convey the toll that family separation had on transnational immigrant families. One of the effective strategies used in the production of the videos is the incorporation of the dramatic sound effect of a clock ticking in the background as activists share their testimonials. This sound effect creates an ephemeral reaction on the part of the viewer, expressing the limitations of time experienced by the undocumented community: time during which immigrants are separated from their loved ones in their home countries, time that undocumented immigrants are not able to spend with their families because of economic obligations. Time, in the transmedia narratives shared by the activists, is a privilege not afforded to undocumented immigrants. But in the case of #BringThemHome, the use of time in the editing of the video also serves as a call for the viewer to support the campaign.

The videos have a raw, grassroots, low-budget production aesthetic. This is what makes their transmedia narratives effective: they are deliberate, direct, and forward with their messaging. The camera angle provides a close-up shot that centers the participant, placing the viewer in an intimate conversation with the activist. There is seriousness and emotion in each one of the activists' voices as they deliver their narrative. These clips are only about a minute and a half in length. As such, part of the effectiveness is that each one of the narratives delivers an impactful message in a short amount of time, leaving the viewer with a lot to process. The transmedia narrative videos consistently include title cards sharing information about the numbers of families experiencing family separation—at the time about 1.7 million. Some of the information cards also share the length of time the activists have been separated from their families, to inform the audience that separations are typically quite lengthy.

Finally, all of the videos end with two concluding title cards. The first title card depicts the "Bring Them Home" logo, which has barbed wire graphically designed across the word "Home," with human silhouettes depicted in bodily positions implying separation, followed by the campaign slogan "DREAMS BEYOND BORDERS." I will take a moment here to provide visual and textual analysis of the logo itself. While it may appear simple, there is much analysis to tease out with regard to the campaign's messaging.

FIGURE 6 "BRING THEM HOME: DREAMS BEYOND BORDERS" logo, National Immigrant Youth Alliance.

The message "DREAMS BEYOND BORDERS" uses, and highlights, terminology that has accrued cultural capital: "DREAMS," deriving from "DREAMers." Here, NIYA strategically uses the DREAMer narrative as a way to expand the definition of DREAMers, emphasizing the idea that it is not only undocumented youth who have dreams. In other words, family separation is experienced across the mixed-status spectrum of undocumented populations. The campaign messaging also points to the idea that "dreams" exist "beyond borders," including for people on the Mexican side of the border. My textual analysis of "beyond borders" is meant to highlight the inequity in our thought process when we think that "dreams," aspirations, hopes, and ideas of progress exist solely on the north side of the border. This messaging contextualizes family separation as a source of trauma and stress not only for undocumented immigrants on the U.S. side of the border, but also for their transnational families residing in their home countries. The barbed wire depicted across the word "HOME" indicates that a sense of place or feeling of home is literally and physically shattered by a physical border and also by restrictive immigration policy that impedes mobility and family reunification.

After this, the second title card appears, fading in from multiple directions to read, "SHOW YOUR SUPPORT . . . FIND OUT HOW," and providing the NIYA website. In a traditional organizing strategy, the videos produced by NIYA provide a call to action, formulating storytelling through the transmedia narratives of their organizers who are embarking on a journey to be reunited with their families in Mexico.

NIYA MEMBERS' SELF-RETURN MIGRATION VIDEOS

VIDEO #1: PUTTING LAW-SCHOOL DREAMS ON HOLD FOR THE MOVEMENT

At the time of the #BringThemHome campaign, Lizbeth Mateo was a twenty-nine-year-old graduate of California State University, Northridge.[20] Mateo self-identifies as Zapotec from the state of Oaxaca, Mexico.[21] Her activist curriculum included fighting for the passage of the California Dream Act and leading student activism in Southern California. She originally connected with undocumented activist leader Mohammad Abdollahi through internet chat groups, where they talked about creating an organization with a national presence, which would later become NIYA. Prior to the #BringThemHome campaign, Lizbeth Mateo had also participated in the widely documented sit-in action at Arizona Republican senator John McCain's office in Tucson, Arizona, during the summer of 2010, which is referenced in chapter 2. After the national Dream Act failed to pass in 2010, NIYA organizers like Mohammad and Lizbeth realized it would take much more radical organizing strategies to truly bring about change. It would take self-sacrifice on the part of the activists and the risk of losing the life they had built in the United States.

Lizbeth had been accepted into law school at Santa Clara University (Santa Clara, California) and was scheduled to begin classes in the fall of 2013. Instead of beginning her law education, she decided to participate in the #BringThem-Home campaign.[22] In the first video published by NIYA on July 17, 2013, Lizbeth announces:

Hi, everyone, this is Lizbeth! I'm making this video from Mexico. I know it's going to sound a little crazy, and to be honest, I still can't believe that I am here.

[Information card appears in the video announcing: "Lizbeth has not seen her family in over 15 years."]

LIZBETH: It's surreal. Hmmm . . . I know you are going to think that I am crazy for doing this, for leaving the U.S., for coming to Mexico, but to be honest, I think it's even crazier that I had to wait fifteen years to see my family.

[Photograph shows Lizbeth with her family in Mexico, all with visible smiles.]

LIZBETH: I did not just do this for my own family, but I did it for the families that have been deported. 1.7 million people have been deported. These are not just 1.7 million people, those are 1.7 million families. Families like mine.

[The narrating voice repeats the phrase "Families like mine" five times.]

[Title card appears, accompanied by dramatic music, textually showcasing "1.7 million families," followed by "Million Families Separated."]

LIZBETH: I came to Oaxaca knowing that the U.S. government might not allow me to go back.

[Video ends with two title cards with the campaign logo, the campaign hashtag, and the NIYA website.][23]

In this beginning statement, "I know it's going to sound a little crazy," Lizbeth addresses the fear and anxiety that any undocumented youth or immigrant would feel when leaving the United States to return to their ancestral home and not knowing if they will be able to return. For many immigrants, the United States is an important destination in their migration journey, and making it there is seen as a privilege and benefit. However, as my analysis of the moving borderlands highlights, entering the United States is only one step of the migration journey. Many immigrants end up additionally migrating to other cities, counties, and states across the United States, in part to escape the encroachment of the moving borderlands. In other words, some undocumented immigrants find that their host cities and states might try to surveil and detain them, as police departments and local institutions can participate with federal agencies like ICE. Navigating a moving borderlands sometimes entails migrating several times across multiple immigration enforcement landscapes. Then, sometimes it leads to the decision by undocumented immigrants to return to their country of birth as retornadxs.

For undocumented youths to suddenly risk everything by returning "home" turned immigration logic on its head. Lizbeth's next statement, which emphasizes the time she has spent separated from her family, poses the question: What is crazier, the fact that she chose to go to Mexico with potentially no possibility of returning to the United States, or the fact that freedom of mobility is limited to specific populations? Lizbeth's video is produced as a transmedia narrative—it is curated, developed as a performance for specific campaign messaging points, and prepared to be showcased across multiple media platforms. The narrative shared across the multiple platforms engages with the question of family separation by asking the viewer to consider the state's role and responsibility in separating families across borders and the cruelty that it represents.

VIDEO #2: MIGRATION AS A HUMAN RIGHT

Like Lizbeth, Marco Saavedra built his life in the United States alongside his parents from the time he was three years old. Saavedra self-identifies as a

Mixtec migrant from Oaxaca, Mexico.[24] Similar to Lizbeth's activist trajectory, Marco had been organizing in favor of the New York Dream Act and linked up with Mohammad Abdollahi to push for federal protection for undocumented communities. Marco's escalation from state organizing in New York to the national level came with NIYA when he was among the individuals who infiltrated detention centers in the U.S. South. Like Jonathan and Isaac, Marco was released from the detention center once the U.S. Department of Homeland Security found that his detention was part of an infiltration strategy coordinated by high-profile activists.

While the legal case from his 2012 infiltration was still pending, Marco chose to join the #BringThemHome campaign. In his check-in video, Marco states:

> Hi, this is Marco. If you're watching this, it's because I'm currently in Mexico. As crazy as that sounds, I decided to come back.
>
> [Title card reading "1.7 million families separated" appears.]
>
> MARCO: I decided to come back because we continually find more and more people that, out of desperation or out of forcefulness, were sent back from the United States to Mexico. We decided to come back, and I made the sacrifice knowingly, because it's a right that everyone deserves.[25]

In this check-in video, Marco reaffirms his determination to be reunited with his loved ones based on the belief that migration should be a human right. When he says, "We decided to come back [to Mexico], and I made the sacrifice knowingly, because it's a right that everyone deserves," he explains that the action was an organizing exercise intended to potentially return more people in the future. This personal sacrifice was being made for a larger cause. Marco's words "we made the sacrifice knowingly" place the organizers in control of their actions and their bodies. They place the immigration debate outside the hands of the nation-state and immigration policy and directly place undocumented organizers at the center and in control of their futures. Marco's words propose that mobility or migration is "a right that everyone deserves," an assertive statement that asks the viewer to again question how the rights of mobility are granted and withheld in the United States.

VIDEO #3: TRANSNATIONAL MOVEMENT—
SUPPORT ON BOTH SIDES OF THE BORDER

The last of the three NIYA activists was Lulu Martínez, who grew up in Chicago, Illinois, and self-identified as undocu-queer.[26] Like Lizbeth and Marco, Lulu grew into social consciousness through student activism and statewide organizing and soon heard of the work that NIYA was doing at the national level. Lulu participated in civil disobedience actions such as marches, sit-ins, and organizing campaigns in the Midwest. They joined the #BringThemHome campaign to bring attention not only to family separation but also to issues of identity for queer undocumented youth on a transnational level. In their transmedia narrative, they share:

My name is Lulu Martínez, and I'm here in la Ciudad de México.

[Title card states: "Lulu has not seen her family in Mexico for over 20 years."]

LULU MARTÍNEZ: I still can't believe that I'm here, and part of me is really, really happy. I got to see where I was born, I got to see where my dad grew up, I got to see my cousins who are my age. I'm really excited that we know that we have a lot of support back home in the U.S.

[Title card reads: "Show your support."]

LULU MARTÍNEZ: Mamá, Papá . . . vamos a regresar. I'm going to come home. I'm going to come home.

[Concluding title cards appear with the Bring Them Home logo and the NIYA website.][27]

Lulu's phase-one action video points the viewer to emotional and personal effects of conducting civil disobedience that go beyond the politics of organizing. Lulu says in an emotional tone, "I still can't believe that I'm here, and part of me is really, really happy." This statement provides the viewer with an emotional, heartfelt view of Lulu's reality. Lulu points to the incredulous feeling they experience at being in their birthplace, a distant point on the horizon for most immigrants residing in the United States.

Beyond the way in which the restrictionist policies of the U.S. immigration system deny freedom of mobility, these immigrants are also barred from their homelands, their roots, and their families. Lulu's testimonial represents a fulfillment that most immigrants residing in the United States will never have access to experiencing. Their expressed feelings represent a moment of peace within the fracturing and fragmentation of an immigrant identity rooted in illegality. The status of illegality placed upon the immigrant body marks them as less deserving of access to elements of human rights, such as their roots, their memories, and their culture.[28] Lulu ends their video by saying, "I am really excited to know that we have a lot of support back home in the U.S. Mamá, Papá . . . vamos a regresar [we are going to return]. I'm going to come home. I'm going to come home." This statement demonstrates the positivity that the organizers felt regarding the possibility of returning to the United States thanks to the organizing efforts they had built with political, media, legal, and allied strategic support.

RETORNADX VIDEOS

The act of becoming a retornadx, self-returning to Mexico, and risking being denied reentry into the United States represented an unprecedented and unorthodox form of organizing for immigrant rights. It was also one of NIYA's most radical modes of organizing and a new, unique strategy to push the physical and legal boundaries of the U.S. nation-state. While the campaign was under way, six individuals, some of whom were retornadxs to Mexico and others of whom were deportees, reached out to NIYA. The six individuals had stories of struggle after returning to their home countries, and they were looking to return to the United States. NIYA incorporated them into the campaign, where they would join with the original three NIYA activists as a way to challenge deportation practices. With these additional six individuals incorporated, the campaign would take on the name "the Dream 9."[29]

In addition to Lizbeth's, Marco's, and Lulu's three videos, NIYA also shared check-in videos from three of the other six participants in the Dream 9 campaign, which included the stories of Luis León, Ceferino Santiago, and Claudia Amaro. It is important to note that these three videos of retornadxs and deportees are typically about one to two minutes longer than those of the three NIYA activists. In my textual analysis of their videos, it is notable that their migration journeys reveal narratives that are not linear but rather fragmented. Their video testimonials inform my (un)documenting approach, revealing that the stories of retornadxs or deportees do not follow a homogeneous storyline or a linear migration path and are therefore harder to fit into one single narrative like the DREAMer narrative. The six testimonials read together show the difference across narratives and identities represented by the #BringThemHome campaign. Rather than including the entire transcript from the three additional check-in videos, I provide a detailed textual analysis of key fragments from their stories.

VIDEO #1: BEYOND HARD WORK FOR ILLEGALIZED YOUTH

The first video is from Luis León, who grew up in North Carolina from the age of five. When he graduated from high school and considered higher education, he learned that the U.S. South had begun passing anti-immigration laws that not only made higher education inaccessible for undocumented youth but also targeted immigrant populations for detention and deportation. In his narrative he shares that he studied hard and applied himself as a student, which earned him important accolades. Luis's story reminds me of what Aurora Chang terms *hyperdocumentation*—undocumented youth earning academic accolades to balance the reality of their undocumented status. The stories of undocumented youth growing up in the United States often involve achieving accomplishments until they reach the point of rites of passage like attending university or college and find out that it is not possible. In his check-in video, Luis shares that his goals during his youth rested on education:

> That was my dream. That's what I worked for thirteen years knowing, the entire time, I was undocumented. I knew I had to push it harder just so I could be successful in the U.S., but when it came time to go to college, it was impossible.[30]

That moment of realization that education was not possible given state and local politics is what sociologist Alexis M. Silver refers to as the "tectonic incorporation model" in her research on undocumented youth in the U.S. South. In *Shifting Boundaries* (2018), Silver speaks of "tectonic plates, sometimes moving them toward incorporation and other times shifting them farther toward the margins," which in the case of retornadxs like Luis led to a return to Mexico to pursue an educational path not possible in the United States.[31] However, the experience of most retornadxs like Luis is that a similar political, financial, and societal challenge exists in trying to access higher education in Mexico. Luis ends his video check-in by stating, "I met here [in Mexico] the Dreamers, and we're fighting for me to come home and to help everybody understand that we got to make it," highlighting that joining the #BringThemHome campaign represents hope for many retornadxs like himself who see their futures in the United States.

VIDEO #2: TRANSNATIONAL FAMILIES' NEEDS

The next two video check-ins are by Ceferino Santiago and Claudia Amaro, whose stories represent the experience of members of the immigrant community who did not fit the molds of the DREAMer narrative. Ceferino also self-identifies with his Indigenous roots as a Zapotec from Oaxaca, Mexico. In his testimonial, Ceferino states, "I left Oaxaca at the age of thirteen. I knew the sacrifice that I was making by leaving my parents. It was a big responsibility for us [Ceferino and his brothers] to raise ourselves, to live without my parents. We had to work and go to school at the same time. It was hard."[32] Ceferino shares that at age thirteen, economic push factors demanded he be placed in the position of an adult by raising himself and his brothers, working hard, and attempting to receive an education. He returned to Oaxaca when his parents needed him home and chose to return to the United States with the #BringThemHome campaign because of the need he felt to go back to Kentucky to help his brothers who stayed behind there. He states, "I took a big risk by leaving Kentucky, just to come visit my parents. There are a lot of people who are in my situation . . . and now, I want to go back home [to] Kentucky, to be with my brothers. But the government of the United States might not want me." The narrative in his video highlights the stress and pressures under which transnational families are placed when they try to have a chance at a dignified life. As the older child, he was made the head of the household at an early age. Ultimately, Ceferino's testimonial and life story differ greatly from those of the three NIYA activists in that he did not have the privilege of education while in the United States, and economic factors led to his return to Mexico.

VIDEO #3: NO PAST, NO PRESENT, CARVING A FUTURE

In Claudia Amaro's video we see that stories of retornadxs and deportees do not have a clear-cut linear trajectory but rather are complex case studies that reflect state pressure and control. As a teenager, Claudia moved with her widowed mother and sisters from Tijuana to Wichita, Kansas, because her father had been violently murdered in Mexico. She states:

> When I was around ten years old, we went to Durango for vacation in spring-time, and my father was killed. That really affected me in different ways. I was the older sister, so I think I grew up a little faster because I had to start think-ing on problems that my mom had. When she actually told me that we were going to move to a different country, we actually moved with many hopes of a different life without being afraid.[33]

Push factors that were out of her family's control compelled them to leave Mexico. She would grow up in Wichita, Kansas, and eventually go on to marry her husband, who was also undocumented. They would eventually welcome a U.S.-born son into their lives, making them a mixed-status family.[34] Her husband was detained after a routine traffic stop on his way to work and turned over to U.S. Immigration and Customs Enforcement. Soon after he was placed in deportation proceedings, Claudia was also arrested while attempting to visit him in detention. The legal and economic battles of fighting her case while being a single mother pushed Claudia out of the United States and forced her back to Mexico to reunite with her family. While in Mexico, she attempted to make the best of the situation and enrolled in a university where she studied to be an engineer. Yet her life was not easy. She mentions that with all of her family's attempts to make the best of their return to Mexico, they were still limited by a lack of educational opportunities. Claudia's son was bullied at school for not speaking fluent Spanish and for being American-born. Claudia speaks to the feeling of being twice removed and displaced by saying, "Lately, I feel that I don't have no past, because where I live right now, I don't have any past. I don't have a present, because I am not happy, and I am not living it. And I don't see a future. So, I just want that back, I want my life back. I want my dreams back." These are the factors that pushed Claudia to connect with NIYA to participate in the #BringThemHome campaign.

NIYA published the promotional videos after the three original NIYA activists had already traveled to Mexico as a way to demonstrate that there was no going back on the campaign and also to raise awareness of what was to come in the action and build public support. Most importantly, the videos were a statement by immigrants in which they reclaimed control of their own lives and their bodies, while seeking to undermine the state-control apparatus that places them in the shadows. The assertive statements by NIYA activists, as well as participants like Luis, Ceferino, and Claudia, demonstrated their willingness to take a bold step to regain control of their lives. The other participants who constituted the Dream 9 were María Inés Peniche, Mario Félix, and Adriana Gil Díaz.[35] The participants were willing to challenge the U.S. government to demonstrate that migration should be a human right and not a privilege predetermined by nationality and citizenship. The Dream 9 transmedia narratives challenged the stories about retornadxs and deportees built by mainstream media, showing that the process of return migration is complex and that physical borders can be trespassed.

CAPTURING THE DEFIANT WALK TO THE BORDER

Shortly after the check-in videos made by the Dream 9 members in Mexico were posted online by NIYA, the nine activists met up in Nogales, Sonora, on the Mexican side of the border, to prepare for the second phase of the campaign: *infiltration*. The initial eight activists (the ninth, Mario Félix, would join at the very last minute) participated in a weeklong boot-camp-style orientation where they were trained by members of the attorney team representing them on interacting with Border Patrol officers, answering questions from the media, and dealing with their arrests and their probable transfer to a detention center.[36] In addition to being trained for their border crossing, the nine activists treated their meeting as a way to get to know each other. They had candlelight vigils where they shared their stories and participated in other bonding exercises that would give them the mental and emotional strength for the second phase. On July 22, 2013, the immigrant activists walked through the legal point of entry on the Mexico-U.S. border at Nogales, Arizona, demanding lawful entry to the United States, petitioning for humanitarian parole on the basis of their request for asylum. Each one of the activists was carrying their asylum papers; these had been carefully crafted and put together by their legal team, which included attorney Margo Cowan.[37]

It is important to analyze the elements of symbolism and performance used by the Dream 9 campaign on its march north toward the Mexico-U.S. border. The activists were hosted by a lawyer-led organization dealing with labor rights in Nogales, Sonora, Mexico, called Soluciones Laborales (Labor Solutions), located within minutes of the Mexico-U.S. border. From Soluciones Laborales the activists marched toward the border, symbolically wearing their caps and gowns, holding hands in solidarity, and followed by a sizable crowd showing their support. The caps and gowns were a common symbol strategically used by NIYA to represent undocumented youth's place in U.S. society.

In this section I use digital photographic archival material produced by NIYA organizers to create transmedia narratives. NIYA strategically used national U.S. media coverage by venues such as *Latino USA*. NIYA also relied on allied coverage by contemplative-activist photographers like Steve Pavey. *Latino USA* used the photography assembled by Pavey to create an audiovisual montage of the Dream 9 that documents their move from Nogales, Sonora, to the Mexico-U.S. border.[38] In many of the photographs that Pavey captured of the event, he represents some of the Dream 9 participants as calm and collected and others as smiling, while none appear worried or in distress.

In Pavey's photo series, we first see the image of three of the nine activists—Lulu, Luis, and María—lined up in single file with steel-beam bars directly behind them. We can understand the steel beams behind them to be the legal entry point on the Mexico-U.S. border, just before they encounter Border Patrol agents. All three of them are wearing graduation caps and gowns. Lulu is captured with their chin up in a proud posture with their glasses glaring. Luis appears to be looking ahead with a feeling of anticipation, perhaps imagining what will come next and their possible interaction with Border Patrol agents. María is directly behind Luis, also looking ahead of the line, but with the difference that she appears with a joyful smile on her face. To Luis's left, we see a hand gripping a midsized video camera with a powerful microphone mounted on top, covering the action closely. Immediately to Luis's and María's right, we see another individual who is covering the action with a photography camera in their right hand and their left hand up in the air holding a cell phone to take photographs, video, or audio of the action. Besides these individuals, there only appears an older woman whose head is peeking over María's left shoulder. We also see a hand resting on Luis's left shoulder in an endearing manner.

Luis is at the center of this photograph. Again, he is wearing a graduation cap and gown aimed at symbolically representing the activists' place in American culture and society. On the left side of his chest, placed right next to his heart, he wears a button with the #BringThemHome logo. The button on each one of the activists' gowns adds an emotional tone to the campaign, as it is symbolically placed next to their hearts. In the photograph, Luis has his

FIGURE 7 "#1542—The Dream 9." Photograph by Stephen Pavey, Hope in Focus Photography. The complete set of photographs of the Dream 9 campaign can be found published on Google Arts and Culture by *Latino USA*. Steve Pavey is the photographer who documented the Dream 9 campaign. He has also documented many other social movements in the United States. His website featuring his work can be found at www.stevepavey.com.

hands in front of his chest holding what appears to be paperwork on a clipboard, and between the fingers of his left hand he is holding what appears to be an identification card whose back is visible. This symmetric composure of Pavey's photograph also conveys critical information to the viewer, revealing that the action was as carefully crafted and assembled as the photograph itself. In other words, the assembly we see speaks to the level of organization and care that NIYA and its allied partners put into the action to ensure its success, as it would have tremendous impacts on the lives of the participants.

The second photograph included in Pavey's montage includes eight of the nine #BringThemHome participants casually leaning back against the Mexico-- U.S. border wall. There are only eight activists because Mario Félix, who would become the ninth participant, did not join the NIYA campaign until moments before the action of walking across the border took place. We only see Mario Félix in the photographs of the point when the activists passed through the official entry point in Nogales, Arizona, and in post-action photographs.

FIGURE 8 "Meet the Dream 9." Photograph by Stephen Pavey, Hope in Focus Photography. Published on Google Arts and Culture by *Latino USA*.

The photograph shows the eight activists standing on a cement base holding the steel beams that compose the Mexico-U.S. border wall. From the viewer's left to right, we see Luis León standing sideways with his face turned toward the camera, followed by María and Adriana, also in profile but embracing each other. María is seen with a smile, as she is in most of the photographs, while Luis and Adriana show half-smiles. Lulu comes next, near the center of the photograph, with one hand down and the other behind them, posing with an outwardly confident attitude. Ceferino is wearing a USC (University of Southern California) band shirt and standing with his arms behind him while staring with an intense look into the camera. Marco has a playful posture, with one arm next to him and the other behind him and a spirited smile; he sports a T-shirt that reads "Education not Deportation." Lizbeth is next to Marco, wearing a white skirt with a purple design, a black top, and a bright purple cardigan, with a confident smile and sunglasses on her head. Finally, on the far right we have Claudia, who is posed sideways facing inward, the opposite of Luis on the far left, giving the photograph a staged, symmetrical composition. Like Lizbeth, Claudia displays a confident smile and wears sunglasses on her head. Overall, the activists are wearing bright-colored clothing that pops

FIGURE 9 "The Day I Met the Dream 9." Photograph by Stephen Pavey, Hope in Focus Photography. This photograph is included in a separate blog post by *Latino USA* titled "The Day I Met the Dream 9," which can be accessed at https://www.latinousa.org/2015/10/15/the-day-i-met-the-dream-9/.

along with the greenery of the trees on the other side of the border wall. The photograph gives the viewer a bright-spirited feeling. Perhaps this was meant to set the tone visually to express the optimism felt right before walking across the border to Nogales, Arizona.

The third photograph again features three of the activists—Lulu, Lizbeth, and Luis—standing on the cement base holding the steel beams that mark the Mexico-U.S. border. However, this time they have their backs to the camera, and Pavey captures a moment in which the three activists are communicating through the border wall with Mohammad Abdollahi and another NIYA ally, who are located on the U.S. side of the wall. Both groups on both sides of the border appear happy and are smiling, communicating in a carefree manner across the steel beams of the border. This photograph is in black-and-white, appearing to show a pinnacle moment in the story of a planned action that involved regular communication and transmedia coverage occurring in both countries. In other words, the photograph conveys the transnational nature of the action required from the activists. The photographer captures these activists organizing in a natural manner across the Mexico-U.S. border, as if suggesting that this is normal for undocumented youth, who are accustomed to living transnational lives.

The fourth photograph in Pavey's montage is again brightly colored and features a close-up of six of the nine activists, who have bright smiles and appear to be walking calmly on the Mexican side of the border. Claudia and Lizbeth are looking toward the camera. Ceferino, María, and Luis are looking away, but they are smiling and observing their surroundings. They appear to be happy with the amount of people that surround them showing their solidarity as they walk toward Nogales, Arizona, the legal entry point to the United States. Even though the photograph is a close-up shot, we can see that there is quite a crowd surrounding them. Among those captured by the photograph is a priest wearing his religious robe, indicating there was also faith-based support for the action. This is not uncommon, as religious institutions have a long history in the (im)migrant and refugee movements in the United States. In the background we see at least one cameraman holding a midsized camera and wearing a distinctive tan journalist vest, representing the wide coverage of the action that occurred on both sides of the border. Finally, many individuals in the background appear to be wearing #BringThemHome pins displayed over their hearts, showing solidarity with the activists, who are also wearing them on their graduation caps.

The next series of photographs is of all of the individual activists except Mario Félix, some with their families; the audiovisual montage provides some individual information on who the Dream 9 are. The photograph used for Mario's profile is a group photo captured after the action concluded with the release of the activists, showing them in front of the Eloy Detention Center in Arizona where they were detained. We see that the photograph was captured right at the moment in which all nine activists are raising their fists proudly in the air, resulting in a blurred effect. We see a sign in the shape of a pillar right behind the activists that reads "Eloy Detention Center," with a large green saguaro to the activists' right that is used as landscaping intended to give an aesthetic effect to the otherwise unappealing location that is the detention center, which is visible in the background to the activists' left. In front of the nine activists, we see a bright blue banner that reads "WE'RE HOME," with the same design as the #BringThemHome logo. However, this time we see the silhouettes within the word "home" appearing to display actions of freedom, in contrast to the #BringThemHome logo, in which the silhouettes struggle with a barbed-wire fence representing the border fence. At the bottom of the banner, additional text reads, "Families Beyond Borders," which serves the call-to-action messaging that its transmedia campaign advocated. Finally, at the top right-hand side of the banner we see NIYA's web address.

This final photograph in *Latino USA*'s coverage is one displaying triumph and post-action success, after the nine activists were released and had accomplished the goals of their action: to challenge family separation and claim the right to mobility for immigrants. The photography montage is a way in which NIYA activists strategically collaborated with journalists and media to produce a public transmedia narrative that conveyed a particular social imaginary: "Families Beyond Borders." The social imaginary constructed through the messaging of NIYA's #BringThemHome campaign provides an alternative vision of transnational family living. NIYA's transmedia narrative invites communities on both sides of the border to reflect on what our world could be if mobility were not only available to a few in the privileged class. NIYA found a cleavage in immigration policy and constructed a campaign to expose the violence that comes with family separation at the hands of the state. The action of self-documenting or (un)documenting, as well as inviting media professionals to support the documentation process, was aimed at exposing the state while also recording undocumented youth's escalating civil-disobedience actions.

PHASE TWO: INFILTRATION

The activists' arrival at the Mexico-U.S. border represented the completion of phase one of the campaign, and the beginning of the second phase of their efforts. The nine individuals were aware that if parole was denied, this could mean a potential ten-year ban from the United States.[39] The activists lined up, and one by one they walked up to immigration officials with their paperwork ready, informing them that they were there to petition for asylum. As they were walking across the border, activists from NIYA, like Mohammad Abdollahi, were waiting for them on the U.S. side and documenting the event to develop it into transmedia narratives produced for the #BringThemHome campaign. As the event was live streamed and shared via media and social media, everyone including the members of the Dream 9 asked themselves the big question: Would they be allowed entry into the United States?[40] To everyone's surprise, the nine activists were allowed entry. Once in the custody of Border Patrol, they were interrogated for hours before being transported in a Border Patrol van to the Eloy Detention Center in Eloy, Arizona.

The Eloy Detention Center is a 1,600-bed facility exclusively for immigration detention, operated by a private company called CoreCivic.[41] The Eloy Detention Center is carefully located out of sight between Phoenix and Tucson, Arizona. Most U.S. detention centers have carefully been assembled and constructed in restricted locations. The common expression "in the middle of nowhere" is a fitting way to describe where contemporary detention centers are established. The nine activists spent a total of seventeen days, from July 22 to August 8, 2013, detained at the Eloy Detention Center.

The infiltration phase of the #BringThemHome campaign used recorded audio calls that were shared widely across social media and diverse media outlets. These audio calls were called "detention check-ins" by NIYA in the transmedia narratives the organization produced. Again, these were preplanned strategies organized by NIYA and their legal representatives to document the activists' experiences inside of the detention center. The NIYA organizers took the detention check-ins and produced video clips that were released publicly via the organization's YouTube channel. The audio calls were the campaign's (un)documenting strategy—they produced audio archival evidence documenting and exposing the human rights violations by the state against immigrant populations held in detention. Prior to Isaac and Jonathan's infiltration action in 2011 and the #BringThemHome action in 2013, the general public in the United States was not widely aware of these violations. The U.S. government had gone to great lengths to document undocumented immigrants in ways that criminalized them and facilitated their detention and deportation, but it chose not to document publicly what happened behind closed doors in detention centers. NIYA's #BringThemHome campaign aimed to document the shadows of detention.

The detention check-in videos served the archival assemblage of evidence. Here I analyze three of these videos. It is worth noting that the audio-call videos were produced in similar fashion to the check-in videos by the activists described above. They include background music and sound effects that set a tone of seriousness. They use images and photographs to provide context, and they include a call to action at the end urging the public to advocate for and support the #BringThemHome campaign. The videos begin with an image of the Eloy Detention Center. While the photograph is on-screen, an operator's voice is heard announcing that an inmate in the facility is making a call and giving the option of accepting it. As part of the planning for the #BringThemHome campaign, the legal team and NIYA had provided the organizers with enough funding to be able to make the calls from inside of the detention center. In the videos, after the operator's voice, a title card appears with information about the call, including the name of the organizer calling, their alien registration number, and the date of the call. The audio starts with a brief statement by the organizer making the call while sliding photographs of the individual appear. One of the questions all the organizers are asked is about the conditions inside of the Eloy Detention Center, to which each organizer answers with critical information. The videos end again by displaying the #BringThemHome campaign logo and finally an advocacy call to support the campaign.

The first video posted by NIYA does not have a date, but based on the content and the timeline of events we can assume it is the first video, because it consists of María Inés Peniche doing a simple initial check-in and letting the public know the activists are well. Here is the transcript of that first detention check-in:

[Phone ringing.]

MARÍA PENICHE: Hi. This is María Peniche. I'm fine. They showered us and we've already been assigned a room and everyone's okay.

[Music.]

MARÍA PENICHE: I'm just calling to give you guys my number. It is 820–593–5698.

[Music.]

MARÍA PENICHE: Thank you, guys. I'll see you soon. Bye. Thank you. Thank you. Thank you. Bye.

[Music.]

[Phone dial tone.][42]

All of the activists had been instructed to call the NIYA organizers and their lawyers on the outside to provide them with their A-number (alien registration number) so that they could get going on their cases toward humanitarian parole. Not wasting time or money, María is quick to inform NIYA organizers and the audience watching the video that the activists have been processed inside of the Eloy Detention Center and that they are settling in.

The second detention check-in audio call published by NIYA did not come until the seventh day of detention, on July 29, 2013, and features Lizbeth Mateo.

PHONE OPERATOR VOICE: A detainee at CCA Eloy Detention Center. This call is subject to recording and monitoring. To accept charges, press one. To refuse charges, press two. Thank you for using Securus. You may start the conversation now.

LIZBETH MATEO: Hello, this is Lizbeth Mateo. I'm at the Eloy Detention Center. I've been in solitary confinement, this is my fourth—actually, this is my fifth solitary confinement [day] and I want my friends and I to come home. I want all nine of us to go home as soon as possible.

The conditions here are not the best. They have women who have been waiting for months to see their asylum officer and to get interviewed. Been here six, seven months, even three years. They're all waiting. One of the ICE officers today told me that there's a reason why they should be waiting because they're all kind of [unintelligible] with interviews. I don't know why they're keeping them here, sometimes with restricted phone calls, they're not able to talk to their families. If they say something, they're sent to solitary confinement and they're really, really scared. If you actually see them, they're absolutely scared to say anything. I don't know what they're doing to these women so that they don't try anything.[43]

Lizbeth's call focuses on calling attention to the particular treatment of women inside of detention centers and the conditions they were experiencing. In particular, the quoted passage further highlights the use of time as a mechanism to effect trauma on the women inside of detention, by not letting them know when they will be let out or have access to communicate with the outside world. The use of time as a form of violence is something that was also corroborated in Jonathan and Isaac's experience during their detention infiltration in Louisiana, mentioned in chapter 2. In Lizbeth's audio call, we see that this particular form of violence was common, along with intimidation of women inmates by the immigration officers inside of the detention center. Lizbeth's call (un)documents the forms of violence that women in detention experience.

This form of systemic gendered violence is not new, but rather a historical continuum, as historians and ethnic studies scholars highlight. Kelly Lytle Hernández's work *Migra!* (2010) historicizes systemic violence against immigrant women and children over time from the period of the bracero program under the Immigrant Naturalization Services (INS) department, which preceded the Department of Homeland Security.[44] From the Border Patrol's history of systemic violence against undocumented immigrant women, we see how historically this behavior is taken to sites like detention centers by the INS, as told in *The Shadow of El Centro* (2021) by Jessica Ordaz. Ordaz argues, "Dominant discourses of masculinity shaped life inside of detention, a part of the larger administrative regimes, where racial and gendered cruelty was weaponized against immigrants."[45] She is able to show this through the archival exploration of detention center handbooks, oral histories, and other administrative documents. Additionally, Ordaz's work explores what she terms a "geography of violence" inside of detention centers, using archival materials that highlight locations such as bathrooms where violence became systematic, and particular sites where violence was inflicted upon detained migrants.[46]

After Lizbeth's detention check-in on day seven, she reported the many stories of women in the center who were abused or raped and who suffered other poor conditions. The activists heard many of these horror stories from other detained immigrant women, until it finally reached a point where María Inés Peniche could not take it anymore, and she got on top of a table and started banging on it with a tray, yelling, "Hunger strike!" To her surprise, many of the women followed her action, yelling, "Hunger strike!" while also banging their trays on the table. María and Lulu were then separated from the group and placed in solitary confinement, where they were given orange jumpsuits, different from the green-colored ones that the nine activists received upon entering the detention center. The orange jumpsuits, according to USCIS, mark detained migrants who are considered dangerous to their own safety and that of the other prisoners.

The different-colored jumpsuits assigned to prisoners can be viewed similarly to the way U.S. Homeland Security uses categories such as "illegal alien" and initiatives such as "Safe Communities" to label immigrant populations in the United States. The orange jumpsuits Lulu and María were made to wear further highlight the ways in which the U.S. immigrant system labels and marks undocumented bodies for management and control. It marks those bodies that are deemed a threat to its forms of discipline and punishment. Activists who are deemed a threat are separated to limit or minimize potential forms of dissident action and rebellion that might extend to other inmates. Activists are treated as if they are a disease that must be contained, quarantined, and then eliminated, as demonstrated by the response to Lulu's and María's actions.[47]

Ahead of the action, NIYA leaders had organized other activists and volunteers from the Phoenix and Tucson area, together with a heavy media presence, to go to the Eloy Detention Center during the nine activists' detention, where they would join demonstrations that would be captured on video. The Dream 9 activists' legal representation regularly visited them throughout the seventeen days they were detained. Furthermore, the nine activists also regularly communicated with fellow activists who were organizing the campaign from outside of the detention center; their conversations were recorded and added to the promotional campaign materials.

NIYA published a third detention check-in audio recording by Claudia Amaro that reported that Lulu and María had been placed in solitary confinement.

OPERATOR: A detainee at CCA, Eloy Detention Center. This call is subject to recording and monitoring. To accept charges, press one. To refuse charges, press two. Thank you for using Securus. You may start the conversation now.

CLAUDIA: This is Claudia from this detention center, Eloy. And this what María and Lulu did, was—was that Sunday? They just stand up on a chair and María and they told the women that they are not alone but they have some helping people outside who care about them and we're going to give away some little papers with some legal numbers. Then they start chanting, like, "Sin papeles, sin miedo" in Spanish, "Undocumented and Unafraid." And "El pueblo unido jamás será vencido" [The pueblo united will never be defeated].

They just did that a couple of times and then an officer came in and asked them to get down. They got down. They put some handcuffs on them and they help isolate them. They treat them real bad. They told them that they didn't know what they were doing and they had made a big mistake [unintelligible] . . . going to get isolated and they would be treated like nobody. Since then, every time, they are just by themselves and every time they have to take them out for some sun and they cuff them and they lock up everybody else and they bring them down in handcuffs.

They tell them they're a special case or they're special move to, so they always [*unintelligible*] . . . next to them. Then it's like we have to go somewhere and they have to place us in a different part or something, they always separate them from everybody else. That's the way they usually [*unintelligible*] . . . all the girls say here they usually tell them when they isolate them that they're nobody, that they are nobody.

Actually, they said one of the other girls, when they get isolated, worse because they check [*unintelligible*] . . . them and they put a white gown on them and they don't listen to them.

OPERATOR: Thank you for using Securus.[48]

Claudia provides detailed narratives of the ways in which the guards tell María and Lulu "that they had made a big mistake" and "that they would be treated like nobody," highlighting the way the officers would make detained migrants feel control over their bodies to the extent of being reduced to less than human. Claudia's detention check-in documents in detail the multiple forms of physical, mental, and verbal violence experienced at the hands of the state through private contractors hired by CoreCivic inside the detention center. In this way, detention centers aim to physically and mentally wear down detained migrants to the point of obedience and to forcefully manage human life. The nine activists experienced the effects of multiple forms of psychological and mental harm.

The Dream 9 activists had training and legal support, but nothing could have prepared them for the multiple forms of trauma they encountered while in detention. In a podcast interview with *Latino USA*, María sobs while reporting that she contemplated suicide many times while in solitary confinement and indicated that the control exerted by the officers made her feel as they had said she would feel "like nobody."[49] The treatment Lulu and María experienced had a severe impact on their mental health during detention and for a long time after their release. Their example shows the ways in which the U.S. immigration system beats and batters undocumented youth activists, both physically and sometimes through severe psychological treatment.

POST-RELEASE REACTIONS

After seventeen days spent in the Eloy Detention Center, from July 22 to August 8, and without any prior notification, the nine activists were transported in a van for over an hour and released in a random parking lot without explanation. Fellow NIYA activists joined them shortly afterward, along with media outlets, to report this bittersweet victory. NIYA had generated enough media and public pressure to get the nine activists released, and they were allowed to remain in the United States while their cases were processed. Their experience with the exploitative immigrant detention system was brought to public attention. Ultimately, the #BringThemHome campaign was able to report on the violent system responsible for the detention, imprisonment, and deportation of immigrants in the United States, and it made it public knowledge, adding to the long-standing tradition of undocumented immigrants who have historically aimed to make the violence experienced at the hands of the state visible and documented.[50]

The nine activists spent seventeen days in a detention center, very little compared with their unrepresented immigrant/refugee counterparts, who typically spend from two months to several years in detention. This demonstrates the level of public awareness that accompanied the campaign. Whereas NIYA activists benefited from the public visibility of their organizing, private corporations like CoreCivic benefit from the invisibility of undocumented bodies. The majority of the refugee/migrant individuals detained at the Eloy Detention Center cannot afford representation, making it extremely difficult for them to gain their release. The longer they are held, the greater the profit for companies contracted by the U.S. government.[51]

NIYA considered the campaign a success and went on to organize the "Dream 30" only four months later with more individuals.[52] This time the campaign took place at the Mexico-U.S. border between Tijuana and San Diego. This campaign focused much more on "non-DREAMer" individuals, ones who were still young but who might not have the privilege of the cap-and-gown symbolic public spectacle of the first campaign, or who did not benefit from DACA. Individuals like Elvira Arellano (chapter 1), who did not fit the DREAMer narrative, later joined with NIYA to reunite families in three other campaigns on the #BringThemHome model. Elvira used her image as a public figure to help bring awareness to the other #BringThemHome initiatives.

Many of the participants in the subsequent Dream 30 campaign included individuals, like Jessica (who only gives her first name in the campaign video), who had been deported at an early age. She was only fourteen years old when her family decided to go back to Mexico after the persecution and pressure exerted by Sheriff Joe Arpaio's administration in Arizona.[53] While her family self-returned to Mexico, Jessica made the difficult choice to stay in Arizona, the place she had grown to call home, until her abrupt deportation. Her video, posted by NIYA in September 2013 and used to announce the Dream 30 campaign, reveals that once in Mexico she received nothing but harassment at school and work. Thus it becomes evident that returning to their home country does not represent a different fate for immigrants; rather, their illegality follows them across nation-states. In this instance, it is not that their illegality is represented in their legal status, because they are citizens of their home countries; rather, their illegality is present in their bodies, their identity, their customs, and their language.

In another video posted by NIYA, a twenty-year-old woman named Ana speaks about the violence her family endured at the hands of local gangs when they returned to Mexico.[54] In an emotionally driven message, she states, "We didn't have to pass through all these bad things," which highlights the difference between growing up in the United States and in Mexico. The idea of a better future, or the "American Dream," is not an idea of privilege for many of the youth who participated in the campaigns, but rather a possibility of escaping the violence of their home countries. In other words, the repressiveness of the U.S. immigration system is not limited to the borders of the nation-state; we can see how the violence and pressure that begins in the United States for retornadxs or deportees can continue to be experienced upon their return to their birth countries.

Similarly, for queer or trans-identified individuals who were part of the Dream 30 campaign, the regulation and control of their bodies through violent means was effected by multiple states and extended to every facet of their lives. Migrations become a necessity of life for undocu-queer migrants. Their migration represents a fleeing from violence at the hands of historically homophobic and transphobic governments in Latin America, Central America, and Mexico. Leaning on Latinx studies scholars exploring homophobia in Latin America, Lawrence La Fountain-Stokes focuses part of his work "Queer Ducks, Puerto Rican Patos, and Jewish-American Feygelekh" (2007) on derogatory terminology associating homosexual identities in Puerto Rico with negative stereotypes in the word pato (duck). La Fountain-Stokes traces these histori-cal stereotypes to colonial times in Puerto Rico, whose family models and sex-ual moralities extend into the present day.[55] Chicanx studies and jotería studies scholar Daniel Enrique Pérez draws on La Fountain-Stokes's work to extend the history of homophobia and transphobia to representations of migrants and immigrants as mariposas (butterflies)—a widely recognized symbol of migration, but also one that can be used to queer migration.[56] Daniel Enrique Pérez draws on Emma Pérez's work on *the decolonial imaginary* to build what he terms a mariposa *imaginary*, which he defines as a third space of conscious-ness where queer-identified individuals can subvert negative stereotypes and terminology existing in Chicanx and Mexican American culture to produce new meanings of empowerment. The work by Latinx and Chicanx studies scholars shows that while there is a history of homophobia in the United States, some of the violence endured by migrants in their home countries also reveals systemic violence both figurative and physical. Many of the migrants are aware that they are not fully escaping violence in the U.S. nation-state, but they understand that this does represent an escape from more overt forms of violence. Migration in this instance is not about simply surviving but living a viable life, one that is not whole, or full, but will always be fragmented by the scars of endured violence.

CONCLUSION: POSTSCRIPT

Activism is a self-sacrificing ritual with the idea of societal change as a goal. The three NIYA activists who participated in the original #BringThemHome campaign, also known as the Dream 9 campaign, sacrificed their mental health and their legal status in the United States. They spent the following years in immigration courts and continued to organize in different capacities. Lizbeth Mateo went on to earn a law degree in 2016 from Santa Clara University. She has applied twice for the DACA program and been rejected because of her trip to Mexico for the #BringThemHome campaign. In 2018, she became the first undocumented individual to be appointed to a statewide post, specifically to an advisory committee for low-income students in California.[57] Marco contin-ues to organize in New York, and his work previous to the #BringThemHome campaign was featured in a documentary titled *The Infiltrators* (2019), which captures infiltration actions he participated in during 2012.[58] Lulu returned to their community in Chicago, where they continue to organize; they are the only reported member of the Dream 9 to have been granted asylum.[59]

The (un)document—or the archive—from the case study of the first #BringThemHome campaign reveals that there is power in numbers for migrants caravanning to request asylum. In culmination, I argue that there are two critical legacies resulting from the #BringThemHome campaigns. First, the power-in-numbers organizing ideology formed the basis for the *migrant caravan* model that was used to organize Central American migrants beginning in 2017. Second, NIYA's 2013 #BringThemHome campaign broadens the possibilities for organizing by social movements due to its transnational nature, which would be represented in the caravans as well.

This chapter contextualizes the #BringThemHome campaign in the second decade of the twenty-first century, when detentions and deportations grew significantly in the United States, which resulted in the political categorization and identification of deportees and retornadxs. NIYA challenged the limitations on immigrant mobility but also highlighted the stories and political action of deportees and retornadxs. After its success with the initial Dream 9 campaign, NIYA went on to organize several additional campaigns, as mentioned just above, in which Elvira Arellano would participate, making her way back to the United States along with other non-DREAMer-identified individuals who included adult women, children, adult men, and transgender individuals. During the seven years Elvira spent in Mexico after her deportation (2007–14), she learned about the Central American migrants coming through Mexico and into the United States while connecting and working with organizations that provided aid and relief to migrants along their journey. This seven-year time period helped Elvira expand her transnational organizing efforts across multiple borders including the border between Mexico and Guatemala (the Central American point of entry). Mexican states themselves serve as borders, as they have begun to adopt their own immigration policies influenced by U.S. states. Elvira helped construct a transnational network of U.S.-based, Mexican-based, and Central America–based organizations to help Central American migrants' journeys.

The #BringThemHome campaign occurred in the context of Mexican immigrants/migrants, but a growing number of migrants during the second decade of the twenty-first century were Central American. A 2017 article by the Pew Research Center reports that the number of migrants from the "Northern Triangle" countries of Central America—Guatemala, El Salvador, and

Honduras—grew after the 2007/8 economic recession in the United States to about 115,000 in 2014.[60] The authors of the article highlight that Central American migration reported growth, while Mexican migration did not. The networks in Mexico, Central America, and the United States helping Central American migrants along their journey paid attention to the #BringThem-Home campaigns organized in 2013 and 2014. The 2014 campaign in which Elvira was directly involved that walked over 130 migrants across the Tijuana–San Diego border entry saw the power in numbers.

The first documented coordinated migrant caravan began on April 9, 2017, during Holy Week—considered a particularly special week for Christian faiths, which are followed widely in the Central American countries where the majority of the migrants were coming from—and was organized by Pueblo Sin Fronteras (A People Without Borders) and supported by other organizations such as La Casa del Migrante (The House of the Migrant). This first caravan was met with both pro- and anti-immigrant rhetoric from the mainstream media. The mass migrant movement resulting from the caravan model, containing hundreds, and at times thousands, of participants, overwhelmed the U.S. immigration system. Migrant caravans became another organizing strategy in which migrants/immigrants (un)documented new possibilities to emphasize the fact that borders are social constructions. As such, the #BringThemHome campaign and the migrant caravans created new social imaginaries across borders.

The #BringThemHome campaign, which envisioned new possibilities for mass migration, needs to be analyzed in the realm of transnational social movements. Scholars typically define social movements in the context of mass movement building; the #BringThemHome campaigns by NIYA never reached massive participation and can be seen as quite small in numbers to be considered a social movement. However, this chapter has demonstrated that the #BringThemHome campaign, along with the other cases in this book, represents a critical moment in undocumented youth movements (UYMs) and their use of transmedia narratives to shift immigrant rights discourse in the United States. Migrant caravans are a legacy of the #BringThemHome campaign that continues to regularly occupy a place in discussions about immigrants, refugees, and asylum in the United States.

NIYA imagined something that was unimaginable at the time—for migrants to return to their home countries and be able to come back to the United States via the legal strategy of petitioning for asylum. I argue that they accomplished their initial aims of challenging family separation, detention, and deportation practices by the U.S. nation-state. But in the process of accomplishing this, they also shifted the strategic possibilities for mass migration. Previous to the #BringThemHome campaign, UYMs were invested in building mass movements in public sites with national and transnational scopes in mind. However, part of my strategic use of "undocumented youth movements" with an *s* is to signify the movements' plurality, heterogeneous nature, and diversity, as well as to reflect the fact that movements change, shift, and adapt over time. Youth "grows up" as well. By the time of the #BringThemHome campaign in 2013, and well into the migrant caravan phase of 2018–20, the majority of the undocumented organizers had been organizing for well over two decades. Many of them did not see themselves as "youth" anymore, but they still wanted to carve out new approaches to defining movement building. The next chapter turns to seasoned undocumented organizers who move their organizing from the streets to nightclubs!

CHAPTER 4

PARTYING AS POLITICAL

Undocumented Artivism and Nightlife Scene Productions as
Alternative Forms of Organizing and Belonging

When they give us a little breathing room, we make the
most of it. We are so grateful that often we forget that
WE DESERVE BETTER.
—YOSIMAR REYES, 2017

ETTING READY FOR A NIGHTCLUB can be a whole process. You must ask yourself a wide range of questions. Are you dressed appropriately to get into the particular venue? Is your wardrobe in line with the aesthetic represented? You also reflect on your positionality and ask: How will you be read based on your race, ethnicity, gender, and sexuality? To extend this last thought process: What body aesthetic is associated with the culture of the venue, and in what ways will your body be read? If you are undocumented, you ask yourself: What documentation do you have for identification, and will your type of ID be accepted at a particular venue? Partying is political. Nightclubs follow hegemonic understandings that regulate certain communities and restrict everyday practices of joy.

The privilege of joy is something that is quite troubling for undocumented youth coming of age across the multiple rites of passage into adulthood. Undocu-poet Yosimar Reyes began conceptualizing the term *undocu-joy*—an aesthetic reminder to undocumented youth to prioritize moments of resistance that push back against the pressures of everyday life as an undocumented immigrant, and to preserve and document joy within the undocumented experience.[1] Yosimar's poem "Share the UndocuJoy!" serves as a call to undocumented communities to remember the strength embodied in our familial resilience, which "makes something out of nothing." They go on to highlight the multiple attacks that undocumented communities face on a daily basis, but at the same time the need to practice seeing beauty in the struggle. The poem by Yosimar was produced as a video by Define American, with DJ Sizzle Fantastic from the artivist movement Cumbiatón among the featured characters performing undocu-joy.[2] For undocumented youth like DJ Sizzle Fantastic, Yosimar Reyes, and Cumbiatón leaders who grew up in California, coming of age was not an easy transition, and they recognized that we must center undocu-joy in our own everyday experiences.

In my memory, coming of age with undocumented status in Los Angeles was not an easy rite of passage. I remember all my friends being excited about transitional moments into adulthood, such as obtaining a driver's license, applying for colleges, and getting into nightclubs for the first time. I was not excited about any of that. Carrying foreign documentation as identification to get into a nightclub will surely earn you stares. Before the Deferred Action for Childhood Arrivals (DACA) program beginning in 2012, and before driver's licenses were authorized for undocumented communities in California in 2015 (through AB 60), undocumented immigrants had no access to a U.S.-based identification card.[3] In most U.S. states, where driver's licenses were not allowed or are still currently not allowed for undocumented immigrants, undocumented communities had to visit their country's consulate to receive an ID containing their photograph, date of birth, and local address. This form of identification is known as a matrícula in Spanish, and it is what I used to get into nightclubs before the DACA program existed and before I qualified for a driver's license.

Many nightclubs did not accept matrículas because they did not recognize them, or simply because they were foreign identification. That moment when the nightclub bouncer holds your foreign identification card and decides whether or not to recognize you as a human being showcases the way the borderlands expand and contract in terms of the monitoring of immigrants in the interior of the nation-state.[4] In a partygoing setting, a nightclub bouncer becomes an agent of the state enforcing not only IDs but also immigration beliefs and practices. And like that nightclub bouncer, other private institutions and their agents also become extensions of the state and are recruited to participate in restricting everyday life for immigrants. Parents can often serve as the first line of defense for the state by warning immigrant children against moving freely into certain spaces that might represent a risk of detention and possible threat of deportation. That is how illegalization moves through undocumented communities in every space of society, including nightclubs. Illegality is what makes partying a political act for undocumented communities. Illegalization is a systematic way in which societal institutions are deliberately tasked with recognizing immigrant bodies and further rejecting their opportunities to participate in societal functions such as partying. Illegality enforced by multiple agents of the state is what restricts undocu-joy or makes it difficult to experience for undocumented communities.

I include my positionality and identity as an undocu-scholar to provide insights into the ways in which undocumented communities organize to resist illegalization. As an undocu-scholar writing from an illegalized perspective, I explore the Cumbiatón nightlife scene through participant observation as well as analysis of digital archives produced by artivists—artists who produce art for purposes of social justice or activism. Having grown up undocumented in the city of Los Angeles and run into many of the social borders that exist for undocumented youth, I am interested in Cumbiatón as a case study in order to analyze and document the ways in which the movement navigates the politics of partying for undocumented and BIPOC (Black, Indigenous, and people of color) communities within neoliberal power structures.

This chapter explores artivism produced by the movement Cumbiatón. When their website was launched, Cumbiatón's mission statement described the movement as "an intergenerational cultural movement which utilizes music and art as a vessel to heal and uplift oppressed hood communities."[5] I analyze the Cumbiatón artivist movement as a nightlife scene creating alternate politics of belonging through an illegalized identity that challenges neoliberal modes of world-making. I argue that the activism produced by undocumented organizers like those of Cumbiatón creates alternative ways of organizing and develops new ways to resist the nation-state. This chapter analyzes the transmedia assemblage of archives produced by Cumbiatón across multiple online platforms such as the Cumbiatón website, its Instagram page, artists' web pages, YouTube videos, and its Flickr page, all functioning as an archival repository. I argue that Cumbiatón's transmedia-based archives detail new ways of documenting immigrant bodies and experiences that are often relegated to the shadows. In this sense, nightclubs become a physical site in the social imaginary where undocumented youth and allied community members can "come out of the shadows" with their immigration status, gender performance, racial, ethnic, and cultural expressions, and sexuality.

Cumbiatón was born and began organizing parties in 2016 in Boyle Heights, California, as a way to process the trauma caused by the large numbers of deportations occurring during President Barack Obama's administration, which actively employed a neoliberal agenda that prioritized certain qualifying undocumented youth for inclusion while criminalizing broader immigrant populations.[6] For almost a decade undocumented youth enjoyed the privilege of the cultural capital they earned through public visibility during the Obama administration, which they exchanged for the level of protection that allowed them to effectively perform civil disobedience and direct forms of activism, as detailed in chapters 2 and 3. Once the forty-fourth president's term ended and the forty-fifth's term started in 2017, there would be a direct attack on undocumented organizers.[7] The Cumbiatón movement was composed of seasoned veterans who had been active in organizing in the early stages of the UYMs and had transitioned into adulthood while continuing to organize for immigrant communities. This chapter represents the struggle of undocumented organizers as a historical continuum, including the Cumbiatón movement along with others referenced in this book who have spent a lifetime in organizing circles. I see this continuum not only in the age and experience of the organizers themselves but also in the ways in which social movements grow and new members bring important changes to push societal boundaries, and in the way power systems change and adapt over time as well. As such, the Cumbiatón movement also represents the knowledge systems of undocumented organizers using the *undocu-knowledge*—pedagogy and praxis that come from the lived experience of being undocumented or formerly undocumented— built over a decade of organizing experience. Over time, undocumented youth used their undocu-knowledge to build movements that aimed to be much more inclusive while demonstrating that mass movement building can take on multiple approaches, including organizing parties.

The Cumbiatón movement represented a direct form of resistance to the forty-fifth U.S. presidential administration, which further marginalized undocumented communities by attacking many of the policies and political measures that had offered these communities a certain level of protection. Cumbiatón organizers designed their movement to be inclusive around issues of immigration status, crafting spaces that were womxn-led, womxn-centered, and womxn-friendly, trans-led, trans-centered, and trans-friendly, and intergenerational, and that had a BIPOC lens in mind.[8] Organizers of the Cumbiatón space recognized that partying is political. My analysis of

Cumbiatón adds to the theorization of illegalization by demonstrating that being "undocumented" is not only about documentation or "papers," as many often think, but also about how illegalization processes restrict mobility in everyday societal spaces such as nightclubs and practices such as the privilege of joy.

This chapter is organized in three sections. Section 1, "Undoing the DREAMer Narrative," provides a brief historical contextualization that transitions from the period of neoliberal power described in chapter 3 to a neoconservative state under the forty-fifth president. In the second section of the chapter I situate the fields of performance studies and critical archival studies, along with the transmedia-based archival productions used in the Cumbiatón movement. In the final section, "Cumbiatón: Partying as Political," I analyze the Cumbiatón case study and outline the politics of partying for undocumented communities.

UNDOING THE DREAMER NARRATIVE: DISRUPTING BELONGING UNDER NEOLIBERAL PARADIGMS

As referenced in chapters 1 and 2, in the early 2000s undocumented youth came to national political prominence under the "DREAMer narrative," a term derived from proposed legislation called the Dream Act that would have given qualifying undocumented youth a pathway to permanent residency. During Barack Obama's 2009–17 presidency, the mixed signals sent by the administration were read by undocumented youth and organizers as a neoliberal exercise in recognizing desirable undocumented youth whose potential for assimilation and incorporation was to be protected. Meanwhile, the larger immigrant population was not only denied access to protection but also further criminalized, persecuted, and deported. Sites of detention and deportation are the focus of chapters 2 and 3, which describe how organizers like Jonathan Perez, Isaac Barrera, and the National Immigrant Youth Alliance (NIYA) escalated their efforts at civil disobedience by organizing inside of detention centers to expose the violence performed by the state against immigrant bodies. If the Obama administration had represented *hope* for a large sector of people of color in the United States, for undocumented organizers it highlighted the business of immigration as a global capitalist enterprise that continued no matter who was at the helm.

The birth of Cumbiatón took place in a moment of neoliberal discourse, when the United States was detaining and deporting immigrant communities at heightened levels under Obama's presidency.[9] While undocumented communities exposed President Obama as "deporter in chief," there was also push-back from white America, which felt that President Obama was not capable of managing dissident populations.[10] I read Forty-Five's ascent to the presidency as a modification of neoliberal political power to include characteristics of centralized power driven by neoconservatism. In fact, David Harvey's work reminds us that "neoconservatism is . . . entirely consistent with the neolib-eral agenda of elite governance, mistrust of democracy, and the maintenance of market freedoms," showing shared values between both political models.[11]

In the first one hundred days of his presidency, Forty-Five began waging a war against immigrant communities at large. Most importantly, he began targeting movement leaders as well as structures and spaces created by social movements to protect undocumented communities under the previous administrations.[12] This was not a coincidence; it was strategic. Undocu-scholar Carolina Valdivia argues that "under the Trump administration we are seeing changes in immigration policy and enforcement that yield a qualitatively dif-ferent experience of what it means to be undocumented in the United States."[13] Through her qualitative research, Valdivia is able to highlight how feelings of uncertainty, vulnerability, stress, and anxiety increased significantly for mixed-status families in the United States.[14] Of course, the administration's tactics were not new, but rather obtained directly from the playbook of other neoconservative U.S. political leaders, like Presidents Ronald Reagan and George H. W. Bush in the 1980s. As such, I argue that Cumbiatón's choice to organize parties transferred direct forms of organizing such as civil disobe-dience to sites located in everyday practices such as producing joy. In other words, Cumbiatón directly challenged Forty-Five's attempt to limit organizing opportunities and took a creative approach to what organizing immigrant/undocumented communities can look like publicly. In a United States moving from neoliberal to neoconservative ideologies, Cumbiatón adopted an illegal-ized identity that trumped a DREAMer narrative logic of inclusion.

Undocumented and formerly undocumented scholars and organizers have spoken out against the exclusionary logic under which the DREAMer nar-rative operated, arguing that the term "DREAMer" is (a) an exclusive term that only accounts for a minority of undocumented populations, (b) an iden-tity associated and tied to legislation rather than culturally relevant identity formations, and (c) a neoliberal construction aimed at seeming to be an inclusive policy of the nation-state while making deservingness the condition for inclusion.[15] For example, in the publication *We Are Not Dreamers*, a book that brought together undocumented and formerly undocumented scholars, theorist Joel Sati highlights what is at stake for activists and undocumented youth in identifying with the positive image that the DREAMer narrative represents when he states, "Examining immigrant rights campaigns and their appeals to legitimacy, without substantive analysis of whether the legislation that results will actually help immigrants, will put an already-compromised community into further, unconscionable harm."[16] I join other undocumented and formerly undocumented scholars who write about these transformations within undocumented movements that speak against and choose not to identify with the term "DREAMer."

I add to the literature on illegality by examining examples in which "illegal" refers not only to documentation, as implied in the popular term "undocumented," but also to the way in which illegal status extends to everyday experiences of restricted mobility, access, and inclusion. As such, by analyzing the literature on illegalization alongside neoliberal interpretations, we can further understand the ways in which a small minority of immigrant youth were prioritized for protection, having their mobility restrictions lifted and being given opportunities to prosper, while the larger immigrant population was faced with stronger restrictions on mobility and vulnerability to deportation. After the defeat of Forty-Five in the polls in October 2020, many people celebrated the transition of the presidency to the Democratic Party with president-elect Joseph R. Biden. However, undocumented organizers saw the affair through a much more critical lens. Undocumented communities remember President Joe Biden in his role as vice president in Barack Obama's administration, which enabled a deportation regime. Undocumented organizers have declared on multiple occasions that they plan to hold the new administration accountable for not only what it does now but also what it continues to do moving forward.[17]

Undocumented organizers identify the neoliberal agenda under Obama's and Biden's administrations as being responsible for deporting friends, family, and community members. Cumbiatón partygoers come from a large mixed-status community in which those wounds have not yet healed. Cumbiatón demonstrated that partying can be a political act by creating an alternative space that combats hegemonic and neoliberal understandings of belonging in everyday spaces, such as nightclubs. As a cultural movement that aims to connect intergenerational audiences, Cumbiatón extended its partying-as-political approach to virtual party events as part of its efforts to educate and embrace community during the global COVID-19 pandemic and the transition to a new presidential administration.

The Cumbiatón movement challenges neoliberal strategies to control immigrants' mobility by crafting spaces where expressions of joy are possible for, and shared by, undocumented immigrant communities that are normally met with exclusion and violence. Exclusion is a form of violence that is real, physical, and embodied. Exclusion is also figurative, represented in neoliberal ideological representations such as the DREAMer identity and narrative, which excludes a majority of the undocumented immigrant community and mixed-status families. As such, the undocumented trans womxn of color and queers of color who led the Cumbiatón movement used their lived experiences in the UYMs to create an organizing realm that was a party space where joy could perform a healing process for immigrants and mixed-status community members whose bodies had been marked by trauma at the hands of the immigration control system.

PERFORMANCE, THE ARCHIVAL BODY, AND TRANSMEDIA-BASED ARCHIVES AS CREATIVE INTERFERENCES

Cumbiatón's website and media productions should be analyzed as an archive. Cumbiatón's website serves not only to document the movement's events but also to archive a repertoire of cultural performances. The website connects one easily to a media repository including a YouTube channel, photographs organized in albums using the Flickr platform, artwork-based flyers with a hyperlink to Cumbiatón's Instagram account, an online store housed on Etsy, and artist/activist profiles that connect to their individual websites and social media or media accounts. Before the website launch, Cumbiatón's Instagram account served as a platform to communicate about its initial parties and to document events. As the movement took shape, Cumbiatón began to actively craft and engage a team that was intentional about documenting the undocumented nightlife experience.

I am interested in exploring the diverse and multiple ways in which Cumbiatón's digital repository captures the experience and practice of joy. I term this approach to documentation a transmedia-based archive. Media scholar Henry Jenkins defines transmedia narrative as "the flow of content across multiple media platforms."[18] As such, I am defining a transmedia-based archive as digital content that is stored and creates a repository across multiple online platforms.[19] I argue that the digital content produced by Cumbiatón organizers is a form of artivism that produces alternate ways of belonging and existing for undocumented and BIPOC communities.[20] Their archival processes and artistic repertoire are embodied in praxis and pedagogy. I draw from undocu-scholar Carlos Aguilar, who refers to this process as *UndocuCrit*, or the ways in which immigration status, social class, gender, and age can activate a reflective process of critical consciousness in undocumented individuals.[21] In this case, Cumbiatón organizers actively use their lived experience to assemble transmedia archives that inscribe immigrant bodies in the public record of U.S. society.

The Cumbiatón movement is significant in that it is led by self-identified undocumented, women-of-color, queer, and trans artivists who see artwork as being intertwined with their political activism. As such, the Cumbiatón case study challenges traditional understandings of archival productions as being divorced from notions of performing identities and disrupts the idea of archives upholding normative constructions of fixed identities. I explore the question: How did Cumbiatón create a unique social and cultural movement that documented the welcoming space it provided for undocumented and BIPOC communities using diverse media platforms? As a participant observer, but most importantly as someone who grew up with undocumented status in Los Angeles, I ask: Is the hype on Cumbiatón's social media truly born out by an inclusive intergenerational and immigrant-friendly nightlife scene? I am interested in exploring the Cumbiatón movement as a performance that was experienced in the embodiment of a musical and aesthetic repertoire carefully curated, assembled, and documented by its artivist leaders. I turn to scholars of performance studies, critical archival studies, and transmedia narratives to begin to construct a transmedia archival framework for the Cumbiatón movement.

The archival turn in the humanities is represented by scholars in diverse fields producing work that critiques the traditional or normative form of archival production. Anthropologist Michel-Rolph Trouillot's work (1995) calls into question Western traditions of knowledge production stemming from historical and philosophical fields in which typically only sources with power or institutional representation were admitted as *evidentials*.[22] Additionally,

Trouillot argues that this imbalance of power stems from colonial times, when subaltern communities were deemed not to possess counterarguments because their appeals did not come from Western-recognized forms of evidence, such as texts in written form.[23] Drawing on Trouillot's work, I see the (un)documents that undocumented youth produce not as whole or complete documents, but rather as fragments of their realities aimed at exposing the power behind multiple sites that document immigrant communities to produce detrimental narratives. Furthermore, the incorporation of new interpretations of archival productions such as performance is important for understanding social movements in the twenty-first century.

Performance studies is useful in my analysis of the Cumbiatón movement because it (a) allows me to situate undocumented communities as knowledge producers; (b) provides a framework for alternate ways of knowing and educating; and (c) provides possibilities of a distinct process of storing or archiving that is not only textual, but also performative, embodied, and media-produced.[24] Archival studies scholars incorporate critical theory to go beyond accepting traditional written texts as the sources of authority in archival production. Jamie Lee's work (2020) is particularly useful in my analysis of Cumbiatón in connecting the way the physical body's parts make a collective "whole" to the way archives are composed of similar corporal parts that work to share a (hi)story. In relation to the Cumbiatón movement, Lee's work on the "archival body" focuses on physical and bodily harm that is a result of societal norms that restrict movement and access based on race, gender, and sexuality.[25] As such, Lee's work pushes toward a queering of the archival record to produce community archives, storytelling, and critical theory.[26]

In my analysis of Cumbiatón, I take a cue from critical archival studies scholars like Jamie Lee to show how the digital world provides alternative opportunities for creating knowledge production in forms such as digital archives. Arely Zimmerman's use of "transmedia testimonio" details the ways in which undocumented youth use media across multiple platforms to craft a counterpublic space. She states, "By taking part and constructing these testimonios, youth enact forms of political agency and contest their illegality."[27] While Zimmerman documents undocumented youth's participatory actions as testimonios, my work on and analysis of the Cumbiatón movement treats these media-based productions as transmedia-based archives that are strategically curated, stored, remixed, and used for educational purposes across immigrant/BIPOC communities.

This chapter is in conversation with Zimmerman's work on transmedia testimonials in analyzing the ways undocumented organizers use multiple platforms to share their uniquely crafted stories. In the next section, I will introduce the Cumbiatón movement as a case study to begin exploring the ways in which performance and the archival body combine to produce transmedia-based archives. In order to explore the creative interferences made by the Cumbiatón movement, we turn to partying as a political act.

CUMBIATÓN: PARTYING AS POLITICAL

The city of Los Angeles, home to the Cumbiatón movement, has a history of racial segregation, discrimination, and sociopolitical dividing lines among its neighborhood constructions.[28] Gaye Theresa Johnson's research on post–World War II Los Angeles investigates the way in which Black and Brown youth created "spatial entitlements," which she defines as "a way in which marginalized communities have created new collectivities based not just upon eviction and exclusion from physical places, but also on new and imaginative uses of technology, creativity, and spaces."[29] Johnson demonstrates how Black and Brown youth extended their spatial entitlements through musical productions in what she terms "sonic spatial entitlements." They did this in two significant ways: (a) creating physical spaces, such as parties, nightclubs, dance halls, educational events, etc.; and (b) holding space through technological media, such as creating radio stations, sharing mixtapes, and creating programming. Using sonic spatial entitlements as a framework, in what follows I demonstrate how undocumented artivists organize community through various modes of technology and create alternate spaces of belonging that produce transmedia archives.

Cumbiatón was born as an organization in 2016, with its first official party in Boyle Heights, a historic Chicanx/Mexican neighborhood in Los Angeles, occurring during the summer of 2017.[30] Boyle Heights is a significant location in that it embodies a site of resistance against another phenomenon of neoliberal modalities: gentrification.[31] Cumbiatón organizers link this process to their mission statement focusing on specific communities—"oppressed hood communities"—that have felt the abandonment and exclusion caused by racial capital models following neoliberal logic. Like the logics of neoliberalism that produce gentrification, Cumbiatón organizers recognize that capital and investment leaving their "oppressed hood communities" is a form of illegalizing space and people. The Cumbiatón movement was founded to reinvest in these communities by crafting spaces of belonging.

The two founders of Cumbiatón met while advocating for immigrant communities' human rights in inner-city Los Angeles. Co-founder Normz La Oaxaqueña is from South Central Los Angeles and serves as the current manager of event production. Second co-founder DJ Sizzle Fantastic grew up in Boyle Heights and is one of the resident DJs. Both are undocu-queer womxn of color who apply intersectional activist methods to organize and imagine the Cumbiatón parties and events.[32] For example, both founders recognized that they needed to be inclusive in their musical selection and knew that the public-facing messaging needed to be intersectional across intergenerational and ethnic communities.[33] I follow the trail of several transmedia-based archives to build my insights into Cumbiatón team members, drawing from several interviews, features, and panel presentations. One of these main sources is the Persist conference organized by the UC Riverside Women's Resource Center, where the group served as featured panelists in 2020.[34]

As the production manager, Normz La Oaxaqueña's duties include booking venues, acts, vendors, and logistics for Cumbiatón events. Normz La Oaxaqueña's organizing background comes from experience in labor organizing with car-wash workers in Los Angeles. In working with mixed-status families, Normz La Oaxaqueña realized the ways in which undocumented communities are illegalized by their labor and are relegated to the shadows. At the Persist conference, Normz La Oaxaqueña declared that Cumbiatón's goal was to "create a space with people coming from similar backgrounds" that was inclusive of people of all generations and intersectional identities. Normz La Oaxaqueña indicates that Cumbiatón started with a minimal production aesthetic to convey a community-oriented, friendly atmosphere. Even as Cumbiatón grew, it continued to prioritize the minimal aesthetic.

I remember that when I walked into my first Cumbiatón event in L.A., my immediate visual impression was that the design elements were minimal in contrast to the bold and deliberate messaging intended to create a welcoming environment. But as I took in and absorbed the party, the messaging and artwork felt like a constant reminder of the inclusive space being carefully crafted, assembled, and curated for the diverse communities in attendance.

There were inflatable balloons with messages that read "Viva La Jotería" (Long Live Queerness), artwork along the entrance with critical messages from the immigrant rights movement, and Cumbiatón banners hanging at key locations. The messaging and aesthetic production of the Cumbiatón sets, while not overwhelming, do serve as sensory reminders of the inclusivity that the movement is assembling. The bright lights, which are strategically coordinated and in sync with the culturally relevant and intergenerational music, are another performance element: they make the diverse participants, from communities who normally do not see themselves reflected in mainstream spaces such as nightclubs, visible to each other.

DJ Sizzle Fantastic co-founded Cumbiatón with the intention of creating a nightlife scene that prioritized a musical selection maintaining an intergenerational outlook and deriving from the perspectives of the people attending the events. As such, the name Cumbiatón comes from the merging of the two musical genres, cumbia and reggaetón. Cumbia music derives from colonial times in Colombia's coastal rural communities of slaves of African descent, who combined the music they brought through their diasporic connections with the music of Indigenous communities.[35] As cumbia grew in popularity in Colombia in the 1940s and 1950s, it began to travel across Latin American countries and was adopted heavily into Mexico's working-class communities. Eventually cumbia made its way to the United States, including Los Angeles. Cumbia parties are hosted by DJs who are responsible for keeping the dance floor going, in what became a popular cultural phenomenon known as sonideros.[36] This phenomenon spread throughout Mexico's coastal cities with heavily Afro-Mexican communities, and into rural Indigenous communities and mixed-ethnic communities in Mexico City, to be fused with norteño influences in northern Mexican cities. With its long-standing history spanning over sixty years, cumbia has remained a favorite among older generations of immigrant communities in the United States, yet it is also popular with a younger audience as it continues to be fused and incorporated into contemporary popular music, including reggaetón.

Instagram is one of the places where we can see how Cumbiatón's leaders are assembling an online transmedia archive to educate, empower, and craft inclusive spaces within immigrant and BIPOC communities. DJ Sizzle Fantastic manages a segment on Cumbiatón's Instagram account called "101," where she provides a brief critical history of the distinct musical selection that makes up Cumbiatón events. One of the "Cumbia 101" archival posts reads:

It was the enslaved people of Africa who were brought by the Spanish conquest to Latin America that preserved the rhythm of the drum, which is the backbone of our beloved Cumbia. Sin Africa no hay Cumbia, without Black resistance there is no drum, without the drum there is no cumbia.[37]

This post provides a brief historical interjection that recognizes the role and importance of Black culture in what is often generalized as Latinx music and cultural production. Cumbiatón began adding the slogan "La Cumbia es Cultura" (Cumbia Music is Culture) to their social media posts as well as messaging in their events to make connections to music derived from the historically marginalized BIPOC communities attending the events.[38]

Reggaetón is another musical genre that derives from Black cultural production in Latin America's Caribbean populations. In their book *Reggaeton*, Raquel Rivera, Wayne Marshall, and Deborah Pacini Hernandez highlight reggaetón's roots in working-class communities and as Black resistance musical production.[39] Speaking of reggaetón's musical genealogy, they state, "For all of its continuities with roots reggae, then, dancehall tends to be associated with a militant blackness and a particular class position and critique, characteristics which have boosted its appeal in 'foreign' contexts, such as the United States, Panama, and Puerto Rico."[40] Reggaetón is much younger than cumbia, with its initial roots stemming from the late 1980s and its prominence in the United States peaking in terms of record sales between 2005 and 2006.

The years 2005 and 2006 are significant in reggaetón's connections to undocumented communities, as 2006 witnessed some of the largest ever immigrant rights demonstrations in major cities across the United States (mentioned in chapter 1).[41] As such, I argue that reggaetón rose to prominence alongside the undocumented youth and immigrant rights movements in the United States. One of my first moments of consciousness as an undocumented youth in college was being part of the national peaceful marches of 2006. I remember first hearing of the organizing of the marches through the Myspace social media platform and on Spanish radio stations on car rides with my parents to school and work. That was a historical moment in the immigrant rights movements that crossed intergenerational lines and was communicated across multiple media platforms. As such, the music that accompanied the movement across intergenerational ranks reflected the cumbias that filled Spanish-language radio stations and the reggaetón classics that filled my Myspace profile page. Reggaetón, with its contemporary growth as a worldwide phenomenon, appeals not only to younger generations of Cumbiatón-goers, but also to those who have been in immigrant rights struggles for multiple generations, such as the leadership of Cumbiatón.

The combination of the sonic fusions of cumbia, reggaetón, hip-hop, rock en español, and other genres typifies DJ Sizzle Fantastic's approach to creating a soundscape that connects multiple generations and produces new social imaginaries. Walking into a Cumbiatón party, it is not uncommon to see young people dancing to reggaetón or hip-hop hymns, and during the next set to see someone who looks like your tía/tío (aunt/uncle) dancing to a traditional cumbia melody, or even your parents' and grandparents' generation breaking out on the dance floor and trying out their moves to grupero/banda sounds blasting from the DJs' ones and twos. At the events I joined, the dance floor never seemed to be empty throughout the night, and the party never ended, because Cumbiatón extended the joy of a party atmosphere onto their online platforms.

Gaye Theresa Johnson emphasizes the fact that sonic spatial entitlements do not always have to be physical locations, but most have a component of physical space fused with a hybrid use of media consisting of elements that can be taken from physical sites and become mobile for individual consumption and engagement, such as albums or cassettes. As such, Cumbiatón also aimed to connect with audiences through their online platforms, which engaged with the community and produced a distinct archival record: a transmedia archive. To achieve this, they turned to other artivist leaders within the undocumented movements and nightlife scene to continue the party both physically and online.

Cumbiatón operated out of Boyle Heights for a year but quickly grew and needed to expand to other cities, bigger venues, and a bigger team. In 2018, DJ Funky Caramelo became a "resident DJ," Paolo Riveros became the "resident visual storyteller," and Julio Salgado became the "artist sin residency."[42] When Salgado and Riveros joined the Cumbiatón team, they brought their experience in art and activism, fusing documentation with art to organize the Cumbiatón space virtually and on-site. The new Cumbiatón team members helped take their archives of the nightlife scene to another level across multiple platforms. Sasha Costanza-Chock describes the merging of activism and social media practice as "transmedia mobilization," which they say "marks a transition in the role of movement communication from content creation to aggregation, curation, remix and recirculation of rich media texts through networked movement formations," allowing undocumented movements to use social media to document and archive their experiences.[43]

DJ Funky Caramelo's role as resident DJ brought new dimensions, using popular education and organizing perspectives that incorporated music as a liberating tool and built a transmedia archive. She started a series on Instagram titled "Resistance Anthems," consisting of DJ sets incorporating popular songs in both English and Spanish that have turned into community anthems. Funky Caramelo used projected images placed strategically behind her while DJing her set, with messages that read, "¡Perreo sin acoso!" (Perreo dancing without harassment!) or "¡Ella perrea sola!" (She dances perreo alone!). I read DJ Funky Caramelo's DJing performance as a strategy that incorporates alternate forms of knowledge production with the aim of being decolonial and tackling patriarchal constructs typically associated with nightlife spaces. Furthermore, her performance must be understood in the context of a repertoire that draws on embodied cultural practices such as dancing, and on lyrics organized to craft new meanings. She draws and captivates the audiences with familiar tunes while simultaneously reminding partygoers to be respectful and to decolonize the dance floor by undoing patriarchal behavior that might be associated with party anthems.

DJ Funky Caramelo's strategic use of technology to project decolonized messages and careful curation of a musical selection represents a perfectly assembled repertoire merging with her dancing body, smile, and voice-over in a performance that produces an affective connection between the performer and the viewer. She simultaneously crafts an inclusive and inviting online atmosphere and promotes a welcoming physical space at the Cumbiatón parties. DJ Funky Caramelo's DJing is a form of performance and archiving and an example of applying intersectional practices through musical production. The "Resistance Anthems" series is a transmedia archive because it uses several media and technology platforms, such as the technological art form of DJing, video recording, music as an educational tool, and the Instagram platform where the archive is stored.

Resident visual storyteller Paolo Riveros documents undocumented communities through the media of photography and filmmaking. A self-identified transgender man from Lima, Peru, Riveros mentions that he spent his early career "documenting gay clubs and trans-friendly night clubs."[44] In the Persist conference panel discussion, he expressed that one of the reasons he was convinced to join the Cumbiatón team was the intersectional leadership of Normz

La Oaxaqueña and DJ Sizzle Fantastic, who prioritized a safe space for queer-identified womxn led by womxn. In the same panel discussion, Riveros provided a gendered and sexual analysis of the ways in which the nightlife scene normalizes patriarchal and heteronormative constructs, from implementation of certain dress codes to fetishization of sexuality. As such, his visual transmedia storytelling aims to capture different portrayals of beauty going against normative constructs of aesthetic representation.

In my analysis of Riveros's work, I read his photography as performing an archival mission to address what Chicanx scholar Francisco J. Galarte (2021) describes as a "continued silencing and erasure of brown trans-narratives within queer, trans, and Chicana/o and Latina/o cultural politics."[45] Galarte's work explores how, even with rising awareness and inclusivity of trans- and queer-identified individuals in mainstream U.S. culture, there still exists a racialized distinction within LGBTQ groups, and there still exist homonationalistic practices of exclusion of LGBTQ individuals with other intersecting identities, such as undocumented communities. Riveros's photography captures the visual stories of Brown and Black trans communities who are normally excluded from mainstream LGBTQ nightlife scenes. Additionally, Riveros's artivism helps provide what Galarte calls "brown trans figurations," in that his visual artwork captures Brown and Black trans individuals in a frame of resistance while assembling their "trans" markers as new figurations. Additionally, Riveros's photographs are one of the mediums in which an online audience can see Cumbiatón's documentation of an intergenerational movement, capturing middle-aged people and elders partying along with youth in the same space and in the same frame.

Glancing through the Cumbiatón albums on the Flickr site provides a window into the diversity captured and archived by Riveros's camera lens. The collage of photographs showcases racial, ethnic, gendered, and sexualized diversity, not in order to check a diversity box but rather to display beauty across multiple body-positive images, cultural genre representations such as goth, punk rock, and hip-hop, cross-dressing, chic fashion, dyed hair, no hair, business-casual style, political T-shirts, cultural or ethnic attire, and bondage, just to name a few recorded images that pop up. Most of the pictures highlight individuals or groups of people smiling, expressing themselves on the dance floor, vibing to the music, and posing for the camera in the unique ways in which they wish to be represented. All capture an image of joy. This is an archival repository centering joy. The photographs, visually analyzed as a collection, represent the opportunity to experience joy without any restriction on mobility in social spaces, which are inherently and traditionally made political by neoliberal logics.

In her work *Producing the Archival Body* (2020), Jamie Lee also talks about the embodied memory of physical bodily injuries as well as societal injuries caused by exclusionary practices. She states, "I recognize my embodied ways of knowing and think about 'cell memory' and how my body tightens, my knees bend, and my back slouches forward when I see something coming toward me," describing our bodily reactions to experienced trauma.[46] Cumbiatón organizers recognized the embodied trauma that undocumented and BIPOC communities experience because of deportation and incarceration practices in neoliberal systems. In that way, the Cumbiatón experience goes beyond the nightlife experience. One thing shared by all the Cumbiatón leadership team is that they all have had to experience detentions and deportations, either their own or those of their families and loved ones.[47] DJ Funky Caramelo talks about her experience of being apprehended by Border Patrol while attending a shoe convention at a location that was deemed a "port of entry."[48] She spent three weeks in a detention center before being released. Upon her release, she was diagnosed with PTSD due to the trauma and stress she experienced while detained.[49] In this way, partying is political: the Cumbiatón scene holds a welcoming space for individuals to process and heal from the trauma of deportation. In the Persist conference panel discussion, DJ Funky Caramelo speaks about taking up DJing full-time as a form of healing through musical creation.

Dancing is the performance of an act of joy. The Cumbiatón parties are assembled from multiple joined pieces that include music, performances, design, artwork, vending, and fashion, which results in the experience or embodiment of joy for undocumented and BIPOC communities who are not always afforded that privilege. While neoliberal logic serves to restrict movement of communities like immigrants, the Cumbiatón movement creates a physical space where everyday joy can be experienced in actions like dancing. Mass movement building, in the Cumbiatón sense, is the creation of an embodied experience that allows for everyday movement across spaces like a nightclub.

Cumbiatón's leaders implement an intersectional approach in defining inclusivity and linking oppressed communities' struggles as related. As such, Cumbiatón's transmedia archival assemblage follows an intersectional methodology that expands the definition of illegalized identity to intersect with the similar but distinct ways in which BIPOC, queer, and transgender communities are illegalized. Woman-of-color and queer-of-color scholarship has pushed for ways to assemble archival productions that go against the grain of traditional academic understandings, using intersectional approaches. Intersectional scholars Sumi Cho, Kimberlé Crenshaw, and Leslie McCall highlight the importance of including an intersectional methodology in their disciplines, stating that "networks provide . . . opportunities to develop content that is substantively identifiable as part of the field and to become familiar with the critical tools and archives that are essential in sustaining a discursive community."[50] These scholars contend that the growth of new forms of knowledge production and new understandings is limited without the practice of intersectional work.

The organizers of Cumbiatón are aware that the deportation regime impacts other communities, not just the immigrant community. Many partygoers who attend Cumbiatón are not undocumented or from an immigrant background but do come from mixed-status families or mixed-status communities that have experienced the trauma of deportation. The University of Southern California's Center for the Study of Immigrant Integration (CSII) estimates that there are "16.7 million people in the U.S. that have at least one unauthorized family member living with them in the same household," and that the three states with the most mixed-status family members are California, Texas, and Nevada.[51] Beyond undocumented communities, the BIPOC members that attend Cumbiatón have also experienced the trauma of coming from the communities that have the highest rates of incarceration. This highlights the importance of Cumbiatón's mission statement of doing intersectional work by holding space for "oppressed hood communities." In creating spaces that are inclusive through intersectional practices and documenting events at these spaces, Cumbiatón uses transmedia approaches to archive the ways in which its participants offer affective resistance to the deportation regime and the prison/detention-industrial complexes that are the result of neoliberal power.

The vendors and apparel at the Cumbiatón events form part of the aesthetic and messaging of the movement. In my exploration of Cumbiatón's transmedia archive, I found many examples where the fusion of T-shirt printing with artwork produces messaging rooted in popular education practices for community use, captured through Paolo Riveros's photography and stored in the Flickr site. In particular, this messaging centers around the abolishment of neoliberal models manifested in the prison/detention-industrial complex. At the one-year-anniversary event, I found a T-shirt sold by a Cumbiatón vendor that calls to abolish "ICE, DHS, Prisons, The Police, Binaries, Landlords, Poverty, The Nation & State," and ends with the message "DefendTheCriminals."[52] I read this T-shirt's message as performing three functions: (a) a call to expose the agencies and institutions that are responsible for furthering a neoliberal world-making process that criminalizes marginalized communities and restricts the mobility of BIPOC peoples; (b) an implicit affirmation that under a neoliberal regime there is no space for reform; and (c) a call to defend the criminals, or illegalized peoples, demonstrating that those labeled "illegal" or "criminals" are products of institutions that seek to make everyday existence for marginalized peoples impossible.

Through transmedia archiving practices, the Cumbiatón team can craft an inclusive space that is not only a physical location but also a digital space that speaks to diverse intersectional audiences. By focusing on intersectional approaches, Cumbiatón challenges neoliberal constructs that selectively prioritize individuals with certain qualifications for incorporation and protection while keeping wider undesirable populations in the shadows.

CONCLUSION

In 2019, Cumbiatón celebrated its two-year anniversary by throwing perhaps one of its biggest parties, at the Globe Theater in Los Angeles.[53] The group's Flickr page captures the magnitude of the two-year-anniversary celebration, showcasing the joy not only of its organizers but also of the participating community upon reaching a milestone for the movement. This anniversary represented an opportunity to celebrate a cultural movement that was born and thrived during one of the most anti-immigrant and racially fervent moments in contemporary U.S. history. Hosting a party at the Globe Theater in Los Angeles represented growth, but most importantly, it represented the level of visibility that Cumbiatón organizers were able to create alongside community members who embraced the space. Over its two years, the movement had grown to represent otherwise marginalized communities that are often relegated to the shadows of society, beginning in Boyle Heights and becoming a national movement with sister-city representation in San Francisco, Seattle, and New York, with queer, transgender, undocumented, and BIPOC leadership.

In this chapter, I have demonstrated how Cumbiatón's approach to the politics of partying has steadily grown the intergenerational cultural movement into a national movement using inclusive intersectional practices that are centered around BIPOC communities. The movement uses photography, video production, artwork, social media, and music as unique activist practices. It was born out of protest against a neoliberal administration and resisted a neoconservative administration that sought to make living impossible for BIPOC communities. Finally, Cumbiatón represents a movement that demonstrates alternate ways of organizing, using everyday forms of resistance as a political tool. Organizers and scholars need to understand that activism can take traditional forms, such as a public rally or demonstration, or it can draw from popular education approaches and organize to bring people together in everyday spaces, such as a nightclub.

CONCLUSION

(Un)documenting the Legacies of the Undocumented Youth Movements

AS A CRITICAL SOCIAL MOVEMENT scholar, I am invested in understanding the processes by which social movements produce new discourse and new forms of knowing that impact our society at large. I argue that the legacy of activism by undocumented youth movements (UYMs) is that they produced alternative ways of organizing and created new ways to resist the nation-state. This includes what I theorize as the process of *(un)documenting*, or the ways in which undocumented youth produced new ways of documenting immigrant bodies and experiences that were often pushed to the shadows. In documenting the undocumented experience, UYMs recenter the margins of the nation-state, making them the center of public information. As scholars, organizers, and community members, using an (un)documenting approach allows us to offer important critiques of the nation-state's tools for managing immigrant bodies that render undocumented populations illegal. In other words, by documenting the immigrant experience in the United States we can hold up a mirror to reflect the ways in which the nation-state produces an "other" that is disposable and not fit for inclusion.

UNDOCUMENTED AND UNAFRAID BEFORE AND AFTER DACA IN TRUMPAMERICA

The case studies featured in this book took place in a neoliberal moment during which the United States detained and deported immigrant communities at heightened levels, while U.S. presidents like George Bush Jr. and Barack Obama appealed to communities of color and Latinx populations with the promise of immigration reform. Undocumented youth saw this as an opportunity to highlight the contradictions produced in a neoliberal structure. In her work on neoliberalism, *Represent and Destroy* (2011), Jodi Melamed argues that nation-state formations are built on liberal discourses based on inclusion/exclusion models.[1] According to Melamed, neoliberal multiculturalism differentiates people by protecting those who are valuable to capitalism and devaluing those who are not.[2] As such, undocumented youth realized that the Deferred Action for Childhood Arrivals (DACA) program instituted in 2012 was a form of representation and protection, but also that it aimed to destroy the rest of the immigrant communities who were not afforded the same privilege, to use Melamed's terminology.

I argue that the first three case studies in my investigation—Elvira Arellano's direct and transnational forms of activism in post-sanctuary organizing, detention center infiltrations by Jonathan Perez and Isaac Barrera, and the #BringThemHome campaigns by the National Immigrant Youth Alliance (NIYA)—occurred in a moment when undocumented youth achieved privileging and protection at the national level based on neoliberal politics of incorporation. And while undocumented youth exposed President Obama as a "deporter in chief," the pushback was also felt from white America, which felt that President Obama was not capable of managing dissident populations.[3] Eduardo Bonilla-Silva's work *Racism Without Racists* (2003) captures the essence of the neoliberal model, and he labels masked racists as "compassionate conservatives."[4] We can see theoretical shifts in Eduardo Bonilla-Silva's work with the political ascendance of our forty-fifth U.S. president; by 2019 he calls for new political directions in his article "Toward a New Political Praxis for Trumpamerica." In this article, Bonilla-Silva argues that "racialization is (a) a continuous, never finished process; (b) affected by racial contestation between the racially subaltern and the dominant race as well as through the agency of individuals."[5] He highlights the way in which racial structures do change and are impacted by many social factors including activists, but he also highlights that political systems do not have an end point and that they also adjust. My analysis of UYMs is in conversation with Bonilla-Silva's analysis of racial systems in charting a shift in political systems toward a new political era in what he terms "Trumpamerica."

Several scholars including Bonilla-Silva argue that our forty-fifth U.S. president ushers in a new political system or a new era that trumps the old one. Taking a cue from Bonilla-Silva, I read Forty-Five's presidency as a return to centralized power driven by neoconservatism. I interpret Forty-Five's rhetoric and his slogan "Build the wall" as appealing to a conservative white-supremacist base that Bonilla-Silva describes as having a desire to restore American institutional control and benefit a small white minority. In his second point related to the theorization of understanding the racial process in the United States, Bonilla-Silva reminds his readers that "systematic 'White supremacy' leads actors to develop material interests that line up with their social location—Whites defend the racial order in various ways," underscoring the investment in preserving racial hierarchies that was behind the election of Forty-Five.[6]

Bonilla-Silva also argues that emotions produce materiality that can lead to political action. And in fact, Bonilla-Silva identifies the use of emotions to make a call to action as one of the principal strategies used by Forty-Five, which resulted in political materiality. Bonilla-Silva makes his own call to action, one that I take up, when he states, "We have many other needs in terms of racial theory that are necessary to develop a political praxis to advance our struggle in this special moment"—that is, we need to develop new theoretical frameworks that contextualize the contemporary political moment.[7] Bonilla-Silva goes on to make three recommendations for developing racial theory that can inform the current political systems: (a) experiential knowledge, (b) racialization of space, and (c) processes in which organizations are racialized.[8] I believe that the case studies I present here reflect crucial lessons and knowledge production with the ability to contest political repression at the levels Bonilla-Silva puts forth as recommendations.

In terms of experiential knowledge, my theorization and positionality as an undocu-scholar amounts to new ways of seeing and analyzing the contributions made by undocumented youth. In particular, when it comes to racialization, I interpret this both as the process by which undocumented youth use race as an organizing principle to ensure inclusion in immigrant rights organizing and also as the way in which, in earlier stages of the immigrant rights movements before the rise of undocumented youth movements, race was the basis for exclusionary practices in organizing spaces. My case studies allow me to analyze the ways in which undocumented youth pushed the limits of organizing by racializing organizing spaces and creating spaces of inclusivity for marginalized undocumented communities. Finally, I read the incorporation of undocumented youth into the "DREAMer narrative" as a way in which organizations were racialized and made acceptable for inclusion in the national body. But most importantly, I also analyze the way in which the radical politics and organizing strategies of undocumented youth activists were deemed a threat and why the forty-fifth presidential administration would target activist leaders.

The shift in political power in 2017 had tremendous impacts on immigrant families and on undocumented youth activists who had been pushing the boundaries of immigration reform. On September 5, 2017, five years after the DACA program had come to life, Forty-Five would announce that he was terminating the program.[9] On many occasions before Forty-Five made this decision about DACA, he had negotiated with immigrant rights leaders by saying that he would leave DACA alone if there was support in turn for his border wall project.[10]

My analysis of Forty-Five's decision to terminate the DACA program is not limited to political action and arguments about the legality of the program. I also read his decision as an attack on radical politics and civil disobedience as developed by undocumented youth activists. In other words, the logic of terminating DACA was based on limiting not only the legal, social, and economic well-being of undocumented youth but also the privilege and protection that allowed undocumented youth to organize and continue to push the boundaries of the nation-state in the ways represented in my case studies. The threat against DACA heightened the risk of losing status for undocumented youth who had attained social, economic, political, and cultural capital. Not only did the threat to end DACA cause a fear of loss of status, but it also put in jeopardy previous modes of organizing using direct forms of activism. I am not saying that Forty-Five's actions against DACA represent the end of direct forms of activism. However, I am arguing that Forty-Five's administration directly attempted to shift and limit undocumented youth's possibilities for conducting civil disobedience. This is what power does: it determines the boundaries of civil and uncivil behavior and pushes back.

As I finish writing this book in 2023, the latest ruling on DACA by the Fifth Circuit Court of Appeals of the United States has declared that the program is unlawful and cannot continue in its current form.[11] Forty-Five lost his reelection campaign in 2020 when Joseph R. Biden was elected to office in a return to a Democratic president. Since taking office, President Biden has aimed to protect the DACA program, without much success given the Fifth Circuit ruling. While President Biden's administration has been received as generally much more favorable toward immigrant populations, undocumented organizers saw his presidency as a return to neoliberal power: restoring order meant the inclusion of certain populations while others were pushed to the shadows, much the same as during the Obama administration, in which Biden served as vice-president. As such, many of the undocumented organizers included in my case studies continue to strategize in new organizations and modalities, and along with the younger generations, to explore what a return to undocumented status without the protections of DACA will represent for undocumented communities.

The end of DACA marks more than two decades of organizing for undocumented youth that encapsulates the lessons described in this book: that the inclusion of a few does not represent true liberation for undocumented communities. Undocumented organizers like Elvira Arellano, Jonathan Perez, Isaac Barrera, the National Immigrant Youth Alliance (NIYA), and Cumbiatón movement leaders continue to construct social imaginaries aimed at undoing physical borders as well as social constructions that continue to oppress immigrant communities worldwide.

(UN)DOCUMENTING: ARCHIVES AND LESSONS FROM UNDOCUMENTED YOUTH ORGANIZING

The first case study here was Elvira Arellano's move to exploring direct forms of activism in sanctuary, which resulted in what we now call the new sanctuary movements (NSMs). Elvira Arellano's case study is significant to undocumented youth movements because she represents the story of undocumented immigrants who did not fit the narrative of the "good immigrant" that took hold in the civility politics discourse and was reinforced by the "DREAMer narrative"—those who were not young people considered worthy of protection and inclusion on the basis of educational merit. Instead, as a single mother and activist, she came to represent the multiple young and older generations of immigrants who were targeted for detention and deportation with the creation of the Department of Homeland Security (DHS) after September 11, 2001. Additionally, Elvira represents a shift toward direct forms of activism in the form of civil disobedience and the strategic use of the body to bring awareness to pressing issues for the undocumented communities; undocumented youth organizers would use these same tactics strategically in the second half of the decade. In chapter 1, I also highlight Elvira's use of media outlets to construct a transmedia narrative and expose her daily experiences in sanctuary so that the general public could see what sanctuary was really like. When she chose to leave sanctuary and participate in direct activism in 2007, she knew she was risking deportation, but she also knew she had to challenge the nation-state in a way that sacrificed her own body and well-being, using her public visibility to bring attention to others who did not have that privilege. The legacy of Elvira's actions is that we now see immigrants who take sanctuary inside of a religious setting using transmedia narratives to bring awareness, support, and empathy to their cases, as well as to put pressure on the U.S. government with mass community support. In other words, with Elvira we see people who were often relegated to the shadows emerging as leaders within the broader immigrant rights movements (IRMs).

Elvira Arellano returned to the United States on March 18, 2014, with the final #BringThemHome campaign organized by the National Immigrant Youth Alliance. She did so after organizing transnationally between the Central America–Mexico borderlands and the Mexico-U.S. borderlands. For seven years she helped Central American refugees making their way north. Two years after her return, the election of Forty-Five to the presidency in 2016 would also have significant effects on the new sanctuary movements in the United States.

Forty-Five campaigned promising a "zero-tolerance" approach to immigration policy that would target immigrant criminals in the United States.[12] Once he took office, immigrant communities learned that his "zero-tolerance" approach really meant making life inhospitable for all undocumented populations living in the United States. Perhaps Forty-Five's "zero-tolerance" immigration rhetoric was most heavily felt at first with the targeting of sanctuary cities and new sanctuary movement leaders. Forty-Five targeted sanctuary cities by cutting federal funding and aid to them. To further extend Forty-Five's definition of "zero-tolerance," his administration dropped the distinction between "high" and "low priority" deportation cases that previous administrations had made, which transferred into leaders of the new sanctuary movements being targeted for deportation. In the Trumpamerica era, "zero-tolerance" meant that everyone eligible for deportation must be placed in deportation proceedings.

The new sanctuary movements continue to adjust, resist, and agitate the new powers that be in the U.S. nation-state. One of the new tenets of the new sanctuary movements is the inclusivity and intersectionality that their younger participants are bringing to the spaces of sanctuary. Traditionally, the Sanctuary Movement tended to have leaders and volunteers who were predominantly Anglo and older in age, and who upheld traditional gender roles. New organizations and organizing efforts include the Black-Brown Alliance in Chicago, composed primarily of three organizations: Organized Communities Against Deportations (OCAD), Mijente, and Black Youth Project 100 (BYP100).[13] This coalition is primarily led by youth of color working with religious congregations to offer sanctuary. This is a distinctly different direction in leadership and approach than that of the Sanctuary Movement of the 1980s.

My second chapter explores the case study of the infiltration of a detention center in Louisiana by Jonathan Perez and Isaac Barrera in 2011. Infiltration actions were unique to the organizing by Jonathan Perez, Isaac Barrera, and NIYA in 2011–13. To date, there have not been other infiltration actions that have taken place in the manner they did during this period of time. However, I argue that the legacy of these infiltrations is that today it is common public knowledge that human rights violations have been happening for a long time inside of detention centers, thanks to the actions by undocumented youth activists like Jonathan Perez and Isaac Barrera. And while there were no additional infiltration actions, the movement's findings, or the (un)documenting by the activists, produced an outcry from the general public and inspired other undocumented youth to focus their activism on a call for the abolishment of systems of control and management.

Undocumented activists like Jonathan Perez and Isaac Barrera continued to organize to shut down detention centers and to work alongside allied lawyers to get undocumented community members out of detention.[14] And in 2018 allies and undocumented immigrant groups rallied behind what would be known as the #AbolishICE movement.[15] This call for action came in response to Forty-Five's family separation policy, which separated children from their parents in detention centers.[16] In chapter 2, I demonstrate that the digital archival materials documented in Jonathan and Isaac's infiltration of detention centers began to expose the U.S. government's illegal actions connected to the mass detainment and deportation of immigrants. I highlight that the digital materials produced in the infiltration action additionally produced the evidence undocumented activists and the general public needed to call for an end to ICE and immigration systems altogether. With the call to #AbolishICE along with a general public outcry against policing in the United States, undocumented youth organizers have linked their struggle more broadly to other oppressed communities across the country and moved toward a political position of abolition. Undocumented youth realize that integration into the United States via citizenship does not guarantee freedom from oppression.

The third chapter's case study was the #BringThemHome campaign organized by the National Immigrant Youth Alliance to challenge family separation, detention, and deportation. The legacy of the first #BringThemHome campaign, and subsequent ones, has been felt at multiple societal levels. Perhaps the biggest lesson to take away from these campaigns, from the perspective of social movements, was the move toward translocal forms of organizing rather than pushing for a bigger national organization, as originally imagined with the formation of NIYA. The (un)documenting of NIYA's case study reveals that the grassroots and direct activism NIYA envisioned was challenging to perform while sustaining a national organizational structure. In other words, their actions and strategies could be better performed in a targeted way by local or state-level organizations that had a certain level of support and a history of working together.

I would argue that the most important legacy of the #BringThemHome campaigns was to provide a model of collective migration, or a coordinated group effort by migrants coming to the Mexico-U.S. border asking for asylum. In recent years, we have seen migrant caravans making their way along transnational migration routes from Central America to the United States in large numbers, including migrants self-identified as Indigenous people, transgender people, children, and young people who seek refuge. The collective action witnessed in the three campaigns that NIYA led, starting with the "Dream 9," growing into the "Dream 30," and finally expanding to the "Dream 150," demonstrated the influence of collective power in the process of requesting asylum through a legal port of entry.[17] In 2018, migrant caravans composed in their majority of Central American refugees made their way north, containing up to several hundred migrants who coordinated their requests for entry to the United States. This coordinated effort by the migrant caravans, and the heightened media attention they received, would be met with violence by Forty-Five's administration when he sent military troops to the border on October 29, 2018, which would result in migrants being pepper-sprayed and denied both entry and the due process required by immigrant law. It was the hope and vision of Trumpamerica to deny entry to migrants and make it difficult for immigrants to live in the United States, but, like each previous administration, Forty-Five's administration would be met by activist groups who resist state pressures. Most importantly, this aspiration of making the United States inhospitable for immigrants is based on false assumptions that these conditions will be worse than those in the migrants' home countries.

Finally, chapter 4 represents new directions and reflections for UYMs in moving toward internal forms of decolonization that result in opportunities for undocu-joy. The Cumbiatón movement that forms the case study in chapter 4 represents two decades of organizing by undocumented youth organizers transitioning into new points of their lives after participating in the movement for many years. Additionally, Cumbiatón represents queer and trans leadership within UYMs, which was there from the beginning of the movements, aimed at creating space for intersectional and intergenerational identities. Cumbiatón leadership aimed to be inclusive not only of undocumented community members but also of other marginalized community members who are impacted by incarceration, displacement, and poverty. I argue that Cumbiatón highlights the politics of partying for undocumented people and people of color growing up in large urban cities where mass movement building can take on new forms like fostering joy through partying.

NOT AN END BUT A CONTINUATION OF BUILDING COLLECTIVE POWER

Undocumented youth activists produced new ways of organizing and resisting punitive immigration systems and policies that aim to control and manage immigrant populations. With the case studies in my research here, I have analyzed the ways in which undocumented youth activists use their bodies to pronounce their resistance and bring attention to the illegalization of immigrant bodies. Through their actions, undocumented youth activists have produced new knowledge formations related to family separations, detention, and deportations that changed the discourse in immigration debates in the United States. I theorize these new ways of understanding immigration systems using an (un)documenting methodology. In my case studies (un)documenting undocumented youth movements, I analyze how activists like Elvira Arellano produce alternate ways of organizing and existing as immigrant women of color. In infiltrating a detention center, Jonathan Perez and Isaac Barrera brought attention to the process by which detention centers violate human rights and render immigrant bodies illegal. And with NIYA's actions in the #BringThemHome campaigns we can see the way collective power organized transnationally can challenge the very physical borders and walls that are often regarded as impenetrable. Finally, with the Cumbiatón movement in chapter 4, we see immigrant rights moving toward collective and individual forms to protect and foster joy for oppressed communities.

Illegalized: Undocumented Youth Movements in the United States illuminates directions and lessons for new generations of undocumented youth activists and projects that aim to fight for social justice in the United States and around the world. The world is a complex place, and the "deportation regime" continues to expand and adapt with new power structures all around the globe. But organizers also learned to resist in new ways based on the lessons of the past, and political power will always be met with a collective power of resistance. It is this call to action that propelled me to write this manuscript as part of my development as an undocu-scholar contributing to building collective power.

NOTES

Preface

1. To learn more about Assembly Bill 540 in California, see https://admission .universityofcalifornia.edu/tuition-financial-aid/tuition-cost-of-attendance/ab-540 -nonresident-tuition-exemption.html.

2. For more information on Assembly Bill 60 (2013), which gave undocumented popula- tions in California access to a driver's license, see the information provided on the State of California Department of Motor Vehicles website: https://www.dmv.ca.gov/portal/ driver-licenses-identification-cards/assembly-bill-ab-60-driver-licenses/.

3. The state of New Mexico offers in-state tuition and state financial aid through Senate Bill 582 (2005); the bill can be accessed here: https://www.nmlegis.gov/Sessions/05 %20Regular/final/SB0582.pdf (accessed May 28, 2022). Driver's licenses in New Mex- ico for undocumented immigrants came in 2019 as part of Senate Bill 278, which can be accessed here: https://www.nmlegis.gov/Sessions/16%20Regular/final/HB0099 .pdf (accessed May 28, 2022). Finally, New Mexico also allows professional licens- ing for undocumented immigrants under Senate Bills 137 (2020) and 219 (2021); see: https://www.nmlegis.gov/Legislation/Legislation?Chamber=S&LegType=B&LegNo =137&year=20 (accessed May 28, 2022); and https://www.nmlegis.gov/Legislation/ Legislation?Chamber=S&LegType=B&LegNo=219&year=21 (accessed May 28, 2022).

4. The original Deferred Action for Childhood Arrivals (DACA) program announcement by President Barack Obama can be found on the White House archival website here: https://obamawhitehouse.archives.gov/the-press-office/2012/06/15/remarks-president -immigration.

5. Aurora Chang, *The Struggles of Identity, Education, and Agency in the Lives of Undocu- mented Students: The Burden of Hyperdocumentation* (San Bernardino, Calif.: Palgrave Macmillan, 2018), ix.

6.   The phrase "in the shadows" refers to the watershed event in undocumented youth move-
       ments organized by the Immigrant Youth Justice League (IYJL) in downtown Chicago,
       Illinois, in 2010. On a model similar to that of "coming out" events in LGBTQ move-
       ments, which empower youth to reveal their sexuality identities, the IYJL organized the
       event to empower undocumented youth to reveal their undocumented status as a means
       of building a local and national community of support. "Coming Out of the Shadows"
       remains a staple event organized across university campuses, organizing spaces, and other
       communities. "In the shadows" also refers to undocumented communities who might
       not feel empowered to "come out of the shadows" about their statuses for various reasons.
       As in my story, "coming out of the shadows" or staying "in the shadows" is seen as a rite
       of passage for many undocumented youth.

7.   To learn more about Aguilar's theorization of "acompañamiento" and "UndocuCrit," see
       Carlos Aguilar, "Undocumented Critical Theory," *Cultural Studies Critical Methodologies*
       19, no. 3 (2018): 152–60.

8.   To read more on their theorization of "the undocumented advantage" and the scientific
       findings of their study, see Germán A. Cadenas and Elizabeth Kiehne, "The Undocu-
       mented Advantage: Intersectional Predictors of Critical Consciousness and Academic
       Performance Among U.S. Latinxs," *Journal of Latinx Psychology* 9, no. 4 (2021): 326–43.

9.   Many others also refer to it as an identity rooted in highlighting the privilege of having
       DACA in comparison to the larger undocumented population.

Introduction

1.   See Sylvia R. Lazos Vargas, "The Immigrant Rights Marches (Las Marchas): Did the
       'Gigante' (Giant) Wake Up or Does It Still Sleep Tonight?," *Nevada Law Journal*, Summer
       2007.

2.   I am using "undocu-scholar" with a hyphen to indicate the intersections of identity in
       which undocu-scholars navigate both in academia and in their communities. For scholars
       writing in and experiencing institutions like academia where we cannot always bring our
       whole selves and identities, the hyphen represents the choices, paths, crossroads, and
       multiple hats we navigate when entering these places. Additionally, these intersections
       are a constant reminder of the doors that have been opened for us by mentors, allies,
       and community members as well as a responsibility to create opportunities for the next
       generation. Finally, as I mention, I do not employ the term "undocu-scholars" exclusively
       for those in academia but instead use it to refer to any community member producing
       knowledge with advocacy efforts for our undocumented immigrant communities.

3.   Similar arguments about UYMs not being homogeneous movements are made in foun-
       dational books including, but not limited to, the following examples: Walter Nicholls,
       *The DREAMers: How the Undocumented Youth Movement Transformed the Immigrant
       Rights Debate* (Stanford, Calif.: Stanford University Press, 2013); Karma R. Chávez, *Queer
       Migration Politics: Activist Rhetoric and Coalitional Possibilities* (Urbana: University of Illi-
       nois Press, 2013); Sasha Costanza-Chock, *Out of the Shadows, Into the Streets! Transmedia
       Organizing and the Immigrant Rights Movement* (Cambridge, Mass.: MIT Press, 2014);
       Kevin Escudero, *Organizing While Undocumented: Immigrant Youth's Political Activism*

Under the Law (New York: New York University Press, 2020); Leisy J. Abrego and Genevieve Negrón-Gonzales, eds., *We Are Not Dreamers: Undocumented Scholars Theorize Undocumented Life in the United States* (Durham, N.C.: Duke University Press, 2020).

4. Speaking of UYMs in the plural is meant to emphasize their heterogeneity—in other words, to highlight that there were several movements and directions rather than to celebrate or appear to speak of a single, unified front. I also read undocumented youth as knowledge producers that merit the claim of developing independent and grassroots movements. I always use the plural form in describing social movements, as women-of-color feminists argue that movements are never singular, one-sided, or one-dimensional, but rather multifaceted and multipurpose, and that they must remain intersectional in all their dimensions.

5. My understandings of "cultural capital" come from Renato Rosaldo and his work: Renato Rosaldo, "Cultural Citizenship, Inequality, and Multiculturalism," in *Latino Cultural Citizenship: Claiming Identity, Space, and Rights*, ed. William V. Flores and Rina Benmayor (Boston: Beacon Press, 1997).

6. Ruben G. Rumbaut, "Generation 1.5, Educational Experiences of," in *Encyclopedia of Diversity in Education*, ed. James A. Banks (Seattle: Sage Publications, 2012).

7. "Plyler v. Doe," Oyez, accessed January 18, 2021, www.oyez.org/cases/1981/80-1538.

8. Leticia "A" v. The Board of Regents of the Univ. of Cal., No. 588–982–4 (Cal. Super. Ct., April 11, 1985) (order granting a permanent injunction against the University of California and California State University systems).

9. The *Leticia "A"* case was brought by a total of five undocumented students who, along with allied legal representatives and organizers, laid the framework for state and local political action, thereby opening the doors of higher education to undocumented youth. In an *Education Week* article published shortly after the ruling on May 8, 1985, we begin to see that education and media outlets as early as the 1980s were formulating a narrative around merit for undocumented youth. Lynn Olson, policy analyst with *Education Week* at the time, states, "The five students represented in Leticia 'A' are all long-time residents of California who were brought to the United States by their parents when they were still children," highlighting the innocence of the children and the conscious decision by their parents. She goes on to add information about one of the plaintiffs, noting, "She graduated from high school with a 3.9 grade-point average on a 4.0-point scale, according to court documents. She now has a grade-point average of 4.0 at the University of California-Los Angeles." For more on the case, see Lynn Olson, "Out-Of-State College Fee for Aliens Said Unconstitutional by a California Court," *Education Week*, May 8, 1985, https://www.edweek.org/education/out-of-state-college-fee-for-aliens-said -unconstitutional-by-a-california-court/1985/05.

10. Larry Gordon, "Cal State Held to In-State Fees for Immigrants: Education: Superior Court Judge's Decision Contradicts Similar California Cases on Whether Undocumented Students Must Pay Higher Non-resident Rate," *Los Angeles Times*, May 21, 1992, https://www.latimes.com/archives/la-xpm-1992-05-21-mn-334-story.html.

11. For more on "civility" and "uncivility" as they relate to political action, see Bernard E. Harcourt, "The Politics of Incivility," *Arizona Law Review* 54, no. 2 (2012): 345–73.

12. Responding to national and local organizing efforts, the Departments of Chicana and Chicano Studies and American Studies at the University of New Mexico (UNM) organized the symposium in the fall of 2012. The original website for the "Everyday Practices of Popular Power: Art, Media, Immigration" event is no longer active; it was originally http://artmediaimmigration.com/. But thanks to the internet digital archiving service Wayback Machine, snapshots of the original website can be recovered with original content. Please consult https://web.archive.org/web/20130826155332/http://artmediaimmigration.com/. Sites like the Wayback Machine inform my interventions in conceptualizing digital archives and counterarchives, which I discuss in this introduction.

13. Chon Noriega is credited with coining the terms "artivist" and "artivism." "Artivist" is defined as an artist who produces artwork with an activist message or for social justice motives. See Chon A. Noriega, *Just Another Poster?* (Los Angeles: The Regents of the University of California Art Museum, 2001).

14. Veronica Vélez, Lindsay Perez Huber, Corina Benavides Lopez, Ariana de la Luz, and Daniel G. Solórzano, "Battling for Human Rights and Social Justice: A Latina/o Critical Race Media Analysis of Latina/o Student Youth Activism in the Wake of 2006 Anti-immigrant Sentiment," *Social Justice / Global Options* 35, no. 1 (111) (2008): 7–27.

15. The official announcement of DACA by President Barack Obama can be found in the White House Office of the Press Secretary archival record here: https://obamawhitehouse.archives.gov/the-press-office/2012/06/15/remarks-president-immigration.

16. In the ten-year history of DACA (2012–22), the program has had up to 832,881 qualifying undocumented youth enrolled, with a significant decline as of 2022 to 590,070, as reported by USCIS: https://www.uscis.gov/sites/default/files/document/data/Approximate%20Active%20DACA%20Receipts%20-%20March%2031%2C%202020.pdf. Not all qualifying undocumented youth have applied; an estimated 1.3 million undocumented youth should have qualified when the program was announced in 2012, according to the American Immigrant Council: https://www.americanimmigrationcouncil.org/research/deferred-action-childhood-arrivals-daca-overview. The over 800,000 undocumented youth that have enrolled represent only a small number of the overall undocumented population, estimated by the Pew Research Center at 10.5 million as of 2017: https://www.pewresearch.org/fact-tank/2020/08/20/key-findings-about-u-s-immigrants/.

17. Nathalie Peutz and Nicholas De Genova, "Introduction," in *The Deportation Regime: Sovereignty, Space, and the Freedom of Movement*, ed. Nicholas De Genova and Nathalie Peutz (Durham, N.C.: Duke University Press, 2010), 3.

18. Peutz and De Genova, "Introduction," 39.

19. Laura Stoller suggests interdisciplinary conversations on archives should regard the production of records as a subject and not focus on documentation solely as sources. For more on this conversation on the archival turn, see Laura Stoller, *Along the Archival Grain: Epistemic Anxieties and Colonial Common Sense* (Princeton, N.J.: Princeton University Press, 2009).

20. For more on the archive and archaeology as analyzed by Foucault, see Michel Foucault, *The Archaeology of Knowledge and the Discourse on Language* (New York: Pantheon Books, 1972).

21. Jacques Derrida, *Archive Fever: A Freudian Impression* (Chicago: University of Chicago Press, 1996).

22. My understanding of undocumented status and legality comes from the foundational work of Aviva Chomsky, *Undocumented: How Immigration Became Illegal* (Boston: Beacon Press, 2014).

23. John-Michael Rivera, *Undocuments* (Tucson: University of Arizona Press, 2021), 15.

24. Emma Pérez, *The Decolonial Imaginary: Writing Chicanas into History* (Bloomington: Indiana University Press, 1999).

25. Alicia Schmidt Camacho, *Migrant Imaginaries: Latino Cultural Politics in the U.S.-Mexico Borderlands* (New York: New York University Press, 2008), 5–6, 17, 30, 160, 165, 198, 314.

26. The video interview was collected by the "Art, Media, Immigration" collective that organized the "Art, Media, Immigration" symposium at the University of New Mexico in 2012. It can be found here: Jonathan Perez and Isaac Barrera, "Jonathan Perez and Isaac Barrera," presentation at the "Everyday Practices of Popular Power: Art, Media, Immigration" symposium, University of New Mexico, November 9, 2012, video, 28:35, https://youtu.be/4ct6lMyFWfM.

27. Chicana scholars have worked toward the development of counternarratives that use alternate records to share stories of communities often left out of the historical record. Maylei Blackwell's work *Chicana Power! Contested Histories of Feminism in the Chicano Movement* (Austin: University of Texas Press, 2011) employs the term "retrofitted memory," aimed at incorporating Chicana voices against traditional narratives of both U.S. history and the Chicano/a Movement. In the definition she offers of retrofitted memory, Blackwell highlights the importance of public memory and its connection to the assemblage of archives that tell dominant stories. Building on Blackwell's work, Anita Huizar-Hernández also introduces the useful term *counterfeit narrative*, which she defines as "an invented narrative that masquerades as true in order to consolidate political, cultural, or economic power." Anita Huizar-Hernández, *Forging Arizona: A History of the Peralta Land Grant and Racial Identity in the West* (New Brunswick, N.J.: Rutgers University Press, 2019).

28. Chicana scholars have been at the forefront of uncovering the multitude of ways in which Chicana women were invested in exploring archival remains left by Chicana women who chose to self-document their own movements as well as interpretations of them. What María Cotera terms a "praxis of resistance" includes the multiple strategic movidas Chicana women used to document opportunities to insert themselves and their agendas into the normative and machista space that was the Chicano Movement of the 1960s. See Dionne Espinoza, María Eugenia Cotera, and Maylei Blackwell, eds., *Chicana Movidas: New Narratives of Activism and Feminism in the Movement Era* (Austin: University of Texas Press, 2018).

29. For more on the complexities of the usage of the term "undocumented" and the the paradoxes, limitations, and challenges related to documentation, see E. Johanna Hartelius,

"'Undocumented and Unafraid'? Challenging the Bureaucratic Paradigm," *Communication and Critical/Cultural Studies* 13, no. 2 (2016): 130–49.

30.   Diana Taylor, *The Archive and the Repertoire: Performing Cultural Memory in the Americas* (Durham, N.C.: Duke University Press, 2003).

31.   Taylor, *Archive and the Repertoire*, 3.

32.   Francesca Polletta and James M. Jasper, "Collective Identity and Social Movements," *Annual Review of Sociology* 27, no. 1 (2001): 283–305.

33.   Maurizio Ferraris, *Documentality: Why It Is Necessary to Leave Traces* (Bronx: Fordham University Press, 2013).

34.   Abrego and Negrón-Gonzales, introduction to *We Are Not Dreamers*, 8.

35.   The term "the 1.5 generation" identifies immigrant children who arrived in the United States at a young age and grew up there during formative periods of their lives. To explore more on the literature of the 1.5 generation, see Rumbaut, "Generation 1.5."

36.   To read more on the core tenets of undocumented youth studies developed in the *We Are Not Dreamers* anthology edited by Leisy J. Abrego and Genevieve Negrón-Gonzales, see their co-authored introduction to the book, 16.

37.   A big influence on my understanding of neoliberal models of inclusion and exclusion and the way those modes operate across diverse communities comes from the work of Sara Ahmed. See Sara Ahmed, *On Being Included: Racism and Diversity in Institutional Life* (Durham, N.C.: Duke University Press, 2012). Another work that informs my interpretation here is Roderick A. Ferguson, *The Reorder of Things: The University and Its Pedagogies of Minority Difference* (Minneapolis: University of Minnesota Press, 2012).

38.   Gabrielle Cabrera, "Disrupting Diversity: Undocumented Students in the Neoliberal University," in Abrego and Negrón-Gonzales, *We Are Not Dreamers*, 66–67.

39.   Cabrera, "Disrupting Diversity," 82–83.

40.   Joel Sati, "'Other' Borders: The Illegal as Normative Metaphor," in Abrego and Negrón-Gonzales, *We Are Not Dreamers*, 25–27.

41.   Carolina Valdivia, "Undocumented Young Adults' Heightened Vulnerability in the Trump Era," in Abrego and Negrón-Gonzales, *We Are Not Dreamers*, 127–45.

42.   Carlos Aguilar, "Undocumented Critical Theory," *Cultural Studies Critical Methodologies* 19, no. 3 (2019): 155.

43.   Pedro Santiago Martínez, Claudia Muñoz, Mariela Nuñez-Janes, Stephen Pavey, Fidel Castro Rodriguez, and Marco Saavedra, *Eclipse of Dreams: The Undocumented-Led Struggle for Freedom* (Chico, Calif.: AK Press, 2020), 16.

44.   For more on the use of the term "DREAMer" in a transnational context and adaptations, see Rafael A. Martínez, "Transnational DREAMer Narratives: Following the Deportation and Return-Migration Trails of Mexican Immigrant Youth," *Aztlán: A Journal of Chicano Studies* 49, no. 2 (2024).

45.   See Jose Antonio Vargas, *Dear America: Notes of an Undocumented Citizen* (New York: Harper Collins, 2018); and Karla Cornejo Villavicencio, *The Undocumented Americans* (New York: One World, 2020).

46.   Reyna Grande and Sonia Guiñansaca, *Somewhere We Are Human* (New York: Harper Via, 2022).

47. Cherry Lou Sy, *Dreaming Out Loud: An Anthology of Migrant Writers,* Volume 4 (New York: Pen America, 2022).

48. See Marsha Kinder, *Playing with Power in Movies, Television, and Video Games: From Muppet Babies to Teenage Mutant Ninja Turtles* (Berkeley: University of California Press, 1991).

49. Henry Jenkins, *Convergence Culture: Where Old and New Media Collide* (New York: New York University Press, 2006), 282.

50. See Costanza-Chock, *Out of the Shadows;* and Arely Zimmerman, "Transmedia Testimonio: Examining Undocumented Youth's Political Activism in the Digital Age," *International Journal of Communication* 10 (2016): 1886–1906.

51. Sasha Costanza-Chock, "Se Ve, Se Siente: Transmedia Mobilization in the Los Angeles Immigrant Rights Movement" (PhD diss., University of Southern California, 2010), 114. On their website, Sasha Costanza-Chock highlights the pronouns they use as "she/her" or "they/them."

52. Rebecca M. Schreiber, *The Undocumented Everyday: Migrant Lives and the Politics of Visibility* (Minneapolis: University of Minnesota Press, 2018), 15.

53. Taylor, *Archive and the Repertoire,* 3.

54. Throughout the book I use the term "Mexico-U.S. border or borderlands" consistently. I separate Mexico from the United States with a hyphen as a theoretical exercise in highlighting the physical and ideological attempt to separate the two nations. Furthermore, the hyphen shows the historical connection as a region. Finally, I write the name of Mexico first to prioritize a "global south" theorization drawing on Latin American traditions as well as to point to Latinx migrants' south-to-north global migration pattern. I follow this direction of theoretical framing from works like that of Roberto D. Hernández, who writes this physical and discursive space as "U-S///Mexico border," writes about the history of "coloniality of power," and treats these new understandings of the borderlands as "epistemic disobedience." See Roberto D. Hernández, *Coloniality of the U-S///Mexico Border: Power, Violence, and the Decolonial Imperative* (Tucson: University of Arizona Press, 2018).

55. The term "post-Trumpamerica" is coined by Eduardo Bonilla-Silva to analyze race in the United States in the time after Forty-Five's presidency. I interpret post-Trumpamerica not as the end of the presidency of Donald Trump, but rather as what his politics represent for U.S. society moving forward. In other words, whether Donald Trump is elected for a second term as president or not in 2024, I see post-Trumpamerica as a political situation that is not going to end with Donald Trump.

56. Beyond the use of "out of the shadows" as an immigrant rights phrase, I also trace the historical genealogy from Chicana author Vicki Ruiz in her work *From Out of the Shadows: Mexican Women in Twentieth-Century America* (New York: Oxford University Press, 1998).

Chapter 1

1. I am choosing to refer to Elvira Arellano using her first name, Elvira, throughout the manuscript for two main reasons: (a) her name became a symbol and, I would argue, a household name related to the immigrant rights struggle, becoming used commonly

during the mid-2000s in media outlets, and she herself states in several interviews that she prefers being called by her first name in media sources; (b) *Elvira* was the name of the biographical documentary depicting her life's trajectory. See Javier Solórzano Casarin, dir., *Elvira* (Grado 5, 2009).

2. Cecilia Menjívar, Leisy J. Abrego, and Leah C. Schmalzbauer, *Immigrant Families* (New York: Polity Press, 2016).

3. Maura I. Toro-Morn and Nilda Flores Gonzalez, "Transnational Latina Mother Activists in the Américas: The Case of Elvira Arellano and Flor Crisóstomo," *Journal of the Motherhood Initiative* 2, no. 2 (2011): 113–28.

4. Ruth Gomberg-Muñoz, *Labor and Legality: An Ethnography of a Mexican Immigrant Network* (New York: Oxford University Press, 2010).

5. The private bill introduced by Representatives Gutiérrez and Durbin, H.R. 3105 (9/16/2003), can be accessed on the U.S. Congress website here: https://www.congress .gov/bill/108th-congress/house-bill/3105?q=%7B%22search%22%3A%5B%22Elvira%22 %2C%22Elvira%22%5D%7D&s=2&r=3.

6. Elvira speaks about the privileges granted under the private bill introduced on her behalf by Representatives Gutiérrez and Durbin of Illinois in an interview with Chicago Independent TV in December 2006. The interview can be found here: Chicago Independent TV, "Chicago Independent TV: Episode 23 (Dec. 2006)—Elvira Arellano, Mark Kirk Sing Along," May 17, 2018, video, 11:33, https://youtu.be/2aXZVOVZMIg.

7. Wendy Cole, "People Who Mattered: Elvira Arellano," *Time*, December 25, 2006, http:// content.time.com/time/specials/packages/article/0,28804,2019341_2017328_2017183 ,00.html.

8. To read more about Elvira Arellano and Flor Crisóstomo in the context of transnational mother activism, see Toro-Morn and Flores Gonzalez, "Transnational Latina Mother Activists." For more on Latina transnational motherhood, see Pierrette Hondagneu-Sotelo and Ernestine Ávila, "'I'm Here, but I'm There': The Meanings of Latina Transnational Motherhood," in *Gender and U.S. Immigration: Contemporary Trends*, ed. Pierrette Hondagneu-Sotelo (Berkeley: University of California Press, 1999).

9. Scott Henkel and Vanessa Fonseca-Chávez write about "civility" in the context of the film *Salt of the Earth*, which provides a complex understanding of civility as it relates to social movements, art, film, and literature in the fields of Chicanx studies and Latinx studies. See their article: Scott Henkel and Vanessa Fonseca-Chávez, "Fearless Speech and the Discourse of Civility in *Salt of the Earth*," *Chiricú Journal: Latina/o Literatures, Arts, and Cultures* 1, no. 1 (2016): 19–38.

10. I am informed in the definition of direct and indirect forms of activism by Veronica Vélez, Lindsay Perez Huber, Corina Benavidez Lopez, Ariana De la Luz, and Daniel G. Solorzano, "Battling for Human Rights and Social Justice: A Latina/o Critical Race Media Analysis of Latina/o Student Youth Activism in the Wake of 2006 Anti-immigrant Sentiment," *Social Justice* 35, no. 1 (2008).

11. Transmedia narratives is a concept used originally in media studies and developed by Henry Jenkins to understand the way in which global society constructs narratives across multiple media platforms, creating diverse and distinct stories. In the anthology edited

by Henry Jenkins, Sangita Shresthova, Liana Gamber-Thompson, Neta Kligler-Vilenchik, and Arely M. Zimmerman, *By Any Media Necessary: The New Youth Activism* (New York: New York University Press, 2016), Arely M. Zimmerman extends the definition of transmedia narratives to the ways in which undocumented youth are creating testimonials using diverse media platforms toward strategic organizing. My use of (un)documenting is in conversation with the work of Zimmerman in thinking of not only the creation of narratives but also the production of digital archives that go on to produce a new understanding of immigrants and undocumented bodies.

12. David Harvey, *A Brief History of Neoliberalism* (New York: Oxford University Press, 2005), 2.

13. Isidro Morales, "The Mexican Crisis and the Weakness of the NAFTA Consensus," *The Annals of the American Academy of Political and Social Science* 550, no. 1 (1997): 130–52.

14. Leo Chavez, *The Latino Threat: Constructing Immigrants, Citizens, and the Nation* (Stanford, Calif.: Stanford University Press, 2008).

15. For more about Elvira's early life and an analysis of her migration journey, see the chapter by Maura I. Toro-Morn, "Elvira Arellano and the Struggles of Low-Wage Undocumented Latina Immigrant Women," in the anthology *Immigrant Women Workers in the Neoliberal Age*, ed. Nilda Flores-González, Anna Romina Guevarra, Maura Toro-Morn, and Grace Chang (Urbana: University of Illinois Press, 2013).

16. To read the analysis provided by Pierrette Hondagneu-Sotelo and Ernestine Ávila on the term "gender-transformative odyssey," please refer to Hondagneu-Sotelo and Ávila, "I'm Here, but I'm There," 253.

17. For more on transnational migration challenges and routes as well as the complication of gender and citizenship, see Rainer Bauböck, *Transnational Citizenship: Membership and Rights in International Migration* (Aldershot, UK: Edward Elgar Publishing Company, 1994); and Maylei Blackwell, Laura Briggs, and Mignonette Chiu, "Transnational Feminisms Roundtable," *Frontiers: A Journal of Women's Studies* 36, no 3 (2015): 1–24. Additionally, on transnational feminisms, see Inderpal Grewal, *Transnational America: Feminisms, Diasporas, Neoliberalisms* (Durham, N.C.: Duke University Press, 2005). See also Irene Vásquez, "Transnational Mexican Women's Radical Organizing Activities on the Borders of the Left of the Twentieth Century," *Border-Lines Journal* 9 (2015): 141–60.

18. For more history and background on maquiladoras, see Norma Iglesias-Prieto, "Maquiladoras," in *Keywords for Latina/o Studies*, ed. Lawrence La Fountain-Stokes, Nancy Raquel Mirabal, and Deborah R. Vargas (New York: New York University Press, 2017).

19. For more on the maquiladora industry and its relation to immigrants and immigration, see the following works: Gloria Anzaldúa, *Borderlands / La Frontera: The New Mestiza* (San Francisco: Aunt Lute Books, 1987); Charles Bowden, *Juárez: The Laboratory of Our Future* (New York: Aperture, 1998); Rosa-Linda Fregoso, *meXicana Encounters: The Making of Social Identities on the Borderlands* (Berkeley: University of California Press, 2003). See also the film: Saul Landau and Sonia Angulo, dirs., *Maquila: A Tale of Two Mexicos* (The Cinema Guild, 2005).

20. Toro-Morn, "Elvira Arellano and the Struggles," 38–55.

21. Joseph Nevins, *Operation Gatekeeper: The Rise of the "Illegal Alien" and the Making of the U.S.-Mexico Boundary* (New York: Routledge, 2002).

22. Nevins, *Operation Gatekeeper*, 6.

23. Toro-Morn, "Elvira Arellano and the Struggles," 44.

24. Nevins, *Operation Gatekeeper*.

25. Harvey, *Brief History of Neoliberalism*.

26. Eithne Luibhéid, *Entry Denied: Controlling Sexuality at the Border* (Minneapolis: University of Minnesota Press, 2002), 17.

27. Luibhéid, *Entry Denied*, xvi.

28. Susan B. Coutin, *Nations of Emigrants: Shifting Boundaries of Citizenship in El Salvador and the United States* (Ithaca, N.Y.: Cornell University Press, 2007), 9.

29. Joel Sati, "'Other' Borders: The Illegal as Normative Metaphor," in *We Are Not Dreamers: Undocumented Scholars Theorize Undocumented Life in the United States*, ed. Leisy J. Abrego and Genevieve Negrón-Gonzales (Durham, N.C.: Duke University Press, 2020).

30. Delia Fernández, "Immigrants (Re)make the City (and the Suburbs): Race, Ethnicity, and Labor," *Journal of Urban History* 47, no. 3 (2021): 687–93.

31. Chicago Independent TV, "Episode 23" (see note 6 above). All of the quotations from interviews with Elvira Arellano used in this chapter reflect her own words in my translation from Spanish into English.

32. Chicago Independent TV, "Episode 23."

33. Elvira mentions her foundations in learning organizing thanks to the scholarship through the CAAELII network in the same interview mentioned previously: see Chicago Independent TV, "Episode 23."

34. Chicago Independent TV, "Episode 23."

35. To read more about mixed-status families, see Menjívar, Abrego, and Schmalzbauer, *Immigrant Families*.

36. The University of Southern California's Immigrant Inclusion and Racial Justice Center (previously named the Center for the Study of Immigration Integration) collects important data and publishes critical reports on the growing number of mixed-status families living in the United States. To learn more about the impacts of family separation through deportation, their website with reports can be found here: https://dornsife.usc .edu/eri/publications/immigrant-inclusion-and-racial-justice-reports/. Silva Mathema is a journalist and researcher who has published several reports on the impacts of family separation and why U.S. citizens should care about immigration issues and deportations. See Silva Mathema, "Keeping Families Together: Why All Americans Should Care More About What Happens to Unauthorized Immigrants," Center for American Progress, March 16, 2017, https://www.americanprogress.org/article/keeping-families-together/.

37. The organization La Familia Latina Unida does not exist any longer; as such, their website is no longer on the web. However, one tool in (un)documenting the digital footprint of activists and organizations is the Wayback Machine website service, which allows users to search websites and online materials that do not exist anymore or have changed over time. The Wayback Machine offers snapshots of websites from specific time periods that create an archive from the web. The Wayback Machine service is useful for researching defunct organizations like La Familia Latina Unida to see snapshots of their websites that do not exist anymore. In this case, the archival snapshot is of a page related to La Familia

Latina Unida's family unity campaign from December 1, 2007, but it captures different motives and reasons for establishing the organization. The snapshot can be accessed here: https://web.archive.org/web/20110923114356/http://www.pueblosinfronteras.org/.

38. Vélez et al., "Battling for Human Rights," 16.

39. "Coming out of the shadows" is terminology that would be adopted by 2010 by the UYMs. More on this term in chapter 2.

40. Teresa Watanabe and Hector Becerra, "500,000 Pack Streets to Protest Immigration Bills," *Los Angeles Times*, March 26, 2006, A1; James Sterngold, "500,000 Throng L.A. to Protest Immigration Legislation," *Los Angeles Times*, May 26, 2006, A1.

41. Associated Press, "Power in Numbers: Nearly 400,000 Fill Downtown Chicago's Streets with Rallying Cry for Immigrant Rights," *Chicago Tribune*, May 2, 2006, 6.

42. Anna Gorman, "Immigrants Demonstrate Peaceful Power," *Los Angeles Times*, May 2, 2006, A1.

43. See Commentary, "Marches Full of Disturbing Irony," *Las Vegas Review-Journal*, May 3, 2006, B8.

44. Multiple scholars have written about the ways in which the May Day marches of 2006 and 2007 represented an opportunity for organizers to take on different forms of activism, including direct and indirect forms. For more on this, see the following books: Amalia Pallares and Nilda Flores-González, ¡Marcha! *Latino Chicago and the Immigrant Rights Movement* (Urbana: University of Illinois Press, 2010); Sasha Costanza-Chock, *Out of the Shadows, Into the Streets! Transmedia Organizing and the Immigrant Rights Movement* (Cambridge, Mass.: MIT Press, 2014). See the following articles as well: Vélez et al., "Battling for Human Rights"; and René Galindo, "Repartitioning the National Community: Political Visibility and Voice for Undocumented Immigrants in the Spring 2006 Immigration Rights Marches," *Aztlán: A Journal of Chicano Studies* 35, no. 2 (2010): 37–64.

45. It's important to note that May 1, 2006, produced the largest number of participants for an immigrant rights march nationwide, but, as often happens with social mass movements, there were previous marches happening during the month of April and after May that led up to and continued the momentum of the May Day marches.

46. The hunger strike started on May 10 and ended on June 1. Here is an article that captures the essence of the hunger strike organized by Elvira and Flor: People's World, "Rally Fights Deportation: Keep Families Together," *People's World*, June 9, 2006, https://www.peoplesworld.org/article/rally-fights-deportation-keep-families-together/.

47. Nilda Flores-González and Ruth Gomberg-Muñoz, "FLOResiste: Transnational Labor, Motherhood, and Activism," in Flores-González et al., *Immigrant Women Workers*.

48. Flores-González and Gomberg-Muñoz, "FLOResiste."

49. Pallares and Flores-González, ¡Marcha!

50. Costanza-Chock, *Out of the Shadows*.

51. The reporter goes on to connect Elvira to Centro Sin Fronteras, which had been working with immigrant families who found themselves in deportation proceedings. Elvira's testimonial can be accessed on YouTube here: Elvira Arellano, "Elvira Arellano Migrantes 1/6," presentation at UACM, June 1, 2010, video, 9:54, https://youtu.be/RbEIq_FXci4.

52. Arellano, "Elvira Arellano Migrantes 1/6."

53. Arellano, "Elvira Arellano Migrantes 1/6."

54. Henry Jenkins, Sam Ford, and Joshua Green, *Spreadable Media: Creating Value and Meaning in a Networked Culture* (New York: New York University Press, 2013).

55. Costanza-Chock, *Out of the Shadows*; Arely Zimmerman, "Transmedia Testimonio: Examining Undocumented Youth's Political Activism in the Digital Age," *International Journal of Communication* 10 (2016): 1886–1906.

56. The history of memoranda on sensitive locations goes back to the Immigration and Naturalization Services (INS) department that existed before the establishment of the current Department of Homeland Security (DHS) in 2002. For the first memorandum, see James A. Puleo, "Enforcement Activities at Schools, Places of Worship, or at Funerals or Other Religious Ceremonies," Immigration and Naturalization Services (May 17, 1993), https://niwaplibrary.wcl.american.edu/wp-content/uploads/2015/IMM-Memo -SensLocationsEnforce.pdf. During the establishment of DHS, the memoranda on "sensitive locations" grew. Here is the full list of memoranda shared by DHS: Memorandum from Julie L. Myers, Assistant Secretary, U.S. Immigration and Customs Enforcement, "Field Guidance on Enforcement Actions or Investigative Activities at or near Sensitive Community Locations," I0029.1 (July 3, 2008); Memorandum from Marcy M. Forman, Director, Office of Investigations, "Enforcement Actions at Schools" (December 26, 2007); Memorandum from James A. Puleo, Immigration and Naturalization Service (INS) Acting Associate Commissioner, "Enforcement Activities at Schools, Places of Worship, or at Funerals or Other Religious Ceremonies," HQ 807-P (May 17, 1993). This policy does not supersede the requirements regarding arrests at sensitive locations put forth in the Violence Against Women Act: see Memorandum from John P. Torres, Director Office of Detention and Removal Operations, and Marcy M. Forman, Director, Office of Investigations, "Interim Guidance Relating to Officer Procedure Following Enactment of VAWA 2005" (January 22, 2007). The most current memorandum: John Morton, "Enforcement Actions at or Focused on Sensitive Locations," Department of Homeland Security (DHS) (October 24, 2011); this last memorandum can be found on the Immigration and Customs Enforcement (ICE) website here: https://www.ice.gov/ doclib/ero-outreach/pdf/10029.2-policy.pdf.

57. Aimee Villarreal Garza, "Sanctuaryscapes in the North American Southwest," in "Sanctuary's Radical Networks," ed. A. Naomi Paik, Jason Ruiz, and Rebecca M. Schreiber, special issue, *Radical History Review* 2019, no. 135 (2019). See the full special issue of the journal for more history of sanctuary in the United States.

58. To read more on a comparative approach between the sanctuary movement in the times of slavery and the Underground Railroad and the modern-day sanctuary movement focused on sheltering immigrants/refugees, read Kathleen L. Villaruel, "The Underground Railroad and the Sanctuary Movement: A Comparison of History, Litigation, and Values," *Southern California Law Review* 60, no. 5 (July 1987).

59. To read more on the topic of sanctuary and conscientious objectors, see Ann Crittenden, *Sanctuary: A Story of American Conscience and Law in Collision* (New York: Grove Press, 1988).

60. This was only a policy, not a law, so the U.S. government was not bound by it legally.

61. Robert Tomsho, *The American Sanctuary Movement* (Austin: Texas Monthly Press, 1987).

62. Hector P. García, *Everyday Rhetoric and Mexican American Civil Rights* (Carbondale: Southern Illinois Press, 2006).

63. A good example of the urgency and dedication of a faith-based community creating space for Central American refugees is detailed in Mario T. García, *Father Luis Olivares, a Biography: Faith Politics and the Origins of the Sanctuary Movement* (Chapel Hill: University of North Carolina Press, 2018).

64. My understanding and use of "illegal subjectivity" comes from Mae Ngai's work. Mae Ngai, *Impossible Subjects: Illegal Aliens and the Making of Modern America* (Princeton, N.J.: Princeton University Press, 2004).

65. To also see some of the anti-immigrant reactions that residents of states like Arizona have had to the historical Sanctuary Movement of the 1980s and afterward, see Geraldo L. Cadava, *Standing on Common Ground: The Making of a Sunbelt Borderlands* (Cambridge, Mass.: Harvard University Press, 2013).

66. Kyle Barron, "Sanctuary: A Movement Redefined," *NACLA Report on the Americas* 49, no. 2 (2017). To read more literature on the Sanctuary Movement in New Mexico, see the novel *Mother Tongue* by Demetria Martínez (New York: One World/Ballantine, 1997).

67. In a public lecture on the sanctuary movement, Marian Bock, sanctuary coordinator for the New Mexico Faith Coalition for Immigrant Rights, highlights the fact that folks in sanctuary are not without fear of harassment and do not have complete protection. They are under the care of the religious institution with which they have taken sanctuary, but in reality, volunteers who work with sanctuary cases are there as caretakers and to report any potential arrest or harassment by Homeland Security. See Rafael Martínez, "Readings and Recollections with Demetria Martinez," *KUNM*, May 31, 2019, audio, 29:46, https://www.kunm.org/public-affairs/2019-05-31/reading-recollections-with-demetria -martinez.

68. For more on the influence of media and reactionary positions on immigrant rights, see L. Chavez, *Latino Threat*.

69. Aurora Chang, along with many of the undocu-scholars I reference and mention in this book, is part of the growing number of researchers, writers, and creative individuals who are writing from a hyperdocumented (Chang's term) or illegalized (as I refer to it) perspective. See Aurora Chang, *The Struggles of Identity, Education, and Agency in the Lives of Undocumented Students: The Burden of Hyperdocumentation* (San Bernardino: Palgrave Macmillan, 2018).

70. This presentation by Elvira was part of a conference organized and recorded by the Universidad Autónoma de la Ciudad de México after her deportation in 2007. See Elvira Arellano, "Elvira Arellano Migrantes 2/6," presentation at UACM, June 1, 2010, video, 9:59, https://youtu.be/nCS-tUvozkw.

71. Raw footage and multiple interviews were captured while Elvira was in sanctuary by individuals and organizations participating in the organization of her sanctuary case. This particular video footage was created by ChicagoTalks, and a YouTube video can be

accessed here: Elvira Arellano, "Interview with Elvira Arellano," video, 4:48, posted April 27, 2007, https://youtu.be/xQ8CYH94MPQ.

72. Arellano, "Interview with Elvira Arellano."

73. Arellano, "Interview with Elvira Arellano."

74. Lisa Marie Cacho, *Social Death: Racialized Rightlessness and the Criminalization of the Unprotected* (New York: New York University Press, 2012).

75. Cacho, *Social Death*, 31–33, 145.

76. SBS/Dateline, "Elvira's Sanctuary—USA," December 2006, posted August 22, 2007, distributed by Journeyman Pictures, video, 15:16, accessed February 18, 2020, https://youtu .be/U3FxdpneL1U.

77. Cacho, *Social Death*, 9, 16, 116, 148, 166–68.

78. Cacho, *Social Death*, 361.

79. Pallares and Flores-González, *¡Marcha!*

80. The full interview was conducted by a Spanish-speaking local media organization from Chicago called Vívelo Hoy. Vívelo Hoy, "Entrevista con Elvira Arellano," accessed January 24, 2020, https://www.youtube.com/watch?v=Pq6Hi5EoW_M&list= PLh3ihWGCrVWZj9TkAkk8RjSSKzl2_o8e1&index=6. The video link no longer exists, as the media organization no longer is active in Chicago. I was able to transcribe the video before the link came down.

81. "Coming out of the shadows" is popular terminology born out of the UYMs that began in a rally in 2010 in Chicago. I contextualize and historicize this terminology in chapter 2 when I address the importance of undocu-queer activism in the IRMs and UYMs.

82. Associated Press, "Mexican Immigration Activist and US-Born Son Deported to Mexico," AP Archive, July 21, 2015, video, 1:50, https://youtu.be/DEpJwokoZWo.

83. Associated Press, "Mexican Immigration Activist."

84. Associated Press, "Mexican Immigration Activist."

85. Ngai, *Impossible Subjects*.

86. See Hondagneu-Sotelo and Ávila, "I'm Here, but I'm There."

87. For more historical examples of immigrant communities and allies challenging growing numbers of detentions and deportations, see Jimmy Patiño, Raza Sí, Migra No: *Chicano Movement Struggles for Immigrant Rights in San Diego* (Chapel Hill: University of North Carolina Press, 2017).

88. For more on the foundational work on "fearless speech," see Michel Foucault, *Fearless Speech*, ed. Joseph Pearson (Los Angeles: Semiotext(e), 2001).

89. Much of my analysis of transnational social movements, including this stage of Elvira's life, is informed by the work by sociologists Jackie Smith and Sidney Tarrow. See Jackie Smith, *Social Movements for Global Democracy* (Baltimore: Johns Hopkins University Press, 2008); Sidney G. Tarrow, *The New Transnational Activism* (New York: Cambridge University Press, 2005); and Sidney G. Tarrow, *Power in Movement: Social Movements and Contentious Politics* (New York: Cambridge University Press, 2011).

90. Vívelo Hoy, "Entrevista con Elvira Arellano."

91. Vívelo Hoy, "Entrevista con Elvira Arellano."

Chapter 2

1. From a profile on the website of the *Huffington Post*, where Jonathan Perez was a contributor from 2012 to 2017: https://www.huffpost.com/author/jonathan-perez. Jonathan and Isaac both use the gender-fluid pronouns *they*, *them*, and *their*, and as such, I use these pronouns to describe them consistently throughout the book. Additionally, where the archives and records do not indicate how an individual chooses to identify, I choose to use gender-neutral pronouns to refer to them.

2. Isaac Barrera talks about their identity in one of the videos I analyze in this chapter: Jonathan Perez and Isaac Barrera, "Jonathan Perez and Isaac Barrera," presentation at the "Everyday Practices of Popular Power: Art, Media, Immigration" symposium, University of New Mexico, November 9, 2012, video, 28:35, https://youtu.be/4ct6lMyFWfM.

3. For information on the Immigrant Youth Coalition, you can visit their Facebook page, found here: https://www.facebook.com/Immigrant.Youth.Coalition/about.

4. Walter Nicholls writes about the "cleavages" and political "gaps" that undocumented youth learned about through their civic engagement in Dream Act activism after the 2006 and 2007 marches. Walter Nicholls, *The DREAMers: How the Undocumented Youth Movement Transformed the Immigrant Rights Debate* (Stanford: Stanford University Press, 2013).

5. I am using the term "direct forms of organizing" as defined by Vélez et al.: "overt political acts of protest that often utilize the physical body as a vehicle for protest." I define both "indirect forms of activism" and "direct forms of activism" and my use of these terms in relation to the escalation of civil disobedience actions by the UYMs in the introduction and chapter 1. See Veronica Vélez, Lindsay Perez Huber, Corina Benavidez Lopez, Ariana de la Luz, and Daniel G. Solórzano, "Battling for Human Rights and Social Justice: A Latina/o Critical Race Media Analysis of Latina/o Student Youth Activism in the Wake of 2006 Anti-immigrant Sentiment," *Social Justice / Global Options* 35, no. 1 (111) (2008).

6. René Galindo, "Repartitioning the National Community: Political Visibility and Voice for Undocumented Immigrants in the Spring 2006 Immigrant Rights Marches," *Aztlán: A Journal of Chicano Studies* 35, no. 2 (Fall 2010).

7. Sasha Costanza-Chock, *Out of the Shadows, Into the Streets! Transmedia Organizing and the Immigrant Rights Movement* (Cambridge, Mass.: MIT Press, 2014).

8. My understandings of "cultural capital" come from Renato Rosaldo and his work: Renato Rosaldo, "Cultural Citizenship, Inequality, and Multiculturalism," in *Latino Cultural Citizenship: Claiming Identity, Space, and Rights*, ed. William V. Flores and Rina Benmayor (Boston: Beacon Press, 1997).

9. See Bernard E. Harcourt, "The Politics of Incivility," *Arizona Law Review* 54, no. 2 (2012): 345–73.

10. Tanya Maria Golash-Boza, *Deported: Immigrant Policing, Disposable Labor, and Global Capitalism* (New York: New York University Press, 2015).

11. Eithne Luibhéid, *Entry Denied: Controlling Sexuality at the Border* (Minneapolis: University of Minnesota Press, 2002).

12. Audre Lorde, *Sister Outsider: Essays and Speeches* (Berkeley, Calif.: Crossing Press, 1984), 132.

13. Dionne Espinoza, María Eugenia Cotera, and Maylei Blackwell, eds., *Chicana Movidas: New Narratives of Activism and Feminism in the Movement Era* (Austin: University of Texas Press, 2018), 2.

14. Karma R. Chávez, *Queer Migration Politics: Activist Rhetoric and Coalitional Possibilities* (Urbana: University of Illinois Press, 2013).

15. José Esteban Muñoz, *Disidentifications: Queers of Color and the Performance of Politics* (Minneapolis: University of Minnesota Press, 1999).

16. Ruth Gomberg-Muñoz, "Undocumented. Unafraid. Unapologetic," *Practicing Anthropology* 38, no. 1 (Winter 2016).

17. In an interview with the *UndocuTalks* podcast, Nicolás González speaks about the birth of the "Undocumented and Unafraid" message as coming from the "Coming Out of the Shadows" event, held for the first time in downtown Chicago in 2010. The interview can be found here: UndocuTalks, "Undocumented, Unafraid: Before and After DACA," season 1, episode 2, February 25, 2018, audio recording, 41:32, accessed September 18, 2019, https://audioboom.com/posts/6692859-undocumented-unafraid-before-after-daca.

18. Nicholas De Genova, "The Queer Politics of Migration: Reflections on 'Illegality' and Incorrigibility," *Studies in Social Justice* 4, no. 2 (2010): 101–26.

19. Galindo, "Repartitioning the National Community."

20. Nico González quoted from UndocuTalks, "Undocumented, Unafraid" (see note 17 above). The original "Coming Out of the Shadows" event from 2010 is no longer available on YouTube, but the Immigrant Youth Justice League does have a video from 2011 that talks about the history of the annual events including the 2011 event: Immigrant Youth Justice League, "IYJL Out of the Shadows 2011," April 2, 2011, video, 8:32, https://youtu.be/bATPoDrxkAA?si=KF1RtoEvCDBRsgh1. Nico uses the gender-fluid pronouns *they*, *them*, and *theirs*.

21. The Immigrant Youth Justice League website, where the information about the first "Coming Out of the Shadows" event was archived and deposited, along with a toolkit on how to organize your own "Coming Out of the Shadows" event, does not exist anymore, as the organization dissolved. But again, thanks to the Wayback Machine, we are able to recover a "snapshot" archive of what the website was and the information that existed there: https://web.archive.org/web/20130313001244/http://www.iyjl.org/comingout2013/.

22. UndocuTalks, "Undocumented, Unafraid" (see note 17 above).

23. A "sit-in" action derives from the civil rights movements in the 1960s and 1970s, when Black activists sat at lunch counters during the segregation period, when Black people were prohibited from entering businesses and other spaces in cities across the U.S. South.

24. Julia Preston, "Illegal Immigrant Students Protest at McCain Office," *New York Times*, May 18, 2010, A15. Also see Stephen Lemons, "John McCain's Tucson Office Protested, Undocumented Activists Arrested (w/ Updates Video)," *Phoenix News Times*, May 17, 2010, https://www.phoenixnewtimes.com/news/john-mccains-tucson-office-protested-undocumented-activists-arrested-w-updates-video-6501999.

25. Preston, "Illegal Immigrant Students Protest," A15.

26. Preston, "Illegal Immigrant Students Protest."

27. NIYA is also the focus of chapter 3.

28. Preston, "Illegal Immigrant Students Protest." Also see Lemons, "John McCain's Tucson Office Protested."

29. For more coverage of the "Dream Act 5," see René Galindo, "Undocumented & Unafraid: The DREAM Act 5 and the Public Disclosure of Undocumented Students as a Political Act," *The Urban Review* 44, no. 5 (2012): 589–611. For state and local coverage, see Lemons, "John McCain's Tucson Office Protested."

30. The term "Dream Act 5" was taken up by many of the media sources I highlight in my citations above. There were a total of five participants in the action; however, the fifth youth who participated in the action had resident status, and the focus was on the undocumented youth who were risking potential deportation. I believe the label of "Dream Act 5" is accurate in that all five of these youth would have qualified for the Dream Act if it had passed, and technically speaking, Raúl Alcaraz could have still faced deportation, as he was a legal resident but not a permanent citizen. This speaks to the vulnerability generated by the mixed status within undocumented youth movements and the way that illegalization operates with respect to immigrant bodies.

31. Julia Preston, "Students Spared amid an Increase in Deportations," *New York Times*, August 8, 2010, https://www.nytimes.com/2010/08/09/us/09students.html.

32. For an example of the support the four activists received from politicians, in this case L.A. mayor Antonio Villaraigosa, see Teresa Watanabe, "Villaraigosa Backs Boycott of Arizona," *Los Angeles Times*, April 30, 2010.

33. For more information, see Julia Preston, "How the Dreamers Learned to Play Politics," *Politico*, September 9, 2017.

34. Laura Corrunker, "'Coming Out of the Shadows': DREAM Act Activism in the Context of Global Anti-deportation Activism," *Indiana Journal of Global Legal Studies* 19, no. 1 (Winter 2012).

35. For other books that focus on states with anti-immigrant legislation and undocumented youth, see Kathryn Abrams, *Open Hand, Closed Fist: Practices of Undocumented Organizing in a Hostile State* (Berkeley: University of California Press, 2022); Alexis M. Silver, *Shifting Boundaries: Immigrant Youth Negotiating National, State, and Small-Town Politics* (Stanford: Stanford University Press, 2018); Lisa Magaña and César S. Silva, *Empowered! ¡Empoderados! Latinos Transforming Arizona Politics* (Tucson: University of Arizona Press, 2021); Reyna Grande and Sonia Guiñansaca, *Somewhere We Are Human* (New York: Harper Via, 2022); Angela S. García, *Legal Passing: Navigating Undocumented Life and Local Immigration Law* (Berkeley: University of California Press, 2019).

36. Jesús Cisneros and Christian Bracho, "Coming Out of the Shadows and the Closet: Visibility Schemas Among Undocuqueer Immigrants," *Journal of Homosexuality* 66, no. 6 (2019): 715–34.

37. You can find the original post on Jonathan's Facebook profile: https://www.facebook.com/photo.php?fbid=10201544510947660&set=a.1447052009320&type=1&theater.

38. For more on "illegalization" and the works I am drawing my understandings from, please see Nicholas De Genova and Nathalie Peutz, eds., *The Deportation Regime: Sovereignty, Space, and the Freedom of Movement* (Durham, N.C.: Duke University Press, 2010); Cecilia

Menjívar and Daniel Kanstroom, *Constructing Illegality in America: Immigrant Experiences, Critiques, and Resistance* (New York: Cambridge University Press, 2013); Leisy J. Abrego, *Sacrificing Families: Navigating Laws, Labor, and Love Across Borders* (Stanford, Calif.: Stanford University Press, 2014).

39. Jotería studies is an academic field that grew organically from both Chicanx and immigrant communities and the academic discipline of Chicanx/Latinx studies with the aim of reclaiming the negative term "joto/a/x," often used to identify queer/LGBTQ community members in Latin America, Mexico, and Latinx Spanish-speaking communities in the United States. For literature on jotería studies, see Gloria Anzaldúa, *Borderlands / La Frontera: The New Mestiza* (San Francisco: Aunt Lute Books, 1987); Cherríe Moraga, *The Last Generation: Prose and Poetry* (Boston: South End Press, 1993); Michael R. Hames-García and Ernesto J. Martínez, eds., *Gay Latino Studies: A Critical Reader* (Durham, N.C.: Duke University Press, 2011); Michael R. Hames-García, "Jotería Studies, or The Political Is Personal," *Aztlán: A Journal of Chicano Studies* 39, no. 1 (Spring 2014).

40. Cherríe Moraga, "Queer Aztlán: the Re-formation of Chicano Tribe," in *Last Generation*, 145–74.

41. For more on futurities and imaginaries along with jotería and consciousness, see the foundational work of Emma Pérez, *The Decolonial Imaginary: Writing Chicanas into History* (Bloomington: Indiana University Press, 1999); and Chela Sandoval, *Methodology of the Oppressed* (Minneapolis: University of Minnesota Press, 2000).

42. Daniel Enrique Pérez, "Jotería Epistemologies: Mapping a Research Agenda, Unearthing a Lost Heritage, and Building 'Queer Aztlán,'" *Aztlán: A Journal of Chicano Studies* 39, no. 1 (2014): 143. Also see Daniel Enrique Pérez, "Toward a Mariposa Consciousness: Reimagining Queer Chicano and Latino Identities," *Aztlán: A Journal of Chicano Studies* 39, no. 2 (2014): 95–127.

43. Juan D. Ochoa, "Shine Bright Like a Diamond: Julio Salgado's Digital Art and Its Use of Jotería," *Social Justice* 42, no. 3–4 (2015).

44. Yvette J. Saavedra, "Of Chicana Lesbian Terrorists and Lesberadas: Recuperating the Lesbian/Queer Roots of Chicana Feminism, 1970–2000," *Feminist Formations* 34, no. 2 (Summer 2022): 99–124.

45. Ochoa, "Shine Bright," 193.

46. The *I Am Undocuqueer* collection by Julio Salgado in which Jonathan Perez was originally included can be found on the artivist's website under the section "Timeline," chronologized under "2012": https://www.juliosalgadoart.com/timeline/.

47. Melissa Autumn White, "Documenting the Undocumented: Toward a Queer Politics of No Borders," *Sexualities* 17, no. 8 (2014): 990.

48. For example, in November 2013, Jonathan made another post on Facebook containing a photograph of themself when younger with a caption reading, "El illegal inocente" (The innocent illegal): https://www.facebook.com/photo.php?fbid=10201606773144176&set=a.1447052009320&type=1&theater.

49. A particular organization that grew as a response to organizing at the intersecions of race and the immigrant rights movements is the UndocuBlack Network. They are also at the

forefront of intermovement coalition building between groups such as Black Lives Matter and immigrant rights organizing. You can find their website here: http://undocublack .org.

50. I follow arguments about citizenship and incorporation into the nation, and colonial and racial trains of thought, similar to those laid out in María Josefina Saldaña-Portillo's work *Indian Given: Racial Geographies Across Mexico and the United States* (Durham, N.C.: Duke University Press, 2016).

51. J. Perez and Barrera, "Jonathan Perez and Isaac Barrera" (see note 2 above). The video interview was made by the "Art, Media, Immigration" collective that organized the "Art, Media, Immigration" symposium at the University of New Mexico in 2012.

52. E. Pérez, *Decolonial Imaginary.*

53. For more on "embodied practice" and performance as archival practice, see Diana Taylor, *The Archive and the Repertoire: Performing Cultural Memory in the Americas* (Durham, N.C.: Duke University Press, 2007), 3–7.

54. Taylor, *Archive and the Repertoire*, 6–7.

55. I have transcribed the three videos I analyze of Jonathan Perez and Isaac Barrera in this section. The textual and visual analysis in this section is derived from these transcriptions.

56. The infiltration video of Jonathan can be found here: Dream Activist, "Undocumented Youth vs. Border Patrol Round 1—Mobile, Alabama," posted November 21, 2011, video, 3:39, https://youtu.be/iA54ErBfZ8E.

57. For more on the national networks created by undocumented youth, including NIYA and Dream Activist, see Rafael A. Martínez, "Counter Culture Youth: Immigrant Rights Activism and the Undocumented Youth Vanguard" (MA thesis, University of New Mexico, 2014).

58. A. García, *Legal Passing*, 134.

59. Jonathan and Isaac, along with NIYA, had begun to organize in anti-immigrant states, beginning with Arizona during the passing of its most widely covered anti-immigrant bill, SB–1070 (2009), which would lead to a political "sunbelt" of anti-immigrant legislation across the southern United States to states like Alabama. Alabama enacted HB 56 (June 9, 2011), a bill that made it legal for local police departments to collaborate with the DHS by contacting ICE to detain and deport undocumented individuals. This series of anti-immigrant legislation stems from the 287(g) program created under IIRIRA (1996), which I mention in chapter 1.

60. Leigh Raiford, *Imprisoned in a Luminous Glare: Photography and the African American Freedom Struggle* (Chapel Hill: University of North Carolina Press, 2013), 13.

61. Dream Activist, "Undocumented Youth vs. Border Patrol."

62. To read more on how Diana Taylor defines and uses "scenarios," see her book *The Archive and the Repertoire*, 29–33.

63. Taylor, *Archive and the Repertoire*, 29.

64. Taylor, *Archive and the Repertoire*, 13.

65. Taylor, *Archive and the Repertoire*, 31.

66. K. Chávez, *Queer Migration Politics*, 15.

67. Taylor, *Archive and the Repertoire*, 31.

68.   The interview was conducted by Chicanx studies scholar Dr. Irene Vásquez and recorded by community filmmaker/documentarian Daniel Sonis, who would be co-organizers of the "Everyday Practices of Popular Power: Art, Media, Immigration" symposium at the University of New Mexico during the fall of 2012. The interview was later uploaded to the "Art, Media, Immigration Net" YouTube channel that formed part of the symposium proceedings and video archive. The video can be accessed here: Irene Vásquez and Daniel Sonis, "Interview w Jonathan Perez and Isaac Barrera 12032011," posted January 27, 2016, video, 31:08, https://youtu.be/g9yXC_Q68gU.

69.   J. Perez and Barrera, "Jonathan Perez and Isaac Barrera" (see note 2 above).

70.   J. Perez and Barrera, "Jonathan Perez and Isaac Barrera."

71.   The year President Obama took office, 2009, the number of deportations was approximately 392,000, and it rose to a record high of approximately 419,000 in 2012. The majority were noncriminal immigrants and from the interior of the country. This is the period during which Jonathan and Isaac were organizing and decided to take their activism toward infiltrating a detention center. Information is from Ana Gonzalez-Barrera, "Record Number of Deportations in 2012," Pew Research Center, January 24, 2014, accessed December 27, 2019, https://www.pewresearch.org/fact-tank/2014/01/24/record-number-of-deportations-in-2012/.

72.   Vásquez and Sonis, "Interview w Jonathan Perez and Isaac Barrera" (see note 68 above).

73.   Vásquez and Sonis, "Interview w Jonathan Perez and Isaac Barrera."

74.   Vásquez and Sonis, "Interview w Jonathan Perez and Isaac Barrera."

75.   Vásquez and Sonis, "Interview w Jonathan Perez and Isaac Barrera."

76.   Mae Ngai, *Impossible Subjects: Illegal Aliens and the Making of Modern America* (Princeton, N.J.: Princeton University Press, 2014).

77.   Jessica Ordaz, *The Shadow of El Centro: A History of Migrant Incarceration and Solidarity* (Chapel Hill: University of North Carolina Press, 2021). Additionally, for more historical narratives on deportation's history and building a deportation regime, see Ethan Blue, *The Deportation Express: A History of America Through Forced Removal* (Berkeley: University of California Press, 2021).

78.   For more on how Ngai and Chomsky are using "illegality," see their books: Ngai, *Impossible Subjects*; and Aviva Chomsky, *Undocumented: How Immigration Became Illegal* (Boston: Beacon Press, 2014).

79.   J. Perez and Barrera, "Jonathan Perez and Isaac Barrera."

80.   J. Perez and Barrera, "Jonathan Perez and Isaac Barrera."

81.   J. Perez and Barrera, "Jonathan Perez and Isaac Barrera."

82.   J. Perez and Barrera, "Jonathan Perez and Isaac Barrera."

83.   Grace M. Cho, *Haunting the Korean Diaspora: Shame, Secrecy, and the Forgotten War* (Minneapolis: University of Minnesota Press, 2008).

84.   I am using the concept of "returning the gaze" stemming from scholarly work on "double consciousness" by W. E. B. Du Bois, Gloria Anzaldúa's understanding of borderlands / la frontera, and also film scholars like Fatimah Rony who talk about the "third eye" and the way filmmakers will create frames where a particular subject will "return the gaze" to the audience.

85.   J. Perez and Barrera, "Jonathan Perez and Isaac Barrera."

86.   J. Perez and Barrera, "Jonathan Perez and Isaac Barrera"; Dylan Rodríguez, "The Political Logic of the Non-profit Industrial Complex," in *The Revolution Will Not Be Funded: Beyond the Non-profit Industrial Complex*, ed. INCITE! (Boston: South End Press, 2007), 21.

87.   Blue-Green, *"Illegal" Lives: Immigrant/Refugee Struggles for Love and Freedom*, curated by Francisco Lefebre, art exhibition, University of New Mexico Art Museum, 2018.

88.   Lazarus Letcher, Blue-Green, Valeria de la Luz, and Mariella Saba, "Human Rights and Intersectional Coalition Building" (public lecture, Mapping Albuquerque Project, University of New Mexico, October 4, 2018).

89.   A scholar working in the critical field of abolition, "border imperialism," and decolonization is Harsha Walia. See Harsha Walia, *Undoing Border Imperialism* (Oakland, Calif.: AK Press, 2013).

Chapter 3

1.   NIYA's website can be found at http://theniya.org.

2.   In their article "Fearless Speech and the Discourse of Civility in *Salt of the Earth*," Scott Henkel and Vanessa Fonseca-Chávez outline the boundaries of "civility" to show that fearless speech requires individuals to "transgress the bounds placed on them." The transgressor must also understand the limitations and possibilities of certain spaces and actions, according to Henkel and Fonseca-Chávez. Scott Henkel and Vanessa Fonseca-Chávez, "Fearless Speech and the Discourse of Civility in *Salt of the Earth*," *Chiricú Journal* 1, no. 1 (2016): 19–38, quotes at 29.

3.   The quote comes from the *Latino USA* podcast episode titled "The Dream 9." The podcast can be accessed here: Latino USA, "#1542—The Dream 9," NPR.org, October 6, 2015, audio, 55:34, https://www.npr.org/2015/10/16/449200924/-1542-the-dream-9.

4.   Latino USA, "#1542—The Dream 9."

5.   Latino USA, "#1542—The Dream 9."

6.   For more information on media coverage of the #BringThemHome campaign, see Esther Yu-His Lee, "'Dream 9' Undocumented Youths Who Crossed the Border Clear First Hurdle to Asylum," *ThinkProgress*, August 6, 2013, accessed April 18, 2018.

7.   For a detailed outline of the course of events following the Dream 9 campaign, see Aura Bogado, "The Dream 9, One Year Later," *Colorlines*, July 22, 2014, https://colorlines.com/article/dream-9-one-year-later/.

8.   The DHS budget is self-reported by the agency on their website by fiscal year. The budget numbers can be found in the document titled "FY 2007 Performance Budget Overview," along with other reports on the DHS website: https://www.dhs.gov/publication/performance-budget-overview-fiscal-year-2007. For the fiscal report on detention and deportations, see DHS, "Immigration Enforcement Actions: 2007," December 2008, https://www.dhs.gov/xlibrary/assets/statistics/publications/enforcement_ar_07.pdf.

9.   Jeffrey S. Passel, D'Vera Cohn, and Ana Gonzalez-Barrera, "Net Migration from Mexico Falls to Zero—and Perhaps Less," Pew Research Center, April 23, 2012, https://www.pewresearch.org/hispanic/2012/04/23/net-migration-from-mexico-falls-to-zero-and-perhaps-less/.

10.   The traditional term used in the literature on self-returned undocumented immigrants was the Spanish masculine term "retornado." One of the recent changes in inclusive scholarship produced by critical scholars is using gender-neutral pronouns in the Spanish terminology—in this case, retornadx, as a means to bring awareness to the queer, transgender, and gender-fluid community who are self-returning to their countries of origin and experiencing violence due to transphobic and homophobic social and political conditions. For more literature on retornadxs, see Jill Anderson and Nin Solis, Los Otros Dreamers (Mexico City: self-published, 2014). Additionally, on deported migrants, see Beth C. Caldwell, *Deported Americans: Life After Deportation to Mexico* (Durham, N.C.: Duke University Press, 2019).

11.   I am drawing from sociologists in social media scholarship who use the term "cleavages" when studying or analyzing the way in which activists find a "political opening" or gaps in policies which they can use as strategies for their campaigns and activism. For more on cleavages as they relate to UYMs, see Walter Nicholls, *The DREAMers: How the Undocumented Youth Movement Transformed the Immigrant Rights Debate* (Stanford, Calif.: Stanford University Press, 2013).

12.   Historians like Mae Ngai have explained the quota system as using racial hierarchies to separate desired populations from undesired populations, with the latter given lower quotas or numbers in comparison to the former. For example, Mexico and Latin American countries, because of their proximity to the United States, were allowed smaller quotas of migrants coming from them to the United States. According to Ngai, the United States claims that the logic behind the quotas is the fact that large numbers of migrants come from those countries, but in reality race can be seen as the true logic. We can see race as a factor, for example, in the fact that Asian countries like China have a lower quota even though they are not in proximity to the United States geographically speaking; a large number of migrants have come from these countries, however, and the United States has historically had racial motives for denying them entry. And certain European countries whose people are white were prioritized in migration quotas. For more on quotas and race, see Mae Ngai, *Impossible Subjects: Illegal Aliens and the Making of Modern America* (Princeton, N.J.: Princeton University Press, 2014).

13.   The organizers were gracious enough to share meeting minutes, reports, and documents that helped with the production of this chapter as a way to understand the insights and internal discussions that led to the planning of the #BringThemHome campaign during the summer of 2013. The (un)documenting process requires a deep dive into the organizational archives of undocumented youth–led organizations like NIYA, which did not see the organization as a sustainable or long-term model because of the nature of their radical activism. Part of the (un)documenting process is to approach organizational archives understanding the pressure, stress, trauma, and concern that went along with even keeping records or archives to leave behind. A paper trail is not typically the goal or mission of an undocumented organizer.

14.   Mimi Thi Nguyen, *The Gift of Freedom: War, Debt, and Other Refugee Passages* (Durham, N.C.: Duke University Press, 2012), 45.

15. A documentary by filmmakers Alex Rivera and Cristina Ibarra focuses on NIYA's infiltration coordination, which included Marco Saavedra and Mohammad Abdollahi's story. Alex Rivera and Cristina Ibarra, dirs., *The Infiltrators* (Chicago Media Project, Naked Edge Films, 2019).

16. To learn more about the infiltration action by Marco Saavedra and Viridiana Martínez with NIYA, see Chris Sweeney, "DREAM Activists to Be Released from Broward Detention Center," *Broward Palm Beach New Times*, August 3, 2012, https://www .browardpalmbeach.com/news/dream-activists-to-be-released-from-broward-detention -center-6437427.

17. Nicholas De Genova and Nathalie Peutz, eds., *The Deportation Regime: Sovereignty, Space, and the Freedom of Movement* (Durham, N.C.: Duke University Press, 2010).

18. Arely Zimmerman, "Transmedia Testimonio: Examining Undocumented Youth's Political Activism in the Digital Age," *International Journal of Communication* 10 (2016): 1886–1906.

19. NIYA's YouTube channel was originally found at https://www.youtube.com/channel/ UCmVedomvjVwWeYZeZ9JJ6Kg/videos. The channel no longer exists, but records of many of the videos posted on it can be found through the Wayback Machine here: https://web.archive.org/web/20190728164955/https://www.youtube.com/channel/ UCmVedomvjVwWeYZeZ9JJ6Kg/videos.

20. I use the reporting by *Latino USA*, which compiled biographic depictions of the Dream 9 activists that can be found here (along with additional journalistic reports and interviews): Latino USA, "The Dream 9," Google Arts and Culture, October 16, 2015, https:// artsandculture.google.com/exhibit/the-dream-9-latino-usa/agIi4BjHN3Z-Lg?hl=en.

21. Bogado, "One Year Later."

22. To read more on Lizbeth Mateo's trajectory before and after law school at Santa Clara University, see Amy B. Wang, "In a First, an Undocumented Immigrant Is Appointed to a Statewide Post in California," *Washington Post*, March 15, 2018, https://www .washingtonpost.com/news/post-nation/wp/2018/03/15/in-a-first-an-undocumented -immigrant-is-appointed-to-a-statewide-post-in-california/#.

23. The full video featuring Lizbeth Mateo was captured and produced by NIYA on their YouTube channel: National Immigrant Youth Alliance (NIYA), "Bring Them Home: Lizbeth Mateo Checking In from Oaxaca, Mexico," July 17, 2013, accessed July 11, 2019, https:// youtu.be/sDUyCszvQgk. This video is no longer available on YouTube.

24. Bogado, "One Year Later."

25. The full video featuring Marco Saavedra was captured and produced by NIYA on their YouTube channel: National Immigrant Youth Alliance (NIYA), "Bring Them Home: Marco Saavedra Checking In from Mexico," July 18, 2013, accessed July 14, 2019, https:// youtu.be/Eb8qooVJ1Ys. This video is no longer available on YouTube.

26. As mentioned in previous chapters, undocu-queer identity refers to the intersection of identifying as undocumented and queer. The term was coined by artivist Julio Salgado.

27. The full video featuring Lulu Martínez was captured and produced by NIYA on their YouTube channel. National Immigrant Youth Alliance (NIYA), "Bring Them Home: Lulu

Martinez Checking In from Mexico City," July 20, 2013, accessed July 14, 2019, https://youtu.be/BAvoS2QdHSg. This video is no longer available on YouTube.

28.   Grace M. Cho, *Haunting the Korean Diaspora: Shame, Secrecy, and the Forgotten War* (Minneapolis: University of Minnesota Press, 2008).

29.   I make the distinction that the name "the Dream 9" was primarily used by the media. NIYA for the most part used the hashtag and name #BringThemHome.

30.   National Immigration Youth Alliance (NIYA), "Luis León," July 23, 2013. This video was originally posted on YouTube (accessed July 16, 2019), but has since been taken down.

31.   Alexis M. Silver, *Shifting Boundaries: Immigrant Youth Negotiating National, State, and Small-Town Politics* (Stanford, Calif.: Stanford University Press, 2018), 11.

32.   The full video featuring Ceferino Santiago was captured and produced by NIYA on their YouTube channel. National Immigrant Youth Alliance (NIYA), "Ceferino Santiago," July 22, 2013, accessed July 14, 2019, https://youtu.be/pQntxIXbhHc. The video is no longer available on YouTube.

33.   The full video featuring Claudia Amaro was captured and produced by NIYA on their YouTube channel. National Immigrant Youth Alliance (NIYA), "Claudia Amaro," July 24, 2013, accessed July 14, 2019, https://youtu.be/9ThRorPMHbQ. The video is no longer available on YouTube.

34.   NIYA, "Claudia Amaro."

35.   *Latino USA* included brief biographies of the Dream 9 participants that can be found in Latino USA, "Dream 9" (see note 20 above).

36.   *Latino USA's* podcast titled "#1542—The Dream 9" followed the activists on the Mexican side of the border and through their crossing of the Mexico-U.S. border. See Latino USA, "#1542—The Dream 9" (see note 3 above).

37.   The attorney representing the Dream 9 activists was interviewed by *Latino USA*. Latino USA, "#1542—The Dream 9."

38.   For the audiovisual montage, see Latino USA, "Dream 9" (see note 20 above).

39.   According to federal policy under IIRIRA, which was passed during President Bill Clinton's administration.

40.   Journalist Aura Bogado, who covered the Dream 9, reports that the action received 10,000 viewers on Ustream live feed. Her article can be found here: Aura Bogado, "Undocumented Activists Take a Giant Risk to Return Home," *Colorlines*, July 23, 2013, https://www.colorlines.com/articles/undocumented-activists-take-giant-risk-return-home.

41.   Information on Eloy Detention Center can be found on the ICE website here: https://www.ice.gov/detention-facility/eloy-detention-center.

42.   National Immigrant Youth Alliance (NIYA), "María Peniche Check-In Video," July 29, 2013. This video was originally posted on YouTube (accessed July 13, 2019) but has since been taken down.

43.   The full audio of Lizbeth Mateo's detention check-in was produced as a video by NIYA. National Immigrant Youth Alliance (NIYA), "Lizbeth Mateo: 'I Don't Know What They've Done to the Women Here . . .'—Eloy Prison," July 30, 2013, accessed July 14, 2019, https://youtu.be/j3AEa-gzZ7E. This video, originally on NIYA's YouTube channel, is no longer available.

44. Kelly Lytle Hernández, *Migra! A History of the U.S. Border Patrol* (Berkeley: University of California Press, 2010).

45. Jessica Ordaz, *The Shadow of El Centro: A History of Migrant Incarceration and Solidarity* (Chapel Hill: University of North Carolina Press, 2021), 159.

46. Ordaz, *Shadow of El Centro*, 160.

47. De Genova and Peutz, *Deportation Regime*.

48. The full audio of Claudia Amaro's detention check-in was produced as a video by NIYA on its YouTube channel: National Immigrant Youth Alliance (NIYA), "A Call from the Eloy Detention Center: Claudia Amaro," July 23, 2013, accessed July 13, 2019, https://youtu.be/DgmVQoeXxYE. This video is no longer available on YouTube.

49. Latino USA, "#1542—The Dream 9."

50. As mentioned in chapter 2, for more historical examples of immigrant resistance and documentation of violence in detention, see Ordaz, *Shadow of El Centro*. See also Lytle Hernández, *Migra!*

51. De Genova and Peutz, *Deportation Regime*.

52. To read more about the Dream 30 campaign and the subsequent third campaign with approximately 150 more participants, see Latino Voices, "150 Undocumented Immigrants to Enter U.S. in Border-Crossing Demonstration," *HuffPost*, March 11, 2014, https://www.huffpost.com/entry/bring-them-home-campaign_n_4940897.

53. The full video featuring Jessica was originally captured and produced by NIYA on their YouTube channel. National Immigrant Youth Alliance (NIYA), "BringThemHome: Jessica 16, Fighting to Come Home to Arizona," September 28, 2013, accessed July 14, 2019, https://youtu.be/KBUkHVxUqM8. The video is no longer available on YouTube.

54. The full video featuring Ana was originally captured and produced by NIYA on their YouTube channel: National Immigrant Youth Alliance (NIYA), "Bring Them Home: Ana, 20, Anxious to Come Home to Arizona!," September 28, 2013, accessed on July 18, 2019, https://youtu.be/JiK6-tuPomk. The video is no longer available on YouTube.

55. Lawrence La Fountain-Stokes, "Queer Ducks, Puerto Rican Patos, and Jewish-American Feygelekh: Birds and the Cultural Representation of Homosexuality," *Centro Journal* 19, no. 1 (2007): 192–229.

56. Daniel Enrique Pérez, "Toward a Mariposa Consciousness: Reimagining Queer Chicano and Latino Identities," *Aztlán: A Journal of Chicano Studies* 39, no. 2 (2014): 95–127.

57. To read more on Lizbeth Mateo's post in California, see Wang, "Undocumented Immigrant Is Appointed."

58. Rivera, *Infiltrators*.

59. To read more on Lulu Martínez's asylum announcement, see Jacqueline Serrato, "Queer Chicagoan Who Turned Herself In to Border Patrol Granted Asylum," *Chicago Tribune*, June 24, 2018.

60. D'Vera Cohn, Jeffrey S. Passel, and Ana Gonzalez-Barrera, "Rise in U.S. Immigrants from El Salvador, Guatemala and Honduras Outpaces Growth from Elsewhere," Pew Research Center, December 7, 2017, https://www.pewresearch.org/hispanic/2017/12/07/rise-in-u-s-immigrants-from-el-salvador-guatemala-and-honduras-outpaces-growth-from-elsewhere/.

Chapter 4

1.   Yosimar Reyes's poem can be found performed for the Define American YouTube channel here: Yosimar Reyes, "Share the UndocuJoy! | Define American," August 22, 2017, video, 3:05, https://youtu.be/V1kkdBjASfc.

2.   For more on undocu-joy, see the website of Elena Calderon, who describes herself as "a former undocumented girl experiencing joy": https://undocujoy.home.blog/2023/05/10/voices-through-collage-and-visual-poems/.

3.   The Deferred Action for Childhood Arrivals (DACA) program is explained and analyzed in the introduction of this book, in the section "Mapping Undocumented Youth Studies," in relation to neoliberal logics of incorporation and exclusion of certain immigration populations.

4.   Kent A. Ono and John M. Sloop, *Shifting Borders: Rhetoric, Immigration, and California's Proposition 187* (Philadelphia: Temple University Press, 2002).

5.   Cumbiatón's website can be accessed here: https://www.cumbiaton.org/. Their website launch was announced on January 30, 2019, on their Instagram account. The announcement can be found here: https://www.instagram.com/p/BtRXYtIBC5p/?igshid=16lr91cmmz20e.

6.   The process of heightened detention and deportation is one detailed throughout the book. In chapter 1, I refer to the 1990s as a period of growth in the neoliberal agenda prioritizing movement of global capital and the beginning of immigration policies restricting mobility and criminalizing immigration to the United States in law. In the 2000s the monitoring of the Mexico-U.S. borderlands moved to the interior of the country after the "9/11" event that led to the tremendous rise of detention and deportations with the establishment of the Department of Homeland Security.

7.   In this book, I use "forty-fifth U.S. president" or "Forty-Five" to refer to the forty-fifth president of the United States of America as a form of resistance in my writing and in praxis. I am inspired to omit the name of the forty-fifth U.S. president as many of the social movements that grew during his presidency chose to, including the undocumented movements that are the focus of this research.

8.   I use the term "womxn" as it is the preferred identifier used by individuals within the Cumbiatón movement, to highlight transgender and gender-fluid representations and to combat the heteronormative interpretations of gender performance traditionally prescribed and often suggested by the word "women." Throughout the book I use preferred gender identifiers when known or identified, and I use gender-fluid identifiers for organizers described in the book.

9.   Ana Gonzalez-Barrera and Jens Manuel Krogstad, "U.S. Immigration Deportations Declined in 2014, but Remain Near Record High," Pew Research Center, August 31, 2016, https://www.pewresearch.org/short-reads/2016/08/31/u-s-immigrant-deportations-declined-in-2014-but-remain-near-record-high/.

10.   Eduardo Bonilla-Silva, "Toward a New Political Praxis for Trumpamerica: New Directions in Critical Race Theory," *American Behavioral Scientist* 63, no. 13 (2019): 1776–88, https://doi.org/10.1177/0002764219842614.

11.   David Harvey, *A Brief History of Neoliberalism* (New York: Oxford University Press, 2005), 82.

12.   For more information on the targeting of immigrant activists under the forty-fifth president's administration, see the following critical journalistic coverage of the topic: John Burnett, "See the 20+ Immigration Activists Arrested Under Trump," *NPR*, March 16, 2018, https://www.npr.org/2018/03/16/591879718/see-the-20-immigration-activists -arrested-under-trump; Gaby Del Valle, "ICE Keeps Arresting Prominent Immigration Activists: They Think They're Being Targeted," *Vice*, August 24, 2019, https://www.vice .com/en/article/ywady5/ice-keeps-arresting-prominent-immigration-activists-they -think-theyre-being-targeted; Nick Pinto, "Across the U.S., Trump Used ICE to Crack Down on Immigration Activists," *The Intercept*, November 1, 2020, https://theintercept .com/2020/11/01/ice-immigration-activists-map/.

13.   Carolina Valdivia, "Undocumented Young Adults' Heightened Vulnerability in the Trump Era," in *We Are Not Dreamers: Undocumented Scholars Theorize Undocumented Life in the United States*, ed. Leisy J. Abrego and Genevieve Negrón-Gonzales (Durham, N.C.: Duke University Press, 2020), 128. Additionally, see Liliana E. Castrellón, Alonso R. Reyna Rivarola, and Gerardo R. López, "We Are Not Alternative Facts: Feeling, Existing, and Resistance in the Era of Trump," *International Journal of Qualitative Studies in Education* 30, no. 10 (2017): 936–45.

14.   Valdivia, "Heightened Vulnerability," 129.

15.   At the eight-year mark of the DACA program's existence, only 643,560 undocumented youth in total have benefited from the program, while the general undocumented population in the United States is closer to 11 million. This general undocumented population does not have access to any level of protection from deportation or opportunities to legally work in the country. Up-to-date DACA numbers can be found on the Department of Homeland Security website here: https://www.uscis.gov/sites/ default/files/document/data/Approximate%20Active%20DACA%20Receipts %20-%20March%2031%2C%202020.pdf. The literature of scholars challenging the DREAMer narrative has grown exponentially. For some of the works and scholars creating this literature, see Karma R. Chávez, *Queer Migration Politics: Activist Rhetoric and Coalitional Possibilities*, Feminist Media Studies Series (Urbana: University of Illinois Press, 2013); Genevieve Negrón-Gonzales, "Undocumented, Unafraid and Unapologetic: Re-articulatory Practices and Migrant Youth 'Illegality,'" *Latino Studies* 12, no. 2 (2014): 259–78, https://doi.org/10.1057/lst.2014.20; and Abrego and Negrón-Gonzales, *We Are Not Dreamers*.

16.   Joel Sati, "'Other' Borders: The Illegal as Normative Metaphor," in Abrego and Negrón-Gonzales, *We Are Not Dreamers*, 25.

17.   For coverage of contemporary demonstrations by undocumented organizers during President Biden's administration, see Franco Ordoñez, "On Immigration, Activists' Demands May Exceed Biden Realities," *NPR*, December 13, 2020, https://www.npr.org/2020/12/ 13/944791054/on-immigration-activists-demands-may-exceed-biden-realities.

18.   Henry Jenkins, *Convergence Culture: Where Old and New Media Collide* (New York: New York University Press, 2006), 282.

19. I am defining my use of the term "transmedia-based archive" here in this chapter while acknowledging that other scholars also use "transmedia-based archive"; my work is very much in conversation with their ongoing work.

20. Chon Noriega is credited with coining the terms "artivist" and "artivism." See Chon A. Noriega, *Just Another Poster?* (Los Angeles: The Regents of the University of California Art Museum, 2001).

21. Carlos Aguilar, "Undocumented Critical Theory," *Cultural Studies Critical Methodologies* 19, no. 3 (2019): 152–60.

22. Michel-Rolph Trouillot, *Silencing the Past: Power and the Production of History* (Boston: Beacon Press, 2015), 13–14.

23. Trouillot, *Silencing the Past*, 4–7.

24. See my treatment and analysis of *The Archive and the Repertoire* by Diana Taylor (Durham, N.C.: Duke University Pess, 2003) earlier in my introduction and subsequent chapters.

25. Jamie A. Lee, *Producing the Archival Body* (New York: Routledge, 2021), 37.

26. One of Lee's major interventions in critical archival studies is to argue that rather than thinking of having a "whole" or complete archive, scholars should think of the idea of having archives go through a process of "unbecoming." Lee's work expands on this notion of "unbecoming" through oral history practices, unpacking the power relations that exist in collaboratively producing an archival record and telling a collective story by means of the interviewer and interviewee relationship. J. Lee, *Producing the Archival Body*.

27. Arely M. Zimmerman, "Transmedia Testimonio: Examining Undocumented Youth's Political Activism in the Digital Age," *International Journal of Communication* 10 (2016): 1887.

28. For more literature on Los Angeles neighborhoods and racial and ethnic divisions, see George J. Sánchez, *Becoming Mexican American: Ethnicity, Culture, and Identity in Chicano Los Angeles, 1900–1945* (New York: Oxford University Press, 1993); Laura Pulido, *Black, Brown, Yellow, and Left: Radical Activism in Southern California* (Berkeley: University of California Press, 2006); Luis Alvarez, *The Power of the Zoot: Youth Culture and Resistance During World War II* (Berkeley: University of California Press, 2009); Daniel Widener, *Black Arts West: Culture and Struggle in Postwar Los Angeles* (Durham, N.C.: Duke University Press, 2010).

29. Gaye Theresa Johnson, *Spaces of Conflict, Sounds of Solidarity: Music, Race, and Spatial Entitlement in Los Angeles* (Berkeley: University of California Press, 2013), 29.

30. The first post by Cumbiatón on their Instagram account @Cumbiatón_la shared their first party using the hashtag #Cumbiatón on May 19, 2017, at First Street Pool & Billiards in Boyle Heights. The post can be seen here: https://www.instagram.com/p/BUP5oJjDYHK/?igshid=1w24toz12j5db.

31. George Lipsitz, *The Possessive Investment in Whiteness: How White People Profit from Identity Politics* (Philadelphia: Temple University Press, 2006). Gentrification has had tremendous impacts on BIPOC and immigrant communities. In a way, neoliberal discourse appears to be welcoming to diversity and accepting of cultural difference by absorbing cultural representation, but it simultaneously displaces people of color. Harvey, in *A Brief History of Neoliberalism*, was among the first to outline the ways in which uneven geog-

raphies developed globally as nation-states adopted the neoliberal state model. At the micro level of cities and neighborhoods, scholars such as George Lipsitz linked these uneven geographies to historic redlining initiatives that used racial capitalist logics to limit mobility of capital into certain locations while using historically marginalized neighborhoods as extractive labor.

32.   Julio Salgado is credited with coining and first using the term "undocuqueer" in his art series *I Am Undocuqueer* in 2012. The term aims to intersect the experiences and identities of being undocumented and queer. The series can be found on Salgado's website, in the "Timeline" section, here: https://www.juliosalgadoart.com/timeline/.

33.   "Intersectionality" is a term coined by law and race scholar Kimberlé Crenshaw while exploring the ways in which the legal system overwhelmingly marginalized and disenfranchised subjects of color whose identities were not accounted for or represented in the legal decision-making process.

34.   I draw on the information shared by the Cumbiatón team members, including how each of the organizers self-identifies, from a conference panel presentation that took place on October 23, 2020: Sizzle Fantastic, Normz La Oaxaqueña, Funky Caramelo, Julio Salgado, and Paolo Riveros, "The Politics of Partying: Undocumented Artists Creating Nightlife Political Spaces Through Music and Art" (panel at the Persist conference, Women's Resource Center, University of California, Riverside, October 23, 2020). I attended the panel presentation and took detailed notes that assisted my development of this chapter. Information on the 2020 Persist conference can be accessed at https://persist.ucr.edu/archives/2020.

35.   For the brief history provided in this section on cumbia, reggaetón, and other Latin American–inspired musical selections in the Cumbiatón movement, I am drawing on Deborah Pacini Hernandez, Oye Como Va! *Hybridity and Identity in Latino Popular Music* (Philadelphia: Temple University Press, 2010).

36.   Sonideros are defined by Deborah Pacini Hernandez as "mobile sound systems enhanced by high-tech light shows, smoke machines, and sonic special effects." She adds that they "have been another key channel for disseminating cumbia throughout the United States." Pacini Hernandez, Oye Como Va, 126. Also see Cathy Ragland, Música Norteña: *Mexican Migrants Creating a Nation Between Nations* (Philadelphia: Temple University Press, 2009), for more history and studies of sonideros.

37.   The Instagram post "Cumbia 101" can be read here: https://www.instagram.com/p/CBjuzfNg8T5/?igshid=14y1610kncif5.

38.   The "La Cumbia es Cultura" slogan first appeared in Cumbiatón's events lineup on June 15, 2018, their "Scumbiatón" event. In their Instagram post, Cumbiatón announced that prints with the "La Cumbia es Cultura" slogan would be available for purchase, and that the first thirty prints would be given free to the first thirty people to enter the event. The Instagram post can be found here: https://www.instagram.com/p/BkDoOyKhUlr/?igshid=gxzt21vybiyg.

39.   Raquel Z. Rivera, Wayne Marshall, and Deborah Pacini Hernandez, eds., *Reggaeton* (Durham, N.C.: Duke University Press, 2009).

40.   Rivera, Marshall, and Pacini Hernandez, introduction to *Reggaeton*, 7.

41. For more information on the immigrant rights marches of 2006, see René Galindo, "Repartitioning the National Community: Political Visibility and Voice for Undocumented Immigrants in the Spring 2006 Immigration Rights Marches," *Aztlán* 35, no. 2 (2010): 37–64.

42. The three additions to the Cumbiatón team—Paolo Riveros, DJ Funky Caramelo, and Julio Salgado—were announced via the Cumbiatón Instagram account. The first to be announced was Julio Salgado; the post can be found here: https://www.instagram.com/p/Bdl5UNXj2Qj/?igshid=qbwhbgrwj5jg.

43. Sasha Costanza-Chock, *Out of the Shadows, Into the Streets! Transmedia Organizing and the Immigrant Rights Movement* (Cambridge, Mass.: MIT Press, 2014), 114.

44. Sizzle Fantastic et al., "Politics of Partying" (see note 34 above).

45. Francisco J. Galarte, *Brown Trans Figurations: Rethinking Race, Gender, and Sexuality in Chicanx/Latinx Studies* (Austin: University of Texas Press, 2021), 8.

46. J. Lee, *Producing the Archival Body*, 37.

47. One common theme expressed by Cumbiatón organizers at the Persist conference is that each one of them has dealt with the trauma of deportation of a loved one among family, friends, organizers, and community members.

48. Sizzle Fantastic et al., "Politics of Partying."

49. This occurred in 2011, before DACA in 2012.

50. Sumi Cho, Kimberlé Williams Crenshaw, and Leslie McCall, "Towards a Field of Intersectionality Studies: Theory, Applications, and Praxis," *Journal of Women in Culture and Society* 38, no. 4 (2013): 794.

51. Silva Mathema, "Keeping Families Together: Why All Americans Should Care About What Happens to Unauthorized Immigrants," Center for American Progress, March 16, 2017, https://www.americanprogress.org/article/keeping-families-together/.

52. The T-shirt designs I am referencing can be found on the Cumbiatón Flickr page in the album "Cumbiatón One Year Anniversary Pt. 2" here: https://www.flickr.com/photos/157517215@N08/albums/72157696333962252.

53. Those images can be accessed here: https://www.flickr.com/photos/157517215@N08/albums/72157710938835703.

Conclusion

1. Jodi Melamed, *Represent and Destroy: Rationalizing Violence in the New Racial Capitalism* (Minneapolis: University of Minnesota Press, 2011).

2. Melamed, *Represent and Destroy*, 42, 138–40, 151–55.

3. Eduardo Bonilla-Silva, "Toward a New Political Praxis for Trumpamerica: New Directions in Critical Race Theory," *American Behavioral Scientist* 63, no. 13 (2019): 1776–88.

4. Eduardo Bonilla-Silva, *Racism Without Racists: Color-Blind Racism and the Persistence of Racial Inequality in America*, 5th ed. (Lanham, Md.: Rowman & Littlefield, 2018).

5. Bonilla-Silva, "Toward a New Political Praxis," 1779.

6. Bonilla-Silva, "Toward a New Political Praxis," 1779.

7. Bonilla-Silva, "Toward a New Political Praxis," 1783.

8. Bonilla-Silva, "Toward a New Political Praxis," 1784.

9. On Forty-Five's announcement about ending DACA, see David Nakamura, "Trump Administration Announces End of Immigration Protection Program for 'Dreamers,'" *Washington Post*, Politics, September 5, 2017.

10. To read more on Forty-Five's announcements about negotiating over DACA in hopes of building a reinforced border wall at the Mexico-U.S. border, see David Jackson, "Trump Offers DACA Protections in Exchange for Border Wall; Democrats Opposed," *USA Today*, Politics, January 19, 2019.

11. U.S. Department of Homeland Security (DHS), "Additional Information: DACA Decision in State of Texas, et al., v. United States of America, et al., 1:18-CV–00068, (SD Texas July 16, 2021) ('Texas II')," U.S. Citizenship and Immigration Services (website), accessed October 5, 2022, https://www.uscis.gov/humanitarian/consideration-of-deferred-action -for-childhood-arrivals-daca/additional-information-daca-decision-in-state-of-texas-et -al-v-united-states-of-america-et-al-118-cv.

12. For further reading on the "zero-tolerance" enforcement policy by Forty-Five's administration, see William A. Kandel, *The Trump Administration's "Zero Tolerance" Immigration Enforcement Policy* (Washington, D.C.: Congressional Research Service, 2018).

13. Yana Kunichoff, "Sanctuary in Your City, in Your Home, in Your Church, in Your School, from Detention, from Deportation, from Displacement, from Police Violence," *In These Times*, May 17, 2017, https://inthesetimes.com/features/sanctuary_cities_movement _trump.html.

14. Jonathan Perez and Isaac Barrera remain active in the Immigrant Youth Coalition (IYC) based out of Southern California. The IYC's website details a full range of campaigns to abolish ICE and efforts to shut down transgender detention. The website can be found here: http://theiyc.org.

15. For more on the #AbolishICE movement, see Peter L. Markowitz, "After ICE: A New Humane and Effective Immigration Enforcement Paradigm," *Wake Forest Law Review* 55, no. 1 (2020): 89–144.

16. This shift in policy was a drastic change to the immigration detention practices that had been in force since the Flores Settlement Agreement of 1993. To read more on family separation and the history of the Flores Settlement Agreement of 1993 in the context of the Trumpamerica era, see Sarah Herman Peck and Ben Harrington, *The "Flores Settlement" and Alien Families Apprehended at the U.S. Border: Frequently Asked Questions* (Washington, D.C.: Congressional Research Service, 2018).

17. For more information on the "Dream 30," with which Elvira Arellano crossed to the United States again, see The Stream Team, "#Dream30 Detained After Public Border Crossing," *Al Jazeera America*, The Stream Blog, September 30, 2015, http://america .aljazeera.com/watch/shows/the-stream/the-stream-officialblog/2013/9/30/-dream30 -detainedafterpublicbordercrossing.html. For more information on the "Dream 150," with which Elvira Arellano also crossed to the United States, see "150 Undocumented Immigrants to Enter U.S. in Border-Crossing Demonstration," *HuffPost*, Latino Voices, March 11, 2014, https://www.huffpost.com/entry/bring-them-home-campaign-_n _4940897.

BIBLIOGRAPHY

Abrams, Kathryn. *Open Hand, Closed Fist: Practices of Undocumented Organizing in a Hostile State.* Berkeley: University of California Press, 2022.

Abrego, Leisy J. *Sacrificing Families: Navigating Laws, Labor, and Love Across Borders.* Stanford: Stanford University Press, 2014.

Abrego, Leisy J., and Genevieve Negrón-Gonzales, eds. *We Are Not Dreamers: Undocumented Scholars Theorize Undocumented Life in the United States.* Durham, N.C.: Duke University Press, 2020.

Aguilar, Carlos. "Undocumented Critical Theory." *Cultural Studies Critical Methodologies* 19, no. 3 (2019): 152–60.

Ahmed, Sara. *On Being Included: Racism and Diversity in Institutional Life.* Durham, N.C.: Duke University Press, 2012.

Alvarez, Luis. *The Power of the Zoot: Youth Culture and Resistance During World War II.* Berkeley: University of California Press, 2009.

Anderson, Jill, and Nin Solis. *Los Otros Dreamers.* Mexico City: self-published, 2014.

Anzaldúa, Gloria E. *Borderlands / La Frontera: The New Mestiza.* San Francisco: Aunt Lute Books, 1987.

Anzaldúa, Gloria E., and Cherríe Moraga. *this bridge we call home: radical visions of transformation.* New York: Routledge, 2002.

Barron, Kyle. "Sanctuary: A Movement Redefined." *NACLA Report on the Americas* 49, no. 2 (2017): 190–97.

Bauboöck, Rainer. *Transnational Citizenship: Membership and Rights in International Migration.* Aldershot, England: Edward Elgar Publishing Company, 1994.

Blackwell, Maylei. *¡Chicana Power! Contested Histories of Feminism in the Chicano Movement.* Austin: University of Texas Press, 2011.

Blackwell, Maylei, Laura Briggs, and Mignonette Chiu. "Transnational Feminisms Roundtable." *Frontiers: A Journal of Women's Studies* 36, no. 3 (2015): 1–24.

Blue, Ethan. *The Deportation Express: A History of America Through Forced Removal.* Berkeley: University of California Press, 2021.

Bonilla-Silva, Eduardo. *Racism Without Racists: Color-Blind Racism and the Persistence of Racial Inequality in America.* Lanham, Md.: Rowman & Littlefield, 2009.

Bonilla-Silva, Eduardo. "Toward a New Political Praxis for Trumpamerica: New Directions in Critical Race Theory." *American Behavioral Scientist* 63, no. 13 (2019): 1776–88.

Bowden, Charles. *Juárez: The Laboratory of Our Future.* New York: Aperture, 1998.

Cabrera, Gabrielle. "Disrupting Diversity: Undocumented Students in the Neoliberal University." In Abrego and Negrón-Gonzales, *We Are Not Dreamers*, 66–86.

Cacho, Lisa Marie. *Social Death: Racialized Rightlessness and the Criminalization of the Unprotected.* New York: NYU Press, 2012.

Cadava, Geraldo L. *Standing on Common Ground: The Making of a Sunbelt Borderlands.* Cambridge, Mass.: Harvard University Press, 2013.

Cadenas, Germán, and Elizabeth Kiehne. "The Undocumented Advantage: Intersectional Predictors of Critical Consciousness and Academic Performance Among U.S. Latinxs." *Journal of Latinx Psychology* 9, no. 4 (2021): 326–43.

Caldwell, Beth C. *Deported Americans: Life After Deportation to Mexico.* Durham, N.C.: Duke University Press, 2019.

Castrellón, Liliana E., Alonso R. Reyna Rivarola, and Gerardo R. López. "We Are Not Alternative Facts: Feeling, Existing, and Resistance in the Era of Trump." *International Journal of Qualitative Studies in Education* 30, no. 10 (2017): 936–45.

Chang, Aurora. *The Struggles of Identity, Education, and Agency in the Lives of Undocumented Students: The Burden of Hyperdocumentation.* San Bernardino: Palgrave Macmillan, 2018.

Chávez, Karma R. *Queer Migration Politics: Activist Rhetoric and Coalitional Possibilities.* Urbana: University of Illinois Press, 2013.

Chavez, Leo. *The Latino Threat: Constructing Immigrants, Citizens, and the Nation.* Stanford, Calif.: Stanford University Press, 2013.

Cho, Grace M. *Haunting the Korean Diaspora: Shame, Secrecy, and the Forgotten War.* Minneapolis: University of Minnesota Press, 2008.

Cho, Sumi, Kimberlé Williams Crenshaw, and Leslie McCall. "Towards a Field of Intersectionality Studies: Theory, Applications, and Praxis." *Journal of Women in Culture and Society* 38, no. 4 (2014): 785–810.

Chomsky, Aviva. *Undocumented: How Immigration Became Illegal.* Boston: Beacon Press, 2014.

Cisneros, Jesús, and Christian Bracho. "Coming Out of the Shadows and the Closet: Visibility Schemas Among Undocuqueer Immigrants." *Journal of Homosexuality* 66, no. 6 (2019): 715–34.

Cisneros, Jesús, Diana Valdivia, Alonso R. Reyna Rivarola, and Felecia Russell. "'I'm Here to Fight Along With You': Undocumented Student Resource Centers Creating Possibilities." *Journal of Diversity in Higher Education* 15, no. 5 (2022): 607–16.

Cornejo Villavicencio, Karla. *The Undocumented Americans.* New York: One World, 2020.

Corrunker, Laura. "'Coming Out of the Shadows': DREAM Act Activism in the Context of Global Anti-deportation Activism." *Indiana Journal of Global Legal Studies* 19, no. 1 (Winter 2012): 143–68.

Costanza-Chock, Sasha. *Out of the Shadows, Into the Streets! Transmedia Organizing and the Immigrant Rights Movement.* Cambridge, Mass.: MIT Press, 2014.

Costanza-Chock, Sasha. "Se Ve, Se Siente: Transmedia Mobilization in the Los Angeles Immigrant Rights Movement." PhD dissertation, University of Southern California, 2010.

Coutin, Susan B. *Nations of Emigrants: Shifting Boundaries of Citizenship in El Salvador and the United States.* Ithaca, N.Y.: Cornell University Press, 2007.

Crittenden, Ann. *Sanctuary: A Story of American Conscience and Law in Collision.* New York: Grove Press, 1988.

De Genova, Nicholas. "The Queer Politics of Migration: Reflections on 'Illegality' and Incorrigibility." *Studies in Social Justice* 4, no. 2 (2010): 101–26.

De Genova, Nicholas, and Nathalie Peutz, eds. *The Deportation Regime: Sovereignty, Space, and the Freedom of Movement.* Durham, N.C.: Duke University Press, 2013.

Derrida, Jacques. *Archive Fever: A Freudian Impression.* Chicago: University of Chicago Press, 1996.

Escudero, Kevin. *Organizing While Undocumented: Immigrant Youth's Political Activism Under the Law.* New York: New York University Press, 2020.

Espinoza, Dionne, María Eugenia Cotera, and Maylei Blackwell, eds. *Chicana Movidas: New Narratives of Activism and Feminism in the Movement Era.* Austin: University of Texas Press, 2018.

Ferguson, Roderick A. *The Reorder of Things: The University and Its Pedagogies of Minority Difference.* Minneapolis: University of Minnesota Press, 2012.

Fernández, Delia. "Immigrants (Re)make the City (and the Suburbs): Race, Ethnicity, and Labor." *Journal of Urban History* 47, no. 3 (2021): 687–93.

Ferraris, Maurizio. *Documentality: Why It Is Necessary to Leave Traces.* Bronx, N.Y.: Fordham University Press, 2013.

Flores-González, Nilda, and Ruth Gomberg-Muñoz. "FLOResiste: Transnational Labor, Motherhood, and Activism." In Flores-González et al., *Immigrant Women Workers,* 262–304.

Flores-González, Nilda, Anna Romina Guevarra, Maura Toro-Morn, and Grace Chang, eds. *Immigrant Women Workers in the Neoliberal Age.* Urbana: University of Illinois Press, 2013.

Fonseca-Chávez, Vanessa. *Colonial Legacies in Chicana/o Literature and Culture: Looking Through the Kaleidoscope.* Tucson: University of Arizona Press, 2020.

Foucault, Michel. *The Archaeology of Knowledge and the Discourse on Language.* New York: Pantheon Books, 1972.

Foucault, Michel. *Fearless Speech.* Edited by Joseph Pearson. Los Angeles: Semiotext(e), 2001.

Foucault, Michel. *The History of Sexuality,* Volume 1: *An Introduction.* New York: Vintage Books, 1980.

Fregoso, Rosa Linda. *meXicana Encounters: The Making of Social Identities on the Borderlands.* Berkeley: University of California Press, 2003.

Freire, Paulo. *Pedagogy of the Oppressed.* New York: Continuum, 2000.

Galarte, Francisco J. *Brown Trans Figurations: Rethinking Race, Gender, and Sexuality in Chicanx/Latinx Studies.* Austin: University of Texas Press, 2021.

Galindo, René. "Repartitioning the National Community: Political Visibility and Voice for Undocumented Immigrants in the Spring 2006 Immigration Rights Marches." *Aztlán: A Journal of Chicano Studies* 35, no. 2 (Fall 2010).

Galindo, René. "Undocumented & Unafraid: The Dream Act 5 and the Public Disclosure of Undocumented Students as a Political Act." *The Urban Review* 44, no. 5 (2012): 589–611.

García, Angela S. *Legal Passing: Navigating Undocumented Life and Local Immigration Law.* Berkeley: University of California Press, 2019.

García, Hector P. *Everyday Rhetoric and Mexican American Civil Rights.* Carbondale: Southern Illinois Press, 2006.

García, María Cristina. *Seeking Refuge: Central American Migration to Mexico, the United States, and Canada.* Berkeley: University of California Press, 2006.

García, Mario T. *Father Luis Olivares, a Biography: Faith Politics and the Origins of the Sanctuary Movement.* Chapel Hill: University of North Carolina Press, 2018.

Golash-Boza, Tanya Maria. *Deported: Immigrant Policing, Disposable Labor and Global Capitalism.* New York: NYU Press, 2015.

Gomberg-Muñoz, Ruth. *Labor and Legality: An Ethnography of a Mexican Immigrant Network.* New York: Oxford University Press, 2011.

Gomberg-Muñoz, Ruth. "Undocumented. Unafraid. Unapologetic." *Practicing Anthropology* 38, no. 1 (Winter 2016): 50–51.

Grande, Reyna, and Sonia Guiñansaca. *Somewhere We Are Human.* New York: Harper Via, 2022.

Grewal, Inderpal. *Transnational America: Feminisms, Diasporas, Neoliberalisms.* Durham, N.C.: Duke University Press, 2005.

Hames-García, Michael R. "Jotería Studies, or The Political Is Personal." *Aztlán: A Journal of Chicano Studies* 39, no. 1 (Spring 2014): 135–42.

Hames-García, Michael R., and Ernesto J. Martínez, eds. *Gay Latino Studies: A Critical Reader.* Durham, N.C.: Duke University Press, 2011.

Harcourt, Bernard E. "The Politics of Incivility." *Arizona Law Review* 54, no. 2 (2012): 345–74.

Hartelius, E. Johanna. "'Undocumented and Unafraid'? Challenging the Bureaucratic Paradigm." *Communication and Critical/Cultural Studies* 13, no. 2 (2016): 130–49.

Harvey, David. *A Brief History of Neoliberalism.* New York: Oxford University Press, 2005.

Henkel, Scott, and Vanessa Fonseca-Chávez. "Fearless Speech and the Discourse of Civility in *Salt of the Earth*." *Chiricú Journal: Latina/o Literatures, Arts, and Cultures* 1, no. 1 (2016): 19–38.

Hernández, Roberto D. *Coloniality of the U-S///Mexico Border: Power, Violence, and the Decolonial Imperative.* Tucson: University of Arizona Press, 2018.

Hondagneu-Sotelo, Pierrette, and Ernestine Ávila. "'I'm Here, but I'm There': The Meanings of Latina Transnational Motherhood." In *Gender and U.S. Immigration: Contemporary Trends*, ed. Pierrette Hondagneu-Sotelo. Berkeley: University of California Press, 1999.

Huizar-Hernández, Anita. *Forging Arizona: A History of the Peralta Land Grant and Racial Identity in the West.* New Brunswick: Rutgers University Press, 2019.

Iglesias-Prieto, Norma. "Maquiladoras." In *Keywords for Latina/o Studies*, edited by Lawrence La Fountain-Stokes, Nancy Raquel Mirabal, and Deborah Vargas, 125–28. New York: New York University Press, 2017.

INCITE!, ed. *The Revolution Will Not Be Funded: Beyond the Non-profit Industrial Complex.* Boston: South End Press, 2009.

Jenkins, Henry. *Convergence Culture: Where Old and New Media Collide.* New York: New York University Press, 2006.

Jenkins, Henry, Sam Ford, and Joshua Green. *Spreadable Media: Creating Value and Meaning in a Networked Culture.* New York: New York University Press, 2013.

Jenkins, Henry, Sangita Shresthova, Liana Gamber-Thompson, Neta Kligler-Vilenchik, and Arely M. Zimmerman. *By Any Media Necessary: The New Youth Activism.* New York: New York University Press, 2016.

Johnson, Gaye Theresa. *Spaces of Conflict, Sounds of Solidarity: Music, Race, and Spatial Entitlement in Los Angeles.* Berkeley: University of California Press, 2013.

Kandel, William A. *The Trump Administration's "Zero Tolerance" Immigration Enforcement Policy.* Washington, D.C.: Congressional Research Service, 2018.

Kelley, Robin D. G. *Freedom Dreams: The Black Radical Imagination.* Boston: Beacon Press, 2003.

Kinder, Marsha. *Playing with Power in Movies, Television, and Video Games: From Muppet Babies to Teenage Mutant Ninja Turtles.* Berkeley: University of California Press, 1991.

La Fountain-Stokes, Lawrence. "Queer Ducks, Puerto Rican Patos, and Jewish-American Feygelekh: Birds and the Cultural Representation of Homosexuality." *Centro Journal* 19, no. 1 (2007): 192–229.

Lazos Vargas, Sylvia R. "The Immigrant Rights Marches (Las Marchas): Did the 'Gigante' (Giant) Wake Up or Does It Still Sleep Tonight?" *Nevada Law Journal,* Summer 2007.

Lee, Erika. *At America's Gates: Chinese Immigration During the Exclusion Era, 1882—1943.* Chapel Hill: University of North Carolina Press, 2003.

Lee, Jamie A. *Producing the Archival Body.* New York: Routledge, 2021.

Lewis Bredbenner, Candice. *A Nationality of Her Own: Women, Marriage, and the Law of Citizenship.* Berkeley: University of California Press, 1998.

Lipsitz, George. *The Possessive Investment in Whiteness: How People Profit from Identity Politics.* Philadelphia: Temple University Press, 2006.

Lorde, Audre. *Sister Outsider: Essays and Speeches.* Crossing Press Feminist Series. Berkeley, Calif.: Crossing Press, 1984.

Lowe, Lisa. *Immigrant Acts: On Asian American Cultural Politics.* Durham, N.C.: Duke University Press, 1996.

Luibhéid, Eithne. *Entry Denied: Controlling Sexuality at the Border.* Minneapolis: University of Minnesota Press, 2015.

Lytle Hernández, Kelly. Migra! *A History of the U.S. Border Patrol.* Berkeley: University of California Press, 2010.

Magaña, Lisa, and César S. Silva. *Empowered!* ¡Empoderados! *Latinos Transforming Arizona Politics.* Tucson: University of Arizona Press, 2021.

Markowitz, Peter L. "After ICE: A New Humane and Effective Immigration Enforcement Paradigm." *Wake Forest Law Review* 55, no. 1 (2020): 89–144.

Martínez, Demetria. *Mother Tongue*. New York: One World/Ballantine, 1996.

Martínez, Rafael A. "Counter Culture Youth: Immigrant Rights Activism and the Undocumented Youth Vanguard." MA thesis, University of New Mexico, 2014.

Martínez, Rafael A. "Transnational DREAMer Narratives: Following the Deportation and Return-Migration Trails of Mexican Immigrant Youth." *Aztlán: A Journal of Chicano Studies* 49, no. 2 (2024): 79–100.

Melamed, Jodi. *Represent and Destroy: Rationalizing Violence in the New Radical Capitalism.* Minneapolis: University of Minnesota Press, 2011.

Melucci, Alberto. *Challenging Codes: Collective Action in the Information Age.* Cambridge, UK: Cambridge University Press, 1996.

Melucci, Alberto. *Nomads of the Present: Social Movements and Individual Needs in Contemporary Society.* Philadelphia: Temple University Press, 1989.

Melucci, Alberto. *The Playing Self: Person and Meaning in the Planetary Society.* Cambridge, UK: Cambridge University Press, 1996.

Menjívar, Cecilia, Leisy J. Abrego, and Leah C. Schmalzbauer. *Immigrant Families.* New York: Polity Press, 2016.

Menjívar, Cecilia, and Daniel Kanstroom. *Constructing Illegality in America: Immigrant Experiences, Critiques, and Resistance.* New York: Cambridge University Press, 2013.

Moraga, Cherríe. *The Last Generation: Prose and Poetry.* Boston: South End Press, 1993.

Morales, Isidro. "The Mexican Crisis and the Weakness of the NAFTA Consensus." *The Annals of the American Academy of Political and Social Science* 550, no. 1 (1997): 130–52.

Muñoz, José Esteban. *Disidentifications: Queers of Color and the Performance of Politics.* Minneapolis: Minnesota University Press, 1999.

Negrón-Gonzales, Genevieve. "Undocumented, Unafraid and Unapologetic: Re-articulatory Practices and Migrant Youth 'Illegality.'" *Latino Studies* 12, no. 2 (2014): 259–78. https://doi.org/10.1057/lst.2014.20.

Nevins, Joseph. *Operation Gatekeeper: The Rise of the "Illegal Alien" and the Making of the U.S.-Mexico Boundary.* New York: Routledge, 2002.

Ngai, Mae. *Impossible Subjects: Illegal Aliens and the Making of Modern America.* Princeton, N.J.: Princeton University Press, 2014.

Nguyen, Mimi Thi. *Gift of Freedom: War, Debt, and Other Refugee Passages.* Durham, N.C.: Duke University Press, 2012.

Nicholls, Walter. *The DREAMers: How the Undocumented Youth Movement Transformed the Immigrant Rights Debate.* Stanford: Stanford University Press, 2013.

Noriega, Chon A. *Just Another Poster?* Los Angeles: The Regents of the University of California Art Museum, 2001.

Ochoa, Juan D. "Shine Bright Like a Diamond: Julio Salgado's Digital Art and Its Use of Jotería." *Social Justice* 42, no. 3–4 (2015): 184–99.

Omi, Michael, and Howard Winant. *Racial Formations in the United States: From the 1960s to the 1990s.* Oxfordshire, England: Routledge, 1994.

Ono, Kent A., and John M. Sloop. *Shifting Borders: Rhetoric, Immigration, and California's Proposition 187*. Philadelphia: Temple University Press, 2002.

Ordaz, Jessica. *The Shadow of El Centro: A History of Migrant Incarceration and Solidarity*. Chapel Hill: University of North Carolina Press, 2021.

Pacini Hernandez, Deborah. *Oye Como Va! Hybridity and Identity in Latino Popular Music*. Philadelphia: Temple University Press, 2010.

Paik, A. Naomi. *Bans, Walls, Raids, Sanctuary: Understanding U.S. Immigration for the Twenty-First Century*. Berkeley: University of California Press, 2020.

Pallares, Amalia, and Nilda Flores-González. *¡Marcha! Latino Chicago and the Immigrant Rights Movement*. Urbana: University of Illinois Press, 2010.

Patiño, Jimmy. *Raza Sí, Migra No: Chicano Movement Struggles for Immigrant Rights in San Diego*. Chapel Hill: University of North Carolina Press, 2017.

Peck, Sarah Herman, and Ben Harrington. *The "Flores Settlement" and Alien Families Apprehended at the U.S. Border: Frequently Asked Questions*. Washington, D.C.: Congressional Research Service, 2018.

Pérez, Daniel Enrique. "Jotería Epistemologies: Mapping a Research Agenda, Unearthing a Lost Heritage, and Building 'Queer Aztlán.'" *Aztlán: A Journal of Chicano Studies* 39, no. 1 (2014): 143–54.

Pérez, Daniel Enrique. "Toward a Mariposa Consciousness: Reimagining Queer Chicano and Latino Identities." *Aztlán: A Journal of Chicano Studies* 39, no. 2 (2014): 95–127.

Pérez, Emma. *The Decolonial Imaginary: Writing Chicanas into History*. Theories of Representation and Difference. Bloomington: Indiana University Press, 1999.

Pérez, William. *American by Heart: Undocumented Latino Students and the Promise of Higher Education*. New York: Teachers College Press, 2012.

Peutz, Nathalie, and Nicholas De Genova. "Introduction." In De Genova and Peutz, *Deportation Regime*.

Polletta, Francesca, and James M. Jasper. "Collective Identity and Social Movements." *Annual Review of Sociology* 27, no. 1 (2001): 283–305.

Pulido, Laura. *Black, Brown, Yellow, and Left: Radical Activism in Southern California*. Berkeley: University of California Press, 2006.

Ragland, Cathy. *Música Norteña: Mexican Migrants Creating a Nation Between Nations*. Philadelphia: Temple University Press, 2009.

Raiford, Leigh. *Imprisoned in a Luminous Glare: Photography and the African American Freedom Struggle*. Chapel Hill: University of North Carolina Press, 2013.

Reyna Rivarola, Alonso R., and Gerardo R. López. "Moscas, Metiches, and Methodologies: Exploring Power, Subjectivity, and Voice When Researching the Undocumented." *International Journal of Qualitative Studies in Education* 34, no. 8 (2021): 733–45.

Rivera, John-Michael. *Undocuments*. Tucson: University of Arizona Press, 2021.

Rivera, Raquel Z., Wayne Marshall, and Deborah Pacini Hernandez, eds. *Reggaeton*. Durham, N.C.: Duke University Press, 2009.

Rodríguez, Dylan. "The Political Logic of the Non-profit Industrial Complex." In INCITE!, *Revolution Will Not Be Funded*, 21–40.

Rodriguez Vega, Silvia. *Drawing Deportation: Art and Resistance Among Immigrant Children*. New York: New York University Press, 2023.

Rosaldo, Renato. "Cultural Citizenship, Inequality, and Multiculturalism." In *Latino Cultural Citizenship: Claiming Identity, Space, and Rights*, edited by William V. Flores and Rina Benmayor. Boston: Beacon Press, 1997.

Ruiz, Vicki L. *From Out of the Shadows: Mexican Women in Twentieth-Century America*. New York: Oxford University Press, 1998.

Rumbaut, Ruben G. "Generation 1.5, Educational Experiences of." In *Encyclopedia of Diversity in Education*, edited by James A. Banks. Seattle: Sage Publications, 2012.

Saavedra, Yvette J. "Of Chicana Lesbian Terrorists and Lesberadas: Recuperating the Lesbian/Queer Roots of Chicana Feminism, 1970–2000." *Feminist Formations* 34, no. 2 (2022): 99–124.

Saavedra, Yvette J. *Pasadena Before the Roses: Race, Identity, and Land Use in Southern California, 1771–1890*. Tucson: University of Arizona Press, 2018.

Saldaña-Portillo, María Josefina. *Indian Given: Racial Geographies Across Mexico and the United States*. Durham, N.C.: Duke University Press, 2016.

Sánchez, George J. *Becoming Mexican American: Ethnicity, Culture, and Identity in Chicano Los Angeles, 1900–1945*. New York: Oxford University Press, 1993.

Sandoval, Chela. *Methodology of the Oppressed*. Minneapolis: University of Minnesota Press, 2000.

Santiago Martínez, Pedro, Claudia Muñoz, Mariela Nuñez-Janes, Stephen Pavey, Fidel Castro Rodriguez, and Marco Saavedra. *Eclipse of Dreams: The Undocumented-Led Struggle for Freedom*. Chico, Calif.: AK Press, 2020.

Sati, Joel. "'Other' Borders: The Illegal as Normative Metaphor." In Abrego and Negrón-Gonzales, *We Are Not Dreamers*, 23–44.

Schmidt Camacho, Alicia. *Migrant Imaginaries: Latino Cultural Politics in the U.S.-Mexico Borderlands*. New York: NYU Press, 2008.

Schreiber, Rebecca M. *The Undocumented Everyday: Migrant Lives and the Politics of Visibility*. Minneapolis: Minnesota University Press, 2018.

Silver, Alexis M. *Shifting Boundaries: Immigrant Youth Negotiating National, State, and Small-Town Politics*. Stanford, Calif.: Stanford University Press, 2018.

Sy, Cherry Lou. *Dreaming Out Loud: An Anthology of Migrant Writers*, Volume 4. New York: Pen America, 2022.

Smith, Jackie. *Social Movements for Global Democracy*. Baltimore: Johns Hopkins University Press, 2008.

Smith, Robert. *Mexican New York: Transnational Lives of New Immigrants*. Berkeley: University of California Press, 2005.

Stoller, Laura. *Along the Archival Grain: Epistemic Anxieties and Colonial Common Sense*. Princeton, N.J.: Princeton University Press, 2009.

Tarrow, Sidney G. *The New Transnational Activism*. New York: Cambridge University Press, 2005.

Tarrow, Sidney G. *Power in Movement: Social Movements and Contentious Politics*. New York: Cambridge University Press, 2011.

Taylor, Diana. *The Archive and the Repertoire: Performing Cultural Memory in the Americas.* Durham, N.C.: Duke University Press, 2003.

Tomsho, Robert. *The American Sanctuary Movement.* Austin: Texas Monthly Press, 1987.

Toro-Morn, Maura I. "Elvira Arellano and the Struggles of Low-Wage Undocumented Latina Immigrant Women." In Flores-González et al., *Immigrant Women Workers,* 38–55.

Toro-Morn, Maura I., and Nilda Flores Gonzalez. "Transnational Latina Mother Activists in the Américas: The Case of Elvira Arellano and Flor Crisóstomo." *Journal of the Motherhood Initiative* 2, no. 2 (2011): 113–28.

Trouillot, Michel-Rolph. *Silencing the Past: Power and the Production of History.* Boston: Beacon Press, 1995.

Valdivia, Carolina. "Undocumented Young Adults' Heightened Vulnerability in the Trump Era." In Abrego and Negrón-Gonzales, *We Are Not Dreamers,* 127–45.

Vargas, Jose Antonio. *Dear America: Notes of an Undocumented Citizen.* New York: Harper Collins, 2018.

Vásquez, Irene. "Transnational Mexican Women's Radical Organizing Activities on the Borders of the Left of the Twentieth Century." *Border-Lines Journal* 9 (2015): 141–60.

Vélez, Veronica, Lindsay Perez Huber, Corina Benavides Lopez, Ariana de la Luz, and Daniel G. Solórzano. "Battling for Human Rights and Social Justice: A Latina/o Critical Race Media Analysis of Latina/o Student Youth Activism in the Wake of 2006 Anti-immigrant Sentiment." *Social Justice / Global Options* 35, no. 1 (111) (2008): 7–27.

Villarreal Garza, Aimee. "Sanctuaryscapes in the North American Southwest." In "Sanctuary's Radical Networks," special issue, *Radical History Review* 2019, no. 135 (2019): 43–70.

Villaruel, Kathleen L. "The Underground Railroad and the Sanctuary Movement: A Comparison of History, Litigation, and Values." *Southern California Law Review* 60, no. 5 (July 1987).

Walia, Harsha. *Undoing Border Imperialism.* Oakland, Calif.: AK Press, 2013.

White, Melissa Autumn. "Documenting the Undocumented: Toward a Queer Politics of No Borders." *Sexualities* 17, no. 8 (2014): 976–97.

Widener, Daniel. *Black Arts West: Culture and Struggle in Postwar Los Angeles.* Durham, N.C.: Duke University Press, 2010.

Zimmerman, Arely. "Transmedia Testimonio: Examining Undocumented Youth's Political Activism in the Digital Age." *International Journal of Communication* 10 (2016): 1886–1906.

INDEX

ABOUT THE AUTHOR

Rafael A. Martínez is an assistant professor of Southwest Borderlands at Arizona State University whose work focuses on immigrant
rights, mixed-status families, and Latinx cultural and historical productions in the Southwest borderlands. He is engaged in public projects
that seek to connect academic work with community development using oral history, transmedia narratives, and creative interferences. His
next academic project uses oral history to share the stories of mixed-
status families who resort to interstate migration.